BrightRED Study Guide

CfE HIGHER

MODERN STUDIES

Caleb Marwick, Heidi Stoutjesdyk
and Derek Timpany

First published in 2021 by:
Bright Red Publishing Ltd
Mitchelston Drive Business Centre
Mitchelston Drive
Kirkcaldy
KY1 3NB

A CIP record for this book is available from the British Library

ISBN 978-1-84948-328-5

With thanks to:
PDQ Digital Media Solutions Ltd (layout), Project One Publishing Solutions (editorial).

Cover design and series book design by Caleb Rutherford – e i d e t i c

Acknowledgements
Every effort has been made to seek all copyright holders. If any have been overlooked, then Bright Red Publishing will be delighted to make the necessary arrangements.

Permission has been sought from all relevant copyright holders and Bright Red Publishing is grateful for the use of the following:

Brian McNeil (CC BY-SA 3.0)1 (p 10); Catherine Bebbington/UK Parliament Copyright (OPL)2 (p 14); UK Parliament Copyright (OPL)2 (p 14); UK Parliament Copyright (OPL)2 (p 16); UK Parliament Copyright (OPL)2 (p 17); Cover of the Enterprise and Regulatory Reform Act 2013 © Crown Copyright (OPL)2 (p 17); Michael Tubi/Shutterstock.com (p 21); TBC/Shutterstock.com (p 22); Colin/Wikimedia Commons (CC BY-SA 4.0)3 (p 24); Image taken from www.scottish.parliament.uk/PublicInformationdocuments/Committees-240613.pdf © Scottish Parliamentary Corporate Body – 2012 (Open Scottish Parliament Licence)4 (p 26); Ninian Reid/Creative Commons (CC BY 2.0)5 (p 27); Image taken from www.scotland.gov.uk/About/People/14944/Scottish-Cabinet/nicolasturgeonmsp © The Scottish Government (OGL)6 (p 28); Image taken from www.flickr.com/photos/scottishgovernment/15844164455 © The Scottish Government (OGL)6 (p 30); Image taken from www.parliament.scot/msps/current-and-previous-msps/jeane-freeman © The Scottish Government (OGL)6 (p 30); Image taken from www.parliament.scot/msps/current-and-previous-msps/maree-todd © The Scottish Government (OGL)6 (p 30); gpointstudio/Shutterstock.com (p 52); gualtiero boffi/Shutterstock.com (p 52); Charts taken from www.ons.gov.uk/employmentandlabourmarket/peopleinwork/earningsandworkinghours/articles/contractsthatdonotguaranteeaminimumnumberofhours/april2018 © Office for National Statistics (OGL)6 (p 54); Logo © Living Wage Foundation (p 56); Cubankite/Shutterstock.com (p 59); Andy Dean Photography/Shutterstock.com (p 60); wgmbh/iStock.com (p 61); Giuseppe Milo (CC BY 2.0)5 (p 65); John Lord (CC BY 2.0)5 (p 70); Extract from "Violent crime in Scotland 'higher than official reports'" from The Scotsman Sept, 2018 (www.scotsman.com/news/politics/violent-crime-in-scotland-higher-than-official-reports-1-4800625). This is copyright of The Scotsman Publications and is being used for this purpose with their kind permission (p 71); George Rex (CC BY-SA 2.0)7 (p 73); Lydia (CC BY 2.0)5 (p 75); Ninian Reid (CC BY 2.0)5 (p 76); Tony Webster (CC BY 2.0)5 (p 78); Paul Birrell (CC BY-SA 2.0)7 (p 82); Sean Hobson/Creative Commons (CC BY 2.0)5 (p 82); DALA Film/VPRO (p 85); Front cover of 'Constitution of the People's Republic of China' © Foreign Languages Press (p 86); Chunhai Cao/iStock.com (p 86); humphery/Shutterstock.com (p 87); Senado Federal (CC BY 2.0)5 (p 89); Pablo Tupin-Noriega (CC BY-SA 4.0)3 (p 89); PromesaArtStudio/iStock.com (p 89); Miaow Miaow (CC BY-SA 3.0)1 (p 90); PaulWong/Shutterstock.com (p 91); Image reproduced by permission of Wealth-X (p 93); Logo © Country Garden Holdings (p 93); Startrooper (CC BY 2.0)5 (p 93); TBC/Shutterstock.com (p 94); dmsl/iStock.com (p 98); Harald Groven (CC BY-SA 2.0)7 (p 99); Tom Wang/Shutterstock.com (p 101); Chensiyuan (CC BY-SA 3.0)1 (p 102); MONUSCO Photos (CC BY-SA 2.0)7 (p 103); 123ArtistImages/iStock.com (p 103); cr8tiveshotz/Shutterstock.com (p 104); Mirko Kuzmanovic/Shutterstock.com (p 105); MemoryMan/Shutterstock.com (p 109); ArnoldPlaton (CC BY-SA 3.0)1 (p 111); Fabio Rodrigues Pozzebom/Agência Brasil (CC BY 3.0 BR)9 (p 113); Embassy of Equatorial Guinea (CC BY-ND 2.0)8 (p 113); Ian Davidson Photography/Shutterstock.com (p 117); Debby Wong/Shutterstock.com (p 118); Emblem of the African Union/Fair Use (p 119); DonkeyHotey (CC BY 2.0)5 (p 121); Valerio Pucci/Shutterstock.com (p 122); TeddyandMia/Shutterstock.com (p 123); Mark Fischer (CC BY-SA 2.0)7 (p 123); Wapcaplet (CC BY-SA 3.0)1 (p 124); Ascannio/Shutterstock.com (p 125); pressureUA/iStock.com (p 125); Kathy Hutchins/Shutterstock.com (p 127); Naresh777/Shutterstock.com (p 127); Niloo138/iStock.com (p 127); Lwp Kommunikáció (CC BY 2.0)5 (p 127); Michal Urbanek/Shutterstock.com (p 131); lev radin/Shutterstock.com (p 135); amagnawa1092/Shutterstock.com (p 136); g0d4ather/Shutterstock.com (p 136); AdrianHancu/iStock.com (p 136); ES3DStudios/Shutterstock.com (p 137); An extract adapted from the article 'More than 75 percent of terrorist attacks in 2016 took place in just 10 countries' by Sophie Chou, 14 July 2017, taken from the website The World (www.pri.org/stories/2017-07-14/more-75-percent-terrorist-attack (p 138); Extract from "Violent crime in Scotland 'higher than official reports'" from The Scotsman Sept, 2018 (www.scotsman.com/news/politics/violent-crime-in-scotland-higher-than-official-reports-1-4800625). This is copyright of The Scotsman Publications and is being used for this purpose with their kind permission (p 142); Infographic from www.gov.scot/publications/recorded-crime-scotland-2018-19/pages/4/ © The Scottish Government (OGL)6 (p 142); Images licenced by Ingram Image (pp 51, 68, 73, 80 & 120).

[1](CC BY-SA 3.0) http://creativecommons.org/licenses/by-sa/3.0/
[2](OPL) Contains Parliamentary information licensed under the Open Parliament Licence. www.parliament.uk/site-information/copyright/open-parliament-licence/
[3](CC BY-SA 4.0) http://creativecommons.org/licenses/by-sa/4.0/
[4]Contains information licensed under the Open Scottish Parliament Licence v2.0 (www.scottish.parliament.uk/FoI/OpenScottishParliamentLicence.pdf)
[5](CC BY 2.0) http://creativecommons.org/licenses/by/2.0/
[6](OGL) Contains public sector information licensed under the Open Government Licence v3.0. (www.nationalarchives.gov.uk/doc/open-government-licence/version/3/)
[7](CC BY-SA 2.0) http://creativecommons.org/licenses/by-sa/2.0/
[8](CC BY-ND 2.0) http://creativecommons.org/licenses/by-nd/2.0/
[9](CC BY 3.0 BR) http://creativecommons.org/licenses/by/3.0/br/deed.en

Printed and bound in the UK.

CONTENTS

INTRODUCTION

DEMOCRACY IN SCOTLAND AND THE UK

SOCIAL ISSUES IN THE UNITED KINGDOM

Social inequality in the UK

Crime and the Law in Scotland

INTERNATIONAL ISSUES

China

Underdevelopment in Africa

USA

INTRODUCTION

INTRODUCING CfE HIGHER MODERN STUDIES

Higher Modern Studies is one of the most popular subjects in the Scottish curriculum. In undertaking Higher Modern Studies you will have opportunities to work collaboratively, while at the same time you will enjoy the freedom to work independently and explore contemporary areas of personal interest.

Choosing Modern Studies at Higher level will provide you with the opportunity to study either *Decision Making in Scotland* or *the United Kingdom*, provide you with an understanding of *Social Inequality* or *Crime and the Law*, and give you an insight into the important role played by a *G20 World Power* or the global impact of a significant *World Issue*.

As well as developing a deeper understanding of international contemporary political and socio-economic issues, you will improve your skills as a critical and reflective thinker. Importantly, you will have the chance to further your research and information-handling skills.

THE BENEFITS OF STUDYING HIGHER MODERN STUDIES

Modern Studies plays a key role in developing political literacy and will help you to develop a number of higher-order thinking skills, such as analysis, synthesis and evaluation. By participating in discussions, delivering presentations, undertaking research activities and collaborating with others, you will develop a range of transferable skills – skills for life, skills for learning and skills for work – which will put you in a strong position to move into college, university or worthwhile employment.

COURSE ASSESSMENT FOR HIGHER MODERN STUDIES

There are three parts or components that make up the Higher Modern Studies course assessment or qualification:

- Component 1 – Question Paper 1 (52 marks).
- Component 2 – Question Paper 2 (28 marks).
- Component 3 – The Assignment (30 marks).

Total marks for course assessment = 110 marks.

External assessment component 1: Question Paper 1

Question Paper 1 will test your knowledge and understanding of the Higher Modern Studies course:

- Section 1 – Democracy in Scotland and the United Kingdom.
- Section 2 – Social Issues in the United Kingdom: **either** Social Inequality **or** Crime and Law.
- Section 3 – International Issues: **either** World Powers **or** World Issues.

Question Paper 1 is worth 52 marks. This constitutes 47% or just under half of the total course assessment marks available. You will be asked to answer **three** extended responses or essay-type questions in this paper. Two questions will be worth 20 marks and the other will be worth 12 marks. In advance of sitting this question paper, you will not know which questions will be worth 20 marks and which questions 12. You will have to prepare to answer 12 or 20 mark questions in any of the three sections of this paper.

You will have 1 hour 45 minutes to complete Question Paper 1. Effective time management is crucial if you wish to secure a top grade. Practising assessment questions under timed conditions is excellent exam preparation.

You will be required to show the examiner the breadth of your knowledge and understanding by giving detailed descriptions and explanations and demonstrating your

contd

ability to analyse and evaluate complex social, political and economic issues. You must include relevant examples throughout your answers and aim to make these as current as possible.

EXTERNAL ASSESSMENT COMPONENT 2: QUESTION PAPER 2

This question paper has a total mark allocation of 28 marks. This is 26% of the overall course assessment.

This question paper allows candidates to demonstrate application of the following higher order thinking skills:

- Explaining the degree of selectivity using a range of sources of information.
- Drawing and supporting complex conclusions using a range of sources of information.
- Evaluating the trustworthiness of a range of sources of information.

This question paper will have **three** questions. You should complete each of them. For more information on Question Paper 2, see p.138.

EXTERNAL ASSESSMENT COMPONENT 3: ASSIGNMENT

The assignment is an opportunity to demonstrate the skills and knowledge gained within the context of a Modern Studies issue with minimum support. The assignment is worth 30 marks (27% of the total course assessment). The assignment has two stages: **research** and **production of evidence**.

The research stage involves investigating your chosen issue and organising and finding sources. You will have approximately eight hours of teaching and learning time to gather relevant information.

The production of evidence involves writing up your report under controlled conditions within 1 hour 30 minutes. You will be allowed to take a Research Evidence sheet into the write up consisting of the information gathered during the research stage. This will be submitted to the SQA for marking along with the assignment and should be no more than two single-sided sheets of A4 paper. This should be mostly used for source information and each source used should be referenced at least once in your assignment. You should not simply copy from the Research Evidence but expand and develop the information presented and, most importantly, you must link to your knowledge of the topic. Synthesis is highly creditworthy.

For more information on the assignment, see pages 8–9.

ONLINE

This book is supported by the BrightRED Digital Zone – log on at www.brightredbooks.net for a world of tests, activities, videos and more.

HOW THIS STUDY GUIDE WILL HELP YOU

This guide will give you the best possible chance of achieving success in the Higher Modern Studies course. It contains information covering each part of the course and will increase your understanding through the provision of high quality descriptions and current exemplification. Here you'll find important facts, key points to remember, useful websites and interesting video clips, with an extensive range of activities. This Study Guide will support both your classroom learning and independent study, and put you in a strong position to succeed in the final external examination. Good luck!

EXAM SKILLS

QUESTION PAPER 1: EXTENDED RESPONSES OR ESSAYS

In Question Paper 1 you will be asked questions drawing on your knowledge and understanding. This paper will last 1 hour and 45 minutes. It is recommended that you limit the amount of time you spend on each question depending on the mark allocation. For example, you should spend more time on a question worth 20 marks than on a question worth 12 marks. Roughly speaking, for every mark in this question paper you will have two minutes of thinking and writing time.

EXTENDED RESPONSES

Extended responses or essays are your opportunity to display your knowledge and understanding, as well as your analysis and evaluation skills. You are expected to answer three essay questions in the exam. You will be given three essay choices to pick from in Section 1 and two options to choose from in Sections 2 and 3. You should **only** answer one of them in each section.

Higher Modern Studies essay questions will start with one of four question stems: **analyse**, **evaluate**, **discuss** and **to what extent**. You should familiarise yourself with each type of question stem.

EXTENDED RESPONSE QUESTIONS: ANALYSE AND EVALUATE (12 MARKS)

There are two question stems that require a 12-mark response: **analyse** and **evaluate**. Each has its own requirements but there are also similarities in how they should be tackled:

- You should have an introduction, a main body and a conclusion.
- Aim to complete at least four paragraphs and provide at least two relevant points of knowledge throughout.
- Each paragraph should describe an issue by making a point, explaining it and providing an example to support it.
- Aim to make an overall balanced argument using terms like 'however' or 'on the other hand' to identify alternative arguments.
- Include a range of points, at least two relevant aspects of knowledge, detailed description or explanation and a range of relevant examples.
- Compare different views, consider possible consequences or make links between factors.
- Aim to spend no longer than 20–25 minutes answering 12-mark questions in an exam.

Analyse questions

You are required to identify parts of an issue, the relationship between these parts and their relationships with the whole issue.

Marks are allocated based on the following criteria:

Knowledge, explanation and exemplification	up to 8 marks
Analysis/evaluation	up to a notional 4 marks

Example:

Analyse the ways in which the views of citizens are represented within the political system of the world power you have studied.

Evaluate questions

You are required to make a judgement based on criteria and determine the value of an idea/statement/opinion. You must make an evaluative comment at the end of each paragraph stating a judgement or conclusion and placing a value on a point.

Example:

Evaluate the effectiveness of parliament in holding the government to account.

EXTENDED RESPONSE QUESTIONS (20 MARKS)

There are two question stems that require a 20-mark response: **discuss** and **to what extent**. Each has its own requirements but there are also similarities in how they should be tackled:

- Use a clear and consistent line of argument throughout.
- Use a clear and sensible structure, include a range of points with detailed explanation and relevant exemplification as well as extended analysis and evaluation.
- Each paragraph should describe an issue by making a point, explaining it and providing an example to support it.
- Aim to make an overall balanced argument using terms like 'however' or 'on the other hand' to identify alternative arguments.
- Include an analytical, balanced conclusion.
- Aim to spend no longer than 40–45 minutes answering 20-mark questions in an exam.

Marks are allocated based on the following criteria:

Knowledge, explanation and exemplification	up to 8 marks
Analysis	up to 6 marks
Structure	up to 2 marks
Conclusions	up to 4 marks

Discuss questions

You will be given a statement to analyse and evaluate. You are required to communicate ideas and information on the issue in the statement made and analyse and evaluate different views on the issue.

Example:

International organisations have been successful in resolving a significant world issue. Discuss with reference to a world issue you have studied.

To what extent questions

You should analyse the issue in question and draw a conclusion or conclusions, making an evaluative judgement that you can support with evidence.

Example:

To what extent have UK Government policies reduced social inequalities?

After you have completed Question Paper 1 you will exit the exam room. Question Paper 2 will start half an hour after the end of Question Paper 1.

QUESTION PAPER 2: SOURCE-BASED SKILLS QUESTIONS

There will be three source-based questions in this paper, totalling 28 marks. The types of source-based skills questions you will meet in Question Paper 2 are fully discussed later in this book. The types of question are:

- Objectivity question – worth 10 marks.
- Conclusions question – worth 10 marks.
- Reliability question worth – 8 marks.

There is no choice of question in Paper 2. You should complete all **three** questions. Please remember that the subject matter in the question may not be something you have studied. However, all the answers to the questions come **entirely** from the sources. There are **no** marks for knowledge.

You will have 1 hour and 15 minutes to complete this paper. Roughly speaking, for each mark, you will have around three minutes of thinking and writing time.

Make sure the evidence is clearly laid out and it is easy for the marker to see where references to sources have been made. The synthesis or combining of evidence from two or more sources to support a point is highly creditworthy.

ONLINE

For example answers to the question types mentioned here, head to www.brightredbooks.net

THINGS TO DO AND THINK ABOUT

Head to the digital zone to look at some more examples of extended response questions.

THE ASSIGNMENT

AN OVERVIEW

The assignment is an opportunity to demonstrate the skills and knowledge gained within the context of a Modern Studies issue with minimum support. It is worth 30 marks. The assignment has two stages: **research** and **production of evidence**.

The research stage involves investigating your chosen issue and organising and finding sources. The production of evidence involves writing up your report under controlled conditions within 1 hour 30 minutes. You will be allowed to take a Research Evidence sheet into the write up, consisting of the information gathered during the research stage. This will be submitted to the SQA for marking along with the assignment and should be no more than two single-sided sheets of A4 paper. This should be mostly used for source information and each source used should be referenced at least once in your assignment. You should not simply copy from the Research Evidence but expand and develop the information presented and, most importantly, you must link to your knowledge of the topic. Synthesis is highly creditworthy.

DON'T FORGET

Make sure the evidence is clearly laid out and that it is easy for the marker to see where references to sources have been made. You are not credited for anything which you copy directly from the Research Evidence sheet during the write up.

WHAT IS REQUIRED IN THE RESEARCH STAGE?

- Identify a Modern Studies issue about which there are alternative views, for example Scottish Independence. Explain, in detail, the possible different courses of action.
- Research the issue using a range of sources of information. You must find these sources yourself.
- Analyse and synthesise information from your chosen sources. Consider at least **two** courses of action related to your chosen issue and provide detailed and synthesised evidence to support your analysis.
- Evaluate the usefulness and reliability of the sources you have chosen. For example, is there evidence of bias in any of them? You must make a clear and comparative judgement of **at least two** of the sources and make a clear statement about reliability.
- Reach a decision about the issue.
- Show detailed knowledge and understanding of the issue to support your decision.
- Show awareness of alternative views and explain why your decision is preferable.
- Organise your information into a report format. Marks are awarded for structure so it is recommended that you use headings to organise your information.

DON'T FORGET

Synthesis means to combine evidence from two or more sources to support a point.

SAMPLE REPORT FORMAT

Subject: State your chosen issue, for example Abolish the Educational Maintenance Allowance (EMA).

Options: Present possible decisions related to your chosen issue, for example abolish EMA, retain EMA or reform EMA.

Author: Your name **Date:**

Recipient: State the government official likely to deal with your report

This format can be expanded upon under each of the following headings to create a report relevant to your chosen issue.

Introduction

Outline the issue you have chosen by describing it and setting it in the context of today's society. You should identify three possible arguments (for, against and an alternative).

Example:

To decide I will evaluate all sides of the argument and come to a balanced conclusion using a range of sources.

contd

Decision

State your decision related to the title or hypothesis of your report.

Example:

Upon reviewing the evidence for each argument I have decided that my original hypothesis .... is the correct decision.

Methodology

Outline **at least two** of the sources used during your research and evaluate their reliability. You must come to a conclusion about which source was the most useful and explain why.

Example:

To investigate my chosen topic I used several different sources to incorporate the best possible evidence. These sources included newspaper articles, website articles, TV programmes and a survey. When conducting my research I found that the .... were useful because they were .... However, they were not entirely reliable because .... I also found that ....

Arguments for

Provide **at least three** arguments with detailed explanations in favour of your decision.

Arguments against and rebuttal

Provide **at least three** arguments that may be presented against your decision and rebut (counter argue against) each using evidence from the sources.

Example:

It has been argued that ...., however, ... Furthermore, ...

Provide **at least two** arguments that would be in favour of the third option you originally stated and rebut them.

Example:

It has also been suggested that ...., however, ...

Conclusion

Finally, summarise the main points in support of your decision in a paragraph.

Example:

Overall, I reached my decision based on the fact that the evidence shows .... The evidence in favour of my decision out-weighs that which supports any alternative views.

ONLINE

Head to www.brightredbooks.net for more topic examples.

THINGS TO DO AND THINK ABOUT

As part of the preparation for your final SQA-assessed assignment, think about a number of different topics that you could research. Before deciding on your final choice of topic, make sure you can locate a range of information so that you can argue for, against and provide an alternative view in your answer.

Again, make sure your evidence is clearly laid out and it is easy for the marker to see where references to sources have been made. The synthesis or combining of evidence from two or more sources to support a point is highly creditworthy. For example:

Topic: Prisoners and the right to vote

Question: Should all prisoners have the right to vote in the UK?

Sources: In favour: https://www.theguardian.com/uk-news/2018/may/14/sturgeon-pressed-allow-prisoners-vote-scottish-elections

Against: http://www.bbc.co.uk/news/uk-politics-20053244

Alternative: https://www.bbc.co.uk/news/uk-politics-41853403

THE UK CONSTITUTIONAL ARRANGEMENT

Decision-making for Scotland and the UK takes place at many levels. Developing an understanding of the way the different elements interact is key to developing your knowledge of Scottish and UK decision-making. There are also the National Assembly for Wales, and the Northern Ireland Assembly, each of which has legislative powers in some areas.

While the UK Parliament has evolved over centuries, the Scottish Parliament began in 1999. As such, the UK Parliament is largely run according to convention (tradition), while the Scottish Parliament was able to define its own procedures and structures. It began life with the **founding principles**.

Accountable	Parliament must answer to the public. The government must answer to the parliament.
Open and encourage participation	Parliament should be accessible. Parliament should involve the people of Scotland wherever possible.
Power sharing	Power is shared between the Scottish Government, Parliament, and people.
Equal opportunities	For all.

The founding principles of the Scottish Parliament

DECISION-MAKING FOR SCOTLAND

Decision-making for Scotland is split between the UK Parliament at Westminster and the Scottish Parliament in Edinburgh. The UK Parliament has responsibility for **reserved matters** – decisions which the UK Parliament makes and which apply to the whole of the UK (including Scotland), and **devolved matters** – decisions which the Scottish Parliament can make for Scotland and which only apply to Scotland.

Reserved matters	Devolved matters
Most benefits and social security	Education and training
Immigration	Health and social services
Defence	Housing
Foreign policy	Income tax
Employment	Law and order
Trade and industry	Local government
Nuclear energy, oil, coal, gas and electricity	Oil/gas extraction
The Constitution	Some welfare benefits

Selected policy areas decided at different levels

THE UK'S CONSTITUTIONAL FUTURE

On 18 September 2014 a referendum was held which asked the people of Scotland whether or not the people of Scotland wanted to become an independent country. After the result was declared, 55.3% of people voted "No" and 44.7% "Yes" to Scottish independence. Crucially, in the run-up to the referendum, all three main UK political parties (Conservative, Labour and Liberal Democrats) promised their support for additional powers for the Scottish Parliament whichever party won the 2015 General Election. This promise became known as the "Vow" and led to the establishment of the Smith Commission.

The Smith Commission, headed by Lord Smith of Kelvin, was asked to investigate further powers for the Scottish Parliament. It reported in late 2014 and its recommendations gave rise to the Scotland Act 2016.

A referendum on the UK's continued membership of the EU was held on 23 June 2016. Although the result was close – 51.8% to leave and 48.1% to remain –the view that the democratic will of the people is for the UK to leave the EU or "Brexit". However, the result highlighted differences between the four countries that make up the UK, with Scotland and Northern Ireland voting to remain but England and Wales voting to leave. Since 2016, the SNP leadership have repeatedly argued that the UK's departure from the EU (31 January 2020) represents a fundamental change to Scotland's constitutional position and that this is reason enough for the people of Scotland to be given a second Scottish independence referendum (sometimes called "Indyref2"). With Northern Ireland also voting to remain within the EU, there is also a view that Britain's exit from the EU may bring a vote on a united Ireland closer.

AREAS OF COOPERATION BETWEEN THE BODIES

Although there have been increasing personal and political differences between the Scottish and UK Governments since devolution, there is a Joint Ministerial Committee (JMC) which facilitates intergovernmental co-operation between Holyrood and Westminster. Over the years, the JMC has promoted co-operation in a diverse range of areas including City Deals, supporting the oil and gas sectors and deploying broadband infrastructure. However, in a 2019 report of the House of Commons Scottish Affairs Committee it was highlighted that the relationship between Scottish and UK Governments had deteriorated markedly and has been characterised since the EU referendum vote by "mutual distrust and political stalemate".

In January 2015, it was announced that the power to change the voting age to 16 would be devolved in time for the 2016 Scottish Election, in a 'fast-track' process. This was in advance of the Scotland Act 2016 being passed by the UK Parliament.

In May 2014, the power to set the cap (limit) on Discretionary Housing Payments was devolved to Scotland. This power allowed the Scottish Government to use some of its budget to offset the effects of the UK Government's ending of the spare room subsidy (the so-called **Bedroom Tax**).

ONLINE TEST

Head to www.brightredbooks.net and test yourself on this topic

AREAS OF CONFLICT BETWEEN THE BODIES

One key area of debate after the Independence Referendum is what the devolution of further powers for Scotland means for decision-making in the UK Parliament. Having Scottish MPs voting for laws which do not apply in Scotland, such as the English education system or health services (while English MPs have no say over devolved matters), has been controversial for decades – this is the so-called **West Lothian Question**, named by West Lothian MP Tam Dalyell in 1977. After the Independence Referendum, four proposals (three Conservative and one Liberal Democrat) were introduced to the UK Parliament about having only 'English votes for English laws' (EVEL). In January 2015, First Minister Nicola Sturgeon said that any SNP MPs would vote on English health laws – something they don't normally do – if it would have an effect on the Scottish budget.

In 2005, the European Court of Human Rights ruled that prisoners should have the right to vote in elections in the UK. Two UK governments failed to deliver this before the 2015 UK General Election. Scottish prisoners were not allowed to vote in the Independence Referendum after the UK Supreme Court threw out two prisoners' attempt to overturn the ban in July 2014. In 2017, a compromise was reached that allows a small number of prisoners to vote ending a twelve-year stand-off between the ECHR and the UK Government.

In May 2012, the Scottish Parliament passed the Alcohol Minimum Pricing Bill, which would set a minimum price of 50p per unit of alcohol. However, The Scotch Whisky Association (which represents 90% of the production industry) successfully brought a case against this legislation, believing the law would break EU free trade law, and the case was referred to the Court of Justice of the European Union in April 2014. However, in November 2017 the UK Supreme Court ruled that minimum unit pricing (MUP) did not breach EU law. MUP came into law 1st May 2018.

In addition, disagreement over the future use of post-Brexit powers looks certain to be an area of widespread dispute between the Scottish and UK governments.

DON'T FORGET

In January 2020, MSPs at Holyrood backed by 64 to 54 a vote for a second Scottish independence referendum. This was rejected by UK Prime Minister Boris Johnson who stated that the 2014 Scottish Independence vote was a "once in a generation" event.

ONLINE

Check out the link at www.brightredbooks.net

DON'T FORGET

In 2021, SNP and Scottish Green Party's representation taken together mean there is majority support in the Scottish Parliament for a second independence referendum or 'Indy2'.

THINGS TO DO AND THINK ABOUT

Research the background to the Alcohol (Minimum Pricing) (Scotland) Act 2012.

1 Essay practice: Analyse the view that the Scottish Parliament has the power to deliver "Scottish solutions to Scottish problems". (12)

THE ROLE OF REPRESENTATIVES

In a representative democracy the electorate give decision-makers the right to speak and act on their behalf. This section details the responsibilities and roles of elected representatives.

As it is a **representative democracy**, the UK's public trusts those they elect to speak and act on their behalf in parliament (UK, Scottish, Welsh or Northern Irish).

PRESSURE ON REPRESENTATIVES

Views of constituents

M(S)Ps are elected to represent their constituents – the people who live in their constituency. If they do not vote and behave in a way in which their constituents are happy with, they may not win re-election. This can conflict with their party's wishes, or indeed their governmental role. Iain Duncan Smith, Work and Pensions Secretary, signed a petition to maintain services at a hospital in his constituency. In cases such as this, M(S)Ps (and government ministers) need to state clearly that they are acting on behalf of their constituents, not the department they are minister of. As M(S)Ps have to represent all of their constituents – even those who did not vote for them – it can be very tricky to keep everyone happy.

Party whips

In the UK Parliament, party whips are MPs or Lords appointed to make sure that enough members of their party vote the way that the leadership wants them to. Every week, whips send out a mailing ('The Whip') to all of their party's members, which contains details of all upcoming parliamentary activities. When the whips require MPs to vote a certain way, they underline the whip with one, two or three lines.

Three-line whips are the most important, and are usually used for significant votes. The closer the vote is likely to be, the more important the job of the whips. If MPs vote against a three-line whip they may be expected to resign from a government position. In some cases, they may be suspended or expelled from the party and have to sit officially as an independent MP until the whip is restored. Expulsion from the party may also mean they can only stand as an independent in the next general election, so parties have a lot of power over the MPs divisions.

Pairing is a convention whereby MPs from opposing parties agree not to vote in agreed **divisions** (votes). This is an informal arrangement, but must be agreed to by the whips (who check that the deal is followed). Whips rarely allow this for important votes.

Personal views

Representatives must balance party pressures against their own beliefs and values. Their own point of view may be very different from that of their constituents, and/or their party's. In July 2018, both David Davis (Minister in charge of Brexit negotiations) and Boris Johnson, (Foreign Secretary) resigned their posts in government as they opposed the Prime Minister's plans for the UK to leave the European Union.

MPs and ministers can also be moved from their government position because of their beliefs. In January 2018 Justine Greening resigned as Education Secretary after reportedly turning down a move to the Department of Work and Pensions, which some commentators viewed as a demotion. Greening, although a supporter of PM Theresa May's Government, is a very independent-minded politician and this may have been the reason behind her proposed move.

FACT 

Junior trade minister Greg Hands resigned from the government to oppose expansion of Heathrow Airport with the proposed building of a third runway. Mr Hands, who represents the Chelsea and Fulham constituency in London, said he had pledged to oppose the new runway at the 2017 election. Mr Hands said after his resignation that he had given a "clear pledge" to vote against expansion and he was keeping his word to his constituents.

VIDEO LINK 

Head to www.brightredbooks.net to watch Baroness Warsi's resignation speech.

PRIVATE MEMBER'S BILLS

One way in which MPs and MSPs can represent their constituents', personal, or party's views is by introducing a **Private Member's Bill** (called a **Member's Bill** in the Scottish Parliament). This allows MPs a chance to limit the government's dominance of the laws made by parliament. In December 2017 the Seat Belts on School Transport (Scotland) Act 2017 received Royal Assent (became law). This Act of the Scottish Parliament requires that motor vehicles provided for the dedicated transport of pupils to and from establishments where they receive primary education or secondary education are fitted with seat belts. Introduced by the SNP's Gillian Martin MSP, it had the support of MSPs from all parties. The Driving Instructors (Registration) Act 2016 was introduced as a Private Member's Bill by Conservative MP Sir David Amiss, MP for Southend West. This Act provided for measures to simplify the registration and deregistration of driving instructors from the Approved Driving Instructor register. It amended certain sections of the Road Traffic Act 1988.

However, Private Member's Bills often fall (are not enacted), or are adopted by the government (such as Neil Findlay's bill on lobbying, discussed later).

DON'T FORGET

In order to be an effective representative, there must be an element of trust and respect from the constituents.

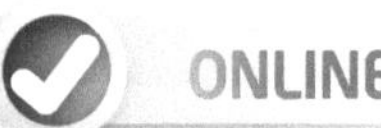

ONLINE TEST

Head to www.brightredbooks.net and test yourself on the role of representatives.

BEHAVE APPROPRIATELY

One of the basic characteristics which people look for in M(S)Ps is that they behave in a way appropriate for public figures. This responsibility has not always been fulfilled. In July 2017 Theresa May ordered the Conservative party's chief whip to suspend an MP who used the N-word at an event during a discussion about Brexit. Anne Marie Morris, the MP for Newton Abbot in Devon, said sorry for causing offence with her use of the word, after a string of opposition politicians accused her of racism. However, the prime minister decided to suspend the whip from Morris after saying the remarks were shocking and unacceptable.

In Scotland, MSPs agreed in June 2018 to exclude former SNP minister Mark McDonald from Holyrood for a month when a report given to the Holyrood standards committee concluded his behaviour towards a parliament worker amounted to sexual harassment. Mr McDonald, who quit as early years minister in November 2017, was found to have sent an "inappropriate" message to the woman. The Aberdeen Donside MSP was barred from entering the Scottish Parliament for a month without pay, the toughest punishment ever handed to a MSP since the Scottish Parliament was founded. MSPs voted by 101 to 0 to support the punishment starting September 2018.

The UK Government passed the Recall of MPs Act (2015), which would trigger a recall petition if an MP is sentenced to prison, or is suspended from the House of Commons for at least 21 sitting days. If 10% of party members eligible to appoint candidates sign the petition, a **by-election** would be held.

ONLINE

The 'Checks and balances in the UK and Scottish political systems' table on www.brightredbooks.net gives an overview of all the checks and balances in each system.

CHECKS AND BALANCES IN THE POLITICAL SYSTEM

Within the UK and Scottish Parliaments, there are a number of checks and balances to prevent excessive dominance by one person or party. You may be aware of a similar system in US politics. Representatives, whether in government or opposition, must play their part in this process. Full discussion of the checks and balances is given elsewhere in the book.

THINGS TO DO AND THINK ABOUT

1 As you work through this chapter, note down examples of the checks and balances in the Scottish and/or UK systems.

ROLE OF THE UK LEGISLATURE: THE PARLIAMENT CHAMBER

MPs are elected to represent their constituents in the House of Commons. Nowhere is this more visible than in the chamber of the House of Commons.

DEBATES

Debates in the House of Commons give MPs the chance to formally discuss bills and deliberate issues brought forward by an MP from the government or opposition. Firstly, the MP in question moves a motion (introduces the subject) in the **First Reading**, and the Speaker repeats this.

ONLINE 

Read about Nigel Dodds being expelled from Commons chamber at www.brightredbooks.net

The motion is then debated by all the MPs who are present. MPs can raise their constituents' concerns during this discussion. MPs take it in turns to speak, and there are strict rules (**Standing Orders**) which the Speaker enforces.

This discussion is often heated, so the Speaker must take charge. MPs who use **unparliamentary language** (not speaking in a manner that the Speaker deems to be appropriate) may be disciplined by the Speaker and/or their party. In July 2013 Nigel Dodds of the Democratic Unionist Party was expelled from the House of Commons for describing the Northern Ireland Secretary's answer to a question as 'deliberately deceptive'. More recently, in April 2016, Labour MP Dennis Skinner was suspended for referring to the then Prime Minister **David Cameron** as 'Dodgy Dave'.

ONLINE 

Read about the Windrush generation, who they are and the problems they face at www.brightredbooks.net

MPs can hold the government to account during these debates, and these can be an occasion when ministers apologise for their earlier actions. In April 2018, the then Home Secretary Amber Rudd apologised to the House of Commons for the "appalling actions" of the Home Office in respect of the Windrush-era citizens who were wrongly threatened with or subject to deportation.

Divisions

Debates may or may not be concluded by holding a **division** (vote). Because the government usually has a majority of seats in the House of Commons, it is expected that the government will win most divisions.

Divisions, however, give MPs from opposition parties, and indeed from within the government, the chance to strongly express their own or their constituents' opposing view. A defeat in a Commons vote can be embarrassing for, and undermine, a Prime Minister. Theresa May's government suffered its first House of Commons defeat on Brexit legislation in December 2017, after MPs narrowly voted in favour of an amendment that guarantees them a say on the final divorce deal.

Divisions do not only affect the government, however. Labour MP Jim Fitzpatrick resigned from the **Shadow Cabinet** the day before this division, as he did not support Ed Miliband's policy on Syria, as he was 'opposed to military intervention in Syria, full stop'.

Other types of debate

Adjournment Debates are general debates which allow MPs to hold debates on a topic without the need to hold a **division**. These can allow MPs to debate government policy

contd

without reaching a decision on it, or allow backbench MPs to raise a constituency issue. There is a 30-minute Adjournment Debate held at the end of each day's sitting.

MPs can request that the House of Commons consider an issue urgently by applying to the **Speaker** for an **Emergency Debate**. However, these are rarely granted. Between May 2012 and September 2014 only 1 out of 6 requests was granted, and that was a debate on 'Royal Charter on Press Conduct' applied for by the then PM David Cameron, although since the election of Theresa May's minority Conservative Government in June 2017 and up to September 2018, a record 13 Emergency Debates have been held covering issues such as the roll out of Universal Credit, Tax Avoidance and Evasion and the war in Syria.

QUESTION TIME

Question Time is an opportunity for MPs to question government ministers about decisions they have made or matters which are under their department's remit. This takes place for one hour, Monday to Thursday, as the first part of parliament's working day. Question Time allows MPs to keep a close check on the government, and the work they are doing. In June 2014, Ian Murray (Labour, Edinburgh South) asked Jenny Willott, Parliamentary Under-Secretary of State for Business, Innovation and Skills, about the government's track record of punishing companies which had broken minimum wage law: 'Just like the Chancellor's hollow promise to increase the national minimum wage to £7, is this not just another example of the government failing to stand up for the lowest paid against rogue employers?'

The minister always has the chance to respond, though, and will usually be very well prepared to answer any question, as they must be submitted three days in advance. In this case, Ms Willott replied fully, mentioning the government was 'increasing fourfold the penalty that employers have to pay'.

Prime Minister's Question Time (PMQs)

For half an hour from midday every Wednesday, it is the turn of the Prime Minister to be questioned by MPs from the opposition and government. The Leader of the Opposition can ask six questions in total, while other MPs may only ask one question (which must be submitted in advance), plus a **supplementary question** on any subject. These supplementary questions in particular give opposition MPs the chance to ask questions which the PM has not seen.

In September 2018, SNP MP Chris Law (Dundee West) asked the then PM Theresa May to commit the UK government to support the introduction of a new direct air service from Heathrow to Dundee by 2021.

However, the Prime Minister has the benefit of extensive research carried out by government departments, who try to ensure that they have a good grounding on any topic which is likely to come up. In the above example, the then PM (Theresa May), whilst welcoming the question, instead chose not to reply directly to what was asked but instead stated that the UK government was working to support investment in Scotland and that once a third runway was completed at Heathrow there would be better connectivity within the UK.

Occasionally, an MP simply seeks to undermine or humiliate the Prime Minister and their government. In February 2013, during the horsemeat scandal, Labour MP Anas Sarwar used PMQs to suggest that the Prime Minister's answers may be '100% bull', much to the other MPs' (and PM's) amusement.

ONLINE

Read more about this by clicking the link 'PMQs: Cameron teased on horsemeat and "100% bull"' at www.brightredbooks.net

DON'T FORGET

Debates and divisions are two of the most high-profile ways in which MPs can represent their constituents.

ONLINE TEST

Want to revise the parliament chamber? Test yourself at www.brightredbooks.net

THINGS TO DO AND THINK ABOUT

1. Watch a recent edition of Prime Minister's Question Time.
   a. Note down the topics they are quizzed upon.
   b. Do they seem to respond successfully?
2. Find a recent example of your MP contributing in the Commons chamber in the ways described above.
3. Essay practice: Analyse the view that parliamentary representatives have few opportunities to represent their constituents in parliament. (12)

ROLE OF THE UK LEGISLATURE: COMMITTEES

SELECT COMMITTEES

Select Committees are responsible for **scrutinising** (examining closely) the work of the government. There are Select Committees in both the Commons and the Lords. Commons Select Committees are usually responsible for a government department, while the Lords' Committees concentrate on four main areas: Europe, science, economics and the UK constitution.

Select Committees have a minimum of 11 members and their Chairs, who are elected by MPs in a secret ballot. The membership of committees (when taken together) is designed to reflect the share of seats in the Commons. The membership of each committee is agreed after each election through negotiations between party whips (sometimes called the **usual channels**). Select Committee membership can, however, be changed between elections. The government would like to have control of all committees in key policy areas, but these negotiations mean it is difficult for any party to have the say it would like to.

A Select Committee

MPs join committees either because they are experienced in that policy area, or it covers an area their constituents have an interest in. Ian Murray MP (Labour, Edinburgh South) has been a member of the Business, Innovation and Skills Committee, Environmental Audit Committee and the Committees on Arms Export Controls.

Commons Select Committees hold **inquiries** into the spending, policies and administration within their policy area. They gather written evidence, and can call for oral evidence. Written evidence can be submitted by anyone, while witnesses are always called by the committee.

Select Committees can summon government ministers to appear and justify actions in their department or indeed their government. This can be a very difficult meeting for the minister, as the issues on which they are questioned are often of high public interest. In July 2018, Employment Minster Alok Sharma was questioned over the Department of Work and Pensions' (DWP) failure to assess Universal Credit's impact on claimants. He was also asked to explain why benefit sanctions was the "only major welfare reform since 2010 that had not been evaluated at all."

FACT

After the 2017 Election, SNP MPs Pete Wishart and Angus MacNeil were appointed as chairs of the Scottish Affairs Committee and Energy and Climate Change Committee respectively.

Even the Prime Minister can be called to appear, if a committee deems it necessary. PM Theresa May was quizzed about Brexit, the economy, social care and sexual harassment when she appeared before the important Parliamentary Liaison Committee chaired by Tory MP Dr Sarah Wollaston in December 2017.

Committees publish their findings on the UK Parliament website, and the government usually has 60 days to reply to the committee's recommendations, either in a self-published report (**Command Paper**), or a memo to the committee.

Committees give the legislature the power to demand answers and responses from the government. However, the government responses are not always to the committee's liking (as in the case study on the next page).

Joint Committees

Joint Committees are made up of MPs and members of the House of Lords. They work in a very similar way to Select Committees. Two Joint Committees – Human Rights, and Statutory Instruments (which examines legislation) – meet regularly.

contd

Case Study: Home Affairs Select Committee and Drugs Policy

In 2012, the Home Affairs Committee decided to investigate UK drugs policy.

22 April: Comedian and former drug addict Russell Brand was called as one of many witnesses. He states: 'What I think we need to do is address the social, mental and spiritual problems that are leading young people, or people of all ages, into taking drugs.'

3 July: Right Hon Kenneth Clarke QC MP, Lord Chancellor and Secretary of State for Justice, gives evidence.

3 December: Committee findings are published, including a recommendation for a 'fundamental review of all UK drugs policy', including exploring the idea of decriminalisation, through the establishment of a Royal Commission.

10 December: Prime Minister David Cameron rejected this proposal, stating:

'I don't support decriminalisation. We have a policy which actually is working in Britain. Drugs use is coming down, the emphasis on treatment is absolutely right, and we need to continue with that to make sure we can really make a difference. Also, we need to do more to keep drugs out of our prisons.'

'These are the government's priorities and I think we should continue with that rather than have some very, very long-term Royal Commission.'

VIDEO LINK

Watch Russell Brand giving evidence at www.brightredbooks.net

ONLINE

Read more about Cameron rejecting calls for a Royal Commission on drugs at www.brightredbooks.net

LEGISLATIVE COMMITTEES

After a bill has had its First and Second Reading, the bill is normally passed to a specially-formed legislative committee for consideration. These may be Public Bill Committees, Private Bill Committees, or general legislative committees. These committees take written evidence (which anyone may submit), and may call for written and/or oral evidence from witnesses. The first witness is usually the government minister of the relevant department.

Legislative Committees have between 16 and 50 members, and membership is shared between the parties in proportion to the number of MPs each party has. This means that overall there is always a government majority of committee members.

MPs can seek to limit the government's power by amending bills which the government puts forward in parliament. These may or may not be accepted by a committee. In June 2012, Ian Murray (Labour, Edinburgh South) proposed an amendment to the government's Enterprise and Regulatory Reform Bill:

'The purpose of our amendments is to make employment tribunals less complicated... Business is demanding that; the trade unions are demanding a simpler and more effective procedure; employers are demanding that, and employees are also demanding it.'

Because the government usually dominates the membership of a committee, it is often difficult for opposition MPs to have their amendments passed. In the above example, Ian Murray's amendment was defeated 13–7, by a Committee chaired by a Conservative MP and attended by 11 Conservative MPs and one Liberal Democrat.

DON'T FORGET

While both Select and Legislative Committees can call witnesses and summon government ministers to testify, only Legislative Committees can directly amend legislation.

THINGS TO DO AND THINK ABOUT

1. Find an up-to-date example of a minister being called as a witness in a Select Committee inquiry.
   - **a** Was the committee supportive of their recent actions?
   - **b** How did the minister cope with the questions?
2. Find examples of your constituency MP acting in committees:
   - **a** asking a question in a select committee
   - **b** proposing an amendment in a legislative committee.
3. Essay practice: Analyse the role of committees in influencing decision-making. You should refer to committees in Scotland or the UK or both in your answer. (12)

ONLINE TEST

How well have you learned about this topic? Head to www.brightredbooks.net and take the test.

ROLE OF THE UK LEGISLATURE: THE HOUSE OF LORDS

Unlike the Scottish Parliament, the UK Parliament has two houses: the House of Commons and the House of Lords. This type of system is called a **bicameral legislature**.

FACT 

Members of the Lords submit about 10 000 written questions to the government annually.

Party/group	Peers	
Conservative	244	Government
Labour	180	Opposition 281
Liberal Democrat	92	
Other Parties	9	
Crossbench	187	Neutral 243
Non-affiliated	49	
Others	7	
Bishops	26	
Total	794	

House of Lords membership (January 2020)

VIDEO LINK 

What is the House of Lords? Watch the clip at www.brightredbooks.net

DON'T FORGET 

Peers are there to add a long-term, experienced opinion to bills, policies and decisions.

ONLINE TEST 

Head to www.brightredbooks.net and test yourself on this topic

MEMBERSHIP OF THE HOUSE OF LORDS

There are around 800 Members of the House of Lords. There are three types of members, or **peers**, all of whom are unelected.

Most members of the Lords are **life peers**, officially appointed by the Queen. They are either recommended by the Prime Minister, or the independent Appointments Commission. Those recommended by the Prime Minister have been called **working peers**, and are expected to frequently attend the House or Lords. Experienced MPs are often appointed as working peers after leaving the House of Commons. The Appointments Commission is an independent body which recommends people based on their expertise, knowledge and experience in a specific area, like health or business. The Commission tries to 'ensure that the House of Lords represents the diversity of the people of the UK.'

Before 1999, most peers inherited their title from a parent, and this title was passed down through the generations. Since 1999, these titles – **excepted hereditary peers** – became life peerages, and upon leaving the house (or dying) each peer's place is filled by an election. Only previous life peers are eligible for election, and those from within the leaving peer's party can vote.

The final 26 peers are **bishops** from the Church of England.

Hereditary peers and working peers will be party-affiliated (either government or **opposition**), while those recommended by the Appointments Commission and bishops will be non-party affiliated: **crossbenchers**.

Lords Reform

Labour, the Conservatives, and the Liberal Democrats all included **reform** of (change to) the House of Lords in their 2010 UK General Election manifestos. The SNP wants to scrap the House of Lords completely. In June 2012, the **Coalition Government** introduced the House of Lords Reform Bill, with the intention of reducing the numbers of peers and introducing an element of election to the appointment of peers. This would have given a House of Lords consisting of 360 elected members (elected to serve one 15-year term in batches of 120, every five years); 90 appointed members; up to 12 Church of England Bishops; and any ministerial members (of the government). However, in August 2012, the then Deputy Prime Minister **Nick Clegg** (Liberal Democrat) announced the Bill would be abandoned, as he saw that it would not pass without the Conservatives guaranteeing it time in the House of Commons in a **programme motion**.

In the period since 2012 there have been minor changes to the House of Lords including legislation covering female bishops (Lords Spiritual Act 2015) and expulsions (House of Lords Expulsion and Suspension Act 2015). Further, an inquiry launched by the Lord Speaker (Burns Report) was held in late 2017 which recommended a reduction in numbers of peers to 600, peers to be appointed for 15-year terms and at least 20% of peers would be independents/crossbenchers. In late 2019, a report in the Financial Times claimed Boris Johnson's Conservative Government was considering radical plans to overhaul the House of Lords. The SNP continue to argue for abolition of the Lords, with Labour under Kier Starmer supporting this position.

contd

THE WORK OF THE HOUSE OF LORDS

The House of Lords exists to work in partnership with the House of Commons, but is independent of it. It assists in making laws, scrutinising bills, and scrutinising the actions of the government.

Making laws

Members of the House of Lords can introduce Private Members' Bills, in the same way that MPs can. If a Private Members' Bill in the Lords is supported by an MP, it can continue in the Commons. Similarly to MP's Members' Bills, it is highly unlikely that Private Members' Bills from the Lords will be granted much time in the Commons. Instead, introducing a Private Member's Bill is used to ensure the topic is debated in the Lords.

Scrutinising bills

The biggest single part of the work of the House of Lords is scrutinising bills, or proposed laws. Around half of the time in the House of Lords is spent doing this. As the UK Parliament is a **bicameral** legislature, and the House of Commons is usually governed by a majority government, the House of Lords performs a crucial role in limiting the power of the UK government. As peers don't have to face re-election, they can give a long-term, expert opinion on legislation, without worrying about the short-term whim of the electorate.

Peers may also join Select Committees, and help investigate proposed new laws. An example of the effectiveness of the Lords in scrutinising government legislation would be during the passing of the EU Withdrawal Bill in 2018. In total, the Lords spent over 160 hours debating the Bill and, in the process, defeated the Government 15 times. Of the 15 amendments proposed by the Lords to the Bill, the Government accepted one and made concessions others.

Since the Parliament Act 1949, the Lords cannot amend or delay Money Bills (bills about taxes or public money). Money Bills will receive Royal Assent even if the Lords doesn't pass them. It also allows for parliament to reintroduce a bill in the next parliamentary session, where it can pass unopposed.

Under the **Salisbury Convention**, the House of Lords does not vote against **manifesto** policies of the government, as this would be seem to directly undermine the wishes of the electorate.

Questions

Peers can keep a close eye on the work of the government by questioning a government spokesperson at Question Time, usually at the start of business on Mondays to Thursdays. Peers can either ask questions in person (up to four each, plus supplementary questions), or submit them in writing.

In September 2018, Lord Ouseley asked: 'What is the assessment of Her Majesty's Government of the increase in the number of children in care and how will the Government ensure that sufficient funding is in place in England and Wales to support the provision of care places?' This question was answered by Lord Agnew, Parliamentary Under Secretary of State for the School System. He said: 'The Government regularly monitor the number of children that come into contact with our child protection system and recognise that the number of children in care has risen. But the Government, as well as giving more money to councils, were improving children's social care through our £200 million Innovation Programme.'

Debates

In debates, peers add their considerable experience to the discussion of government proposals. In December 2014, Lord Alan Sugar spoke in the debate during the Second Reading of the government's Small Business, Enterprise and Employment Bill, stating: 'This Bill does not go far enough in offering practical, common-sense solutions for small businesses.' Famous from his TV show *The Apprentice*, Lord Sugar was appointed as an expert on business. His criticism made the government re-examine the details of the bill.

Motions of no confidence

The House of Lords can also debate a **motion of no confidence** in the government. This has only happened once in the modern era. In December 1993, an opposition **motion of no confidence** was defeated 95–282.

THINGS TO DO AND THINK ABOUT

1. Find a recent example of the House of Lords:
   - **a** introducing a bill
   - **b** voting on a bill
   - **c** asking a government minister a question.
2. Essay practice: Evaluate the importance of the House of Lords in decision-making in the UK. (12)

ROLE OF THE UK EXECUTIVE: THE PRIME MINISTER

The Prime Minister is the person asked by the monarch (Queen) to form the government after a UK General Election. By **convention** (what normally or traditionally has happened), the Queen will ask the leader of the party which wins most seats to form the government. With the resignation of Theresa May in response to her government's failure to pass a European Union withdrawal bill, Boris Johnson took over as Prime Minister on 24 July 2019, comfortably winning the Conservative Party leadership election. After the snap general election of December 2019, the Conservative Party won the election with a huge parliamentary majority of 80.

ONLINE 

Check out the Queen's Speech from December 2019 at the State Opening of Parliament at www.brightredbooks.net

FACT 

The State Opening of Parliament usually takes place in May or the first week of June.

FACT 

Margaret Thatcher appointed an average of 18 peers per year; Tony Blair an average of 37; Theresa May an average of 20.

POWERS OF THE PRIME MINISTER

Once appointed into the position, the Prime Minister has a range of powers.

Leader of government

The Prime Minister is responsible for the overall direction of the UK Government. At the start of each parliamentary session, or after each election, the Queen delivers the **Queen's Speech** at the State Opening of Parliament. This speech is actually written by the government, and outlines their proposed policies and legislation. The December 2019 Queen's Speech was dominated by legislation to deliver Brexit. In total there were 26 bills including several relating to Brexit and its impact on agriculture, fisheries and immigration. Other bills will propose changes in relation to domestic abuse, the environment, town centres, and education and the NHS in England and Wales.

However, these bills must pass through full parliamentary **scrutiny**, including the committee system, before becoming law.

Appointment

The Prime Minster has the power to choose whom they wish to appoint as members of the Cabinet. Usually, the winning party has a majority of seats, and the Cabinet will all be appointed from one party. However, when there is a coalition or joint party government, as there was between 2010-2015, Conservative Prime Minister David Cameron had to negotiate with his Liberal Democrat coalition partner, Nick Clegg (who was depute PM), about which MPs should be appointed to which government departments.

The Prime Minister can also appoint **life peers** to the House of Lords. This allows the Prime Minister to alter the balance of power within the House of Lords to a certain extent. There are often allegations of **cronyism** (appointing friends or allies), such as when David Cameron appointed Michael Farmer a life peer in August 2014. Farmer has donated nearly £6.5m to the Conservatives, and is the party treasurer. When Theresa May was PM she repeatedly stated she wanted to put an end to allegations of cronyism in the honours system. However, on her resignation in 2019 she handed out a number of peerages, knighthoods and other honours to her closest aides and several Conservative Party backers. For example, David Brownlow, who donated more than £2m to the Conservatives, was made a lord.

Representing the UK

The Prime Minister is responsible for representing the UK to the rest of the world. This can be in official or unofficial roles. For example, in July 2017, Theresa May met directly with the leaders of the other 28 NATO countries at a summit in Brussels to discuss current issues affecting the defence organisation.

contd

LIMITS TO THE PRIME MINISTER'S POWERS

The Prime Minister's powers rely on he or she maintaining an image as a strong and competent leader. There are a number of ways this can be called into question.

Prime Minister Boris Johnson

Prime Minister's Questions (PMQs)

For half an hour from noon every Wednesday, the Prime Minister is quizzed by MPs from the Opposition and their own government's party or parties. This is seen as the most confrontational aspect of the UK Parliament's work, leading to heated debates mainly between the leader of the Opposition and the Prime Minister. Questions for PMQs can be submitted by any MP up until three days before PMQs. The session usually starts with the **open question**, a routine question about the Prime Minister's plans for that day. The MP who asked this question is then allowed to ask a **supplementary question**: their real question. Many MPs will submit the open question each week, so if their name is drawn they can ask a question on any topic.

The **Leader of the Opposition** is permitted to ask six questions in total in each session and is the only MP allowed to ask further questions on different topics. The Leader of the Opposition and MPs use PMQs as an opportunity to undermine the Prime Minister and his or her government. In theory, the Prime Minister will not know the topic of any supplementary question, nor any question the Leader of the Opposition will ask. However, the Prime Minister has the benefit of extensive research carried out by government departments (within the Civil Service), who try to ensure that he or she has a good grounding on any topics likely to come up.

Motion of no confidence

To effectively lead the government and the country, the Prime Minister must be trusted to do the job in the proper fashion. While Parliament obviously contains many opponents of the Prime Minister and government, they rarely officially question their position.

Under the Fixed Term Parliaments Act 2011, the wording of a **motion of no confidence** is set as 'That this House has no confidence in Her Majesty's Government'. If this is passed by a majority of voting MPs, the Prime Minister has 14 days to form a new government, or an early General Election is called. The most recent example of a **motion of no confidence** having an impact was the ending of the Labour Government of 1979 by one vote (and subsequent Conservative victory). In January 2019, Theresa May's Government saw off a motion of no confidence by 325 votes to 306.

DON'T FORGET

A Prime Minister's success depends on them being seen as competent in the eyes of parliament, their government and party, and the British public.

Leadership challenges

One limit to the power of the Prime Minister is challenges to their leadership from within their party or government. As parties often include individuals with opposing political views relating to specific issues, a Prime Minister must work to balance these opposing views, be they in cabinet, government or across their party. When PM, Theresa May struggled to keep on side those in the Conservative Party who want the UK to leave the EU ('Brexiteers') and those who wish the UK to stay in the EU or continue to have close relations with the EU ('Remainers'). In July 2018, the differences between Brexiteers and Remainers surfaced spectacularly with the resignation of several Conservative MPs from Cabinet and Government in protest at May's proposed relationship with the EU after Brexit (the Chequers blueprint). By September, at least 50 Conservative MPs (European Research Group) met and openly discussed how they could force Theresa May to stand down.

FACT

The 2018 Queen's Speech was cancelled to give MPs more time to deal with Brexit laws.

THINGS TO DO AND THINK ABOUT

1 Review the progress of the bills in the 2019 Queen's Speech: http://www.youtube.com/watch?vMN4pNOTToOg

   a What bills were proposed?

   b Did all the proposed bills pass?

2 Essay practice: Analyse the view that Parliament has little opportunity to control the powers of the Prime Minister. (12)

ONLINE TEST

Test your knowledge of the Prime Minister's role at www.brightredbooks.net

ROLE OF THE UK EXECUTIVE: THE UK GOVERNMENT

The UK Government is responsible for making and carrying out policies on the reserved powers. Depending on the share of seats after each election, the government will either be a **coalition** (made up of members from more than one party), **minority** (made up of one party which has fewer than half the seats in parliament) or **majority** (where the winning party has more than half the seats in parliament). After the 2019 General Election, the Conservatives had an 80 seat majority government.

ONLINE 

Who's who in Boris Johnson's cabinet? Follow the link at www.brightredbooks.net to find out.

Alister Jack

THE CABINET

The Cabinet is the central decision-making body of the UK Government. It is made up of the Prime Minister and other senior ministers (usually called **Secretaries of State**), who are each responsible for the work of a government department. Cabinet members are usually MPs. Cabinet meetings take place once a week, usually in 10 Downing Street but occasionally elsewhere.

The Prime Minister can appoint whomever they like to be in their Cabinet, based on their expertise in that subject area. If the government is a majority government, the ministers will all be members of the same party. For example, Robert Buckland, Lord Chancellor and Secretary of State for Justice, was a lawyer with extensive experience before entering politics. In February 2020, there were 22 people in Boris Johnson's cabinet including Alister Jack, Secretary of State for Scotland. Two of the cabinet – Baroness Evans of Bowes Park and Baroness Nicky Morgan – are peers in the House of Lords

If the government is in coalition (like the Conservative–Liberal Democrat government of 2010–2015), then the Cabinet will be made up of members of both parties. The Rt Hon **Vince Cable** MP (Liberal Democrat, Twickenham) was the Business Secretary for five years.

Junior ministers

The Prime Minister also appoints junior ministers, who assist the Secretaries of State by taking responsibility for a particular area within a department. In December 2019, Douglas Ross was appointed Parliamentary Under-Secretary of State for Scotland.

POWERS OF THE UK GOVERNMENT

FACT 

A confidence-and-supply agreement is one whereby another party will support the government in motions of confidence or budget votes, by either voting in favour of the government or abstaining.

The main power of the UK Government is to propose legislation, called **Government Bills**. Usually, the UK Government is elected with a majority, and so can deliver the majority of its manifesto commitments. The Conservative Government elected in December 2019 is expected to pass most if not all of its legislative programme given its large 80 seat majority. This was not the case with Theresa May's 2017 minority Conservative Government. At that time the Conservatives entered into a confidence deal with Northern Ireland's Democratic and Unionist Party (DUP) to support the government.

Under a coalition, both (or all) parties in government have to agree to policy before it can be introduced. This may be problematic as it may involve compromises to be made between the coalition partners' differing manifesto policies on the area, or trade-offs to be made as regards a different policy area. David Cameron was aware of the difficulties of coalition government, and stated in 2013: 'I prefer a more decisive form of government.'

In coming up with policy, Secretaries of State and junior ministers are each supported by staff in the **Civil Service**. The Civil Service is divided into departments, agencies, and non-departmental government bodies (NDPBs). Civil servants (those who work for the Civil Service) are not party-affiliated and so their expertise is not lost if one party

contd

loses a General Election. There are more than 430 000 civil servants who work for the UK Government overall.

Collective responsibility

Most decisions regarding government departments are agreed either in Cabinet committees, discussions and negotiations between departments, or in meetings between the Prime Minister and the relevant minister. Cabinet, therefore, is somewhat of a rubberstamp of pre-arranged decisions. If two (or more) ministers disagree about a decision, they may take it to Cabinet, but only in exceptional circumstances.

The UK Government operates on the basis of **collective responsibility**. This means that once a decision has been made by the government, all members of the government have to support this decision and, in the main, this is what happens. To protect this, the minutes (written record) of Cabinet meetings are kept secret on a 'need to know' basis.

Almost since becoming Prime Minister, Theresa May struggled to ensure collective cabinet responsibility. Following the divisive EU referendum vote of June 2016, a split within the Cabinet emerged over what form Brexit should take. Many "Remainers" within the cabinet leant towards a 'soft' Brexit where the UK retains close links with the EU, has access to the single market and stays within the customs union, while most "Brexiteers" favoured a 'hard' Brexit where the UK makes a clean break from the EU to allow the UK control over its borders, to make its own trade deals and to apply only UK law within this country. In July 2018, May moved to restore cabinet collective responsibility by telling ministers they would face the sack if they diverged from the soft-Brexit plan.

Find out more about Brexit at the Digital Zone www.brightredbooks.net/subjects

Vince Cable tells Lib Dem conference Tories have reverted to 'nasty party' (2013): www.brightredbooks.net

However, in reasserting her authority, May forced the resignation of two of her cabinet ministers – David Davis, Secretary of State for the UK Exiting the EU and Foreign Secretary, Boris Johnson. Both Davis and Johnson believed her EU Brexit plan was wrong and rather than support collective cabinet responsibility they chose to resign. Thereafter, a number of other Conservative MPs also resigned their office. After his election as Conservative Party leader and then Prime Minister in July 2019, Johnson made it absolutely clear that anyone who wished to be in the Cabinet would have to fully back his Brexit plan. This decision resulted in 17 members of Theresa May's former senior ministers being axed or stepping down.

CHECKS ON THE GOVERNMENT

There are many ways in which the legislature (parliament) can scrutinise the UK Government, limiting its power.

Motions of no confidence

MPs who are not satisfied with the actions in, or abilities to perform, their role, they can put forward a **motion of no confidence** in a government minister or junior minister. In October 2014, there was a **motion of no confidence** in Lord Freud, Parliamentary Under-Secretary for Welfare Reform, after he suggested that disabled workers could be paid less than the minimum wage. The **motion of no confidence** was defeated by 302–243 votes. In January 2019, Theresa May's Government saw off a motion of no confidence by 325 votes to 306

Question Time

Question Time is an opportunity for MPs to question Ministers and Parliamentary Under-Secretaries probing questions about the areas they are responsible for. This takes place at the start of each day's sitting, Monday to Thursday. Which government department answers questions is decided by a rota called the Order of Oral Questions.

Urgent Questions can also be asked to a minister when the Speaker agrees it is in the public interest. Shadow Health Secretary, Jonathon Ashworth, asked an urgent question on the Government's strategy to tackle childhood obesity in June 2018.

The success of a government depends on its effective delivery of policy, and strength of leadership and of party unity.

Test your knowledge of the role of the UK Government at www.brightredbooks.net/subjects

THINGS TO DO AND THINK ABOUT

1 Keep an eye on any Cabinet reshuffles. Who keeps their job, and who is moved on?
2 Find an edition of Ministerial Question Time on **Hansard**.
   a What are the ministers asked? **b** How well do they answer the questions?
3 Evaluate the effectiveness of MPs in scrutinising government. You should refer to parliamentary representatives in Scotland or the United Kingdom or both in your answer. (20)

ROLE OF THE SCOTTISH LEGISLATURE: THE PARLIAMENT CHAMBER

MSPs are elected to represent their constituents in the Scottish Parliament. The most high-profile way they can do this is in the Scottish Parliament Chamber.

DEBATES

Debates in the Scottish Parliament give MSPs the chance to formally discuss bills and consider issues brought forward by an MSP from the government or opposition, or from a committee.

Firstly, the Presiding Officer introduces the topic of the debate, and requests that MSPs press their 'request-to-speak' buttons. The Presiding Officer decides who will speak in a debate, and for how long, based on the number of MSPs who wish to contribute. By contributing to a debate, MSPs can raise their constituents' concerns during this discussion.

If the discussion becomes heated, the Presiding Officer will enforce the rules of parliament. In February 2016, after a rowdy session of First Minister's Questions, the Presiding Officer wrote to Labour MSP Neil Findlay warning him about his conduct after he called the First Minister a "liar". Neil Findlay asked to withdraw his "unparliamentary" remark but said he wanted to replace it with "dishonest". Findlay was told any repeat of his behaviour and language would mean an automatic referral to the Standards, Procedures and Public Appointments Committee.

ONLINE 

Find out about Neil Findlay being given a warning by the Presiding Officer at www.brightredbooks.net

MSPs can hold the government to account during these debates, raising issues which seek to highlight the government's failings, or undermine their achievements. In August 2018, Neil Findlay MSP (Labour Lothian) introduced motion (Question S5W-18468) which asked the Scottish Government about the steps it was taking to address concerns that further education institutions were receiving adequate funding for student support. The question was answered by Richard Lochhead MSP (Moray) and Minister for Further Education, Higher Education and Science, who replied that the Scottish Government is supporting Further Education students with record levels of support.

Parliamentary votes

DON'T FORGET 

Debates and votes are two of the most high-profile ways in which MSPs can represent their constituents.

Decisions in the Scottish Parliament, in a debate or on a bill, are made by a vote. Unlike the UK Parliament, MSPs vote using digital consoles. Almost all votes are held at **Decision Time**, held at 5pm when parliament meets on Mondays to Thursdays, or noon when it meets on a Friday. Votes are held on most of the issues discussed that day.

Because the Scottish Government is usually a coalition or minority government, it normally has to rely on the support of other parties and other MSPs to allow it to win votes at Decision Time. However, in the two plus years between the May 2016 Scottish Parliament election and September 2018, the SNP minority Scottish government lost one vote in the parliament (on the use of standardised national tests for pupils in primary one, Sept. 2018). The success of the SNP Government in getting its legislative programme through parliament is partly explained by the fact that the SNP Government sit just three MSPs short of an overall majority, but also because the SNP Government have managed to secure support from other parties when taking decisions e.g. securing the support of the Scottish Green Party in respect of the Scottish Government budget for 2018–19.

ONLINE 

Find out more about the passing of the Scottish Parliamentary Budget for 2018–19 at www.brightredbooks.net

In contrast, the majority government formed by the SNP after the 2011 General Election allowed unprecedented opportunities for one-party dominance.

Parliamentary votes do allow MSPs from opposition parties, and indeed from within the government, to strongly express their or their constituents' opposing view.

In September 2013, three SNP MSPs (Christine Grahame, chair of the Justice Committee, Sandra White and Stewart Maxwell) rebelled and voted against a government motion to deduct any imprisoned MSP's pay by 90% for the time of their imprisonment.

contd

Members' business debates

Business debates take place on a motion proposed by an MSP who is not a minister or a Cabinet secretary. These usually highlight local issues which may not otherwise gain national attention. These are given 45 minutes at the end of each day's sitting, and no votes are taken. In September 2018, Scottish Green Party Joint Leader Patrick Harvie (Glasgow), used a Members' Business Debate to congratulate ApparelXchange, a Glasgow-based social enterprise, which aims to promote reuse and recycling of school uniforms to reduce costs to families and prevent the waste of resources.

QUESTION TIME

General Question Time and Portfolio Question Time are opportunities for MSPs to question Cabinet secretaries and government ministers about decisions they have made or matters which are under their department's remit. The MSPs who get to ask a question are selected randomly by computer from all those who have submitted their names by noon on the Monday. The MSP must submit their question by noon on the Wednesday. Question Time allows MPs to keep a close check on the government, and the work they are doing. In August 2018, Conservative Liz Smith MSP (Mid Scotland and Fife) asked the Scottish Government whether parents of P1 pupils were entitled, in law, to withdraw their children from standardised national tests.

The minister always has the chance to respond, though, and will usually be very well prepared to answer any question, as they must be submitted in advance. In this case, John Swinney MSP (Perthshire North), Deputy First Minister and Cabinet Secretary for Education and Skills, answered by saying that virtually all aspects of the Scottish curriculum and its delivery are not provided for in legislation. This means standardised tests cannot be seen as compulsory. However, he continued by saying that there isn't a legal right for parents or carers to withdraw their children from the tests. To that end, if parents or carers had concerns about the tests they should discuss these with the school.

First Minister's Question Time (FMQs)

For half an hour from 12 noon every Thursday, it is the turn of the First Minister to be questioned by MSPs. This is seen as the most confrontational aspect of the Scottish Parliament's work, and can lead to fiery debates, primarily between the opposition party leaders and the First Minister.

Questions for FMQs that week can be submitted by any MSP at any point between the end of the previous FMQs and noon on the Monday. The Presiding Officer selects the questions based on a number of criteria, including that 'a reasonable political balance between the parties is maintained over time', and how often an MSP has asked questions before. MSPs are permitted to ask follow-on questions, which the First Minister will not have read in advance. However, the First Minister has the benefit of extensive research carried out by government departments, who try to ensure that they have a good grounding on any topic which is likely to come up

Opposition party leaders and MSPs often seek to undermine or humiliate the First Minister and their government. In March 2018, Scottish Liberal Democrat leader Willie Rennie challenged First Minister Nicola Sturgeon on what he claimed was delayed spending on mental health care services for young people in Scotland. He asked whether or not she had mental health service waiting times "under control". In her robust reply, the First Minister admitted mental health services for young people were in need of improvement but the Minister for Mental Health was meeting with a number of health boards and other groups to plan for an improvement in the delivery of future services.

THINGS TO DO AND THINK ABOUT

1 Watch a recent edition of First Minister's Question Time.
   a Note the topics they are quizzed upon.
   b Do they seem to respond successfully?
2 Find a recent example of your MSP contributing in the chamber in the ways described above.
3 Essay practice: Analyse the view that parliamentary representatives have few opportunities to represent their constituents in parliament. (12)

Test yourself on this topic at www.brightredbooks.net

ROLE OF THE SCOTTISH LEGISLATURE: COMMITTEES

Committees play a vital role in the work of the Scottish Parliament. The Scottish Parliament is **unicameral** (has only one house) so the committees are even more important than they are in the UK Parliament.

Committees are heavily involved in scrutinising the laws that government or MSPs want to make, and do this to make sure that the decisions made are the best possible for Scotland.

Mandatory	Subject
Standards, Procedures and Public Appointments Committee	Economy, Energy and Fair Work Committee
Finance and Constitution Committee	Education and Skills Committee
Public and Post Legislative Scrutiny Audit Committee	Health and Sport Committee
Environment, Climate Change and Land Reform Committee	Justice Committee
Equality and Human Rights Committee	Justice Sub-Committee on Policing
Public Petitions Committee	Local Government and Communities Committee
Rural Economy and Connectivity Committee	Rural Affairs, Climate Change and Environment Committee
	Social Security Committee

Selected Scottish Parliament Committees [September 2016]

2011–2016	2016–2021
Delegated Powers and Law Reform	Culture, Tourism, Europe and External Affairs
Finance	Environment, Climate Change and Land Reform Committee
Justice	Equalities and Human Rights Committee
Education and Culture	Finance and Constitution Committee
European and External Relations	Local Government and Communities Committee
Local Government and Regeneration	Pow of Inchaffray Drainage Commission (Scotland) Bill Committee
Rural Affairs, Climate Change and Environment	Social Security Committee
Infrastructure and Capital Investment	Standards, Procedures and Public Appointments Committee
8 out of 15	*8 out of 18*

SNP Committees conveners

TYPES OF COMMITTEE

Committees are formed after each Scottish General Election. **Mandatory committees** must be formed to cover the same policy area after every election. **Subject committees** may be slightly different after each election, according to government priorities. For example, education fell under the remit of the Education and Culture Committee in the 4th Session (2011–2016) but fell under the Education and Skills committee in the 5th session 2016–2021.

There can also be **Bill Committees**, formed when a specific bill does not fit clearly within the remit of one of the other committees. The Referendum (Scotland) Bill Committee was formed in October 2012, with a remit to consider matters relating to the referendum. In October 2014 (after the referendum), it became the 'Devolution (Further Powers) Committee'. More recently, the Hutchesons' Hospital Transfer and Dissolution (Scotland) Bill Committee was established in April 2017. It will see the transfer of the property, rights, interests and liabilities of the Royal Incorporation of Hutchesons' Hospital in Glasgow to a successor and repeal the Hutchesons' Hospital Act 1982.

MEMBERSHIP OF COMMITTEES

Each committee in the Scottish Parliament is made up of between five and 15 MSPs, although in practice, most have between seven and nine members. The membership of committees (when taken together) is designed to reflect the share of seats in the Scottish Parliament. The membership of each committee is proposed by the **Parliamentary Bureau** (the Presiding Officer and a representative from each party with five or more MSPs), but must be approved by a parliamentary vote.

Each committee also has a **convener** who leads each meeting. The committee members choose the convener from a party recommended by the Parliamentary Bureau and approved by the parliament. The allocation of converierships is also designed to reflect the share of seats in parliament. There is also a **Conveners Group**, chaired by the Presiding Officer. In April 2018, the Conveners Group called First Minister Nicola Sturgeon for questioning on the government's legislative programme.

MSPs join committees either because they are experienced in that policy area, or it covers an area their constituents have an interest in. For example, former Modern Studies teacher and Conservative Liz Smith MSP (Mid Scotland and Fife) is a member of the Education and Skills Committee as she has experience of working in Scottish education and a personal interest in education matters.

As the Additional Member System makes it very likely that coalition or minority governments will be formed after each election, committees can provide a very effective check on government. In such cases, the government will have a minority of committee members (overall) and conveners.

contd

However, the majority SNP Government (2011–2016) was able to dominate committees in terms of membership of key committees (like Economy, Energy and Tourism), and convenerships. Arguably, this meant that the Scottish Government is not under as much scrutiny as previous governments have been.

COMMITTEE INQUIRIES

Committees hold **inquiries** into the spending, policies and administration within their policy area. They may go on a fact-finding mission, or hold a hearing away from the Scottish Parliament if they feel it will benefit their work. Committees gather written evidence, and can call for oral evidence from witnesses. Written evidence can be submitted by anyone, while witnesses are always called by the committee.

Committees can summon a government minister to appear and justify actions in their department or indeed their government. This can be a very difficult meeting for the minister, as the issues they may be questioned on are often of high public interest. In May 2018, John Swinney MSP, Cabinet Secretary for Education and Skills was closely questioned on the attainment and achievement of school-aged children experiencing poverty and the success government policies to address this issue.

John Swinney Deputy First Minister of Scotland

Case Study – Scottish Government renewable energy targets

In 2012, the Economy, Energy and Tourism Committee decided to investigate the Scottish Government's 2020 renewable energy targets.

25 April: Donald Trump, American business tycoon and star of the American TV show *The Apprentice* was called as one of many witnesses. He claims that the placing of offshore wind turbines around Scotland's coast (including near his multi-million pound Aberdeenshire golf resort) will damage tourism.

20 June: Fergus Ewing, Minister for Energy, Enterprise and Tourism, gives evidence.

23 November: Committee findings are published. The report raised a concern that 'from the evidence we received, there is a risk that the 2020 target may not be met'.

In its formal response to the Committee report, the Scottish Government states that its updated figures, in particular as regards renewable heating, show that greater progress towards the targets had been made: 'This puts us firmly on course to achieve our 2020 target.'

VIDEO LINK

Watch John Swinney giving evidence on the attainment and achievement of school-aged children experiencing poverty to committee at www.brightredbooks.net

COMMITTEES AND LEGISLATION

Committees in the Scottish Parliament have an absolutely crucial role to play in the legislative process. As the Scottish Parliament is a unicameral legislature, committees have a great responsibility over the validity of legislation. Besides the committee responsible for the bill, only the parliament sitting together will review the details of each bill, and they only have a limited time to do this.

As soon as a bill is introduced, it is referred to the committee which will examine it, called the **lead committee**. They may also consult with other committees with an interest in the bill's subject. At this early stage, the committee will take preliminary evidence and recommend whether or not parliament should agree to the **general principles** of the bill, which determines whether it should be given any parliamentary consideration. For example, under Stage 1 of the Marriage and Civil Partnership (Scotland) Bill, which legalised same-sex marriage in Scotland, the committee heard from witnesses including the director of Stonewall Scotland (a gay rights charity) and the Church of Scotland.

If parliament agrees to the general principles of the bill, the lead committee will begin to examine every aspect of the bill in minute detail.

VIDEO LINK

Watch Donald Trump giving evidence at www.brightredbooks.net

DON'T FORGET

Committees in Scotland are particularly important, as there is no second chamber (like the UK House of Lords) which reviews bills.

THINGS TO DO AND THINK ABOUT

1 Find examples of your constituency MSP, or one of your list MSPs, acting in committees:

a Asking a committee witness a question.

b Proposing an amendment in a committee.

2 Essay practice: Analyse the view that committees of the Scottish Parliament have an important role in the decision-making process. (12)

ONLINE TEST

How well have you learned about this topic? Head to www.brightredbooks.net and take the test.

ROLE OF THE SCOTTISH GOVERNMENT: THE FIRST MINISTER

FACT 

Election of Nicola Sturgeon as First Minister: 19 November 2014

Candidate	Party	Votes
Nicola Sturgeon	SNP	66
Ruth Davidson	Conservative	15
Abstain		39

OVERVIEW

The First Minister is elected by MSPs after each Scottish Election (or if the First Minister leaves office) but is officially appointed by the Queen. Nicola Sturgeon was elected First Minister of Scotland in November 2014 after Alex Salmond stood down following the independence referendum. All Labour, Liberal Democrat and Green MSPs in attendance chose to **abstain** (not vote).

All five full-time First Ministers so far have been the leader of the largest party in parliament.

Name	Party	Term	Reason for leaving
Donald Dewar	Labour	May 1999 – October 2000	Died in office
Henry McLeish	Labour	October 2000 – November 2001	Resigned over Officegate (controversial office expenses)
Jack McConnell	Labour	November 2001 – May 2007	Party came second in 2007 Election
Alex Salmond	SNP	May 2007 – November 2014	Resigned after referendum defeat
Nicola Sturgeon	SNP	November 2014 -	

Scotland's First Ministers

POWERS OF THE FIRST MINISTER

Once elected (and appointed) to their position, the First Minister has a range of powers.

Leader of government

The First Minister is responsible for the overall direction of the Scottish Government. After each election, being appointed to the role, or at another key point in the parliament session, the First Minister will publicly announce the overall plans of their government. After the 2016 Scottish Parliament election, the SNP was returned as the largest party with Nicola Sturgeon continuing as First Minister. Included in her 15 bill 2016-17 legislative programme were a Child Poverty Bill, a Domestic Abuse Bill and a Social Security Bill.

However, these bills must pass through full parliamentary scrutiny, including the committee system, before becoming law. In September 2010, the minority SNP Government led by Alex Salmond dropped plans for an independence referendum before the 2011 election (a 2007-election manifesto pledge), realising it would not make it through a parliamentary vote.

Cabinet appointment

The First Minister has the power to appoint members of the Cabinet. These nominations must be approved by a parliamentary vote before they are appointed in the role. Nicola Sturgeon announced her first Cabinet on 21 November 2014, but these appointments only became official when parliament approved of the nominations some days later.

First Minister Nicola Sturgeon

In appointing a **coalition** government (for example, 1999–2003 and 2007), the First Minister has to negotiate with the leader(s) of their junior coalition partner(s) about whom should be appointed, and to which roles.

If the First Minister presides over a minority government, there can be a risk of their nominations to Cabinet being outvoted. At the parliamentary sitting where appointments are debated, all other party leaders are given the opportunity to voice their opposition to their appointments. When Alex Salmond's first government appointments were debated in May 2007, opposition leaders moved amendments calling for the removal of John Swinney and Richard Lochhead. However, there is little chance of opposition parties agreeing on alternative candidates for these roles, who they could then persuade the First Minister to nominate for appointment. The opposition is largely symbolic, and opposition parties rarely vote against appointments; choosing instead to **abstain** (not vote).

contd

In June 2018, FM Nicola Sturgeon reshuffled her cabinet and expanded the number of ministers from 10 to 12. One MSP who continued in his post was John Swinney MSP who retained his post as Cabinet Secretary for Education and Deputy First Minister.

Representing Scotland

The First Minister of Scotland is responsible for representing Scotland to the rest of the world. This can be in official or unofficial roles.

In October 2017, Nicola Sturgeon met with the Irish Prime Minister Leo Varadkar to discuss the impact of Brexit on Ireland and Scotland. A year earlier, in June 2016, she had previously met with EU officials including EU Commission President Jean-Claude Juncker.

On the other hand, any criticism of the Scottish Government lands squarely with the First Minister. For example, in February 2016, the Scottish Government was criticised by a number of MSPs from other parties for allowing publicly owned Prestwick airport to be used for US frontline military operations. However, Nicola Sturgeon stated that it had no part to play in Prestwick's decisions and that military flights were a matter for aviation authorities controlled by the UK government.

LIMITS TO THE FIRST MINISTER'S POWERS

The First Minister's powers rely on them maintaining an image as a strong and competent leader. There are a number of ways this can be called into question.

First Minister's Questions (FMQs)

The First Minister must face tough questions from opposing MSPs at First Minister's Questions every Thursday in the parliament chamber. An unsuccessful showing at FMQs, in the full light of the media, would make the First Minister seem incapable of doing their job well.

Motion of no confidence

In order to effectively lead the government and the country, the First Minister must be trusted to do their job in the proper fashion. While the Scottish Parliament obviously contains many opponents of the First Minister, they rarely officially question their position.

If the first minister or any Scottish government minister is believed to have broken parliamentary rules or intentionally misled parliament, then a No Confidence Motion can be debated. In 2020, John Swinney, Deputy FM and Cabinet Secretary for Education and then in 2021 FM Nicola Sturgeon, were both subject to a no confidence vote. However, in both instances the no confidence vote failed to attract majority parliamentary support.

Leadership challenges

One possible limit to the power of the First Minister would be challenges to their leadership from within their party or government. The potential for this is much greater when there is a coalition government, as the government and Cabinet will not be united by party loyalty to one leader. However, even in the case of Henry McLeish's resignation as First Minister in a Lab–Lib coalition government, the Liberal Democrats supported him throughout the scandal.

THINGS TO DO AND THINK ABOUT

1 Using the Scottish Parliament's website (https://external.parliament.scot/parliamentarybusiness/Bills/72402.aspx), describe three pieces of recent SP legislation and three pieces of current SP legislation.

2 Find out why the Conservatives proposed a motion of no confidence in Henry McLeish.

3 Essay practice: Evaluate the importance of the First Minister in decision-making in Scotland. (12)

VIDEO LINK

Watch Alex Salmond's resignation at www.brightredbooks.net

VIDEO LINK

Watch Nicola Sturgeon's acceptance speech after being re-elected as First Minister in May 2016 at www.brightredpublishing.net

DON'T FORGET

A First Minister's success depends on them being seen as competent in the eyes of parliament, their government and party, and the Scottish public.

ONLINE TEST

Head to www.brightredbooks.net and test yourself on your knowledge of the role of the First Minister.

ROLE OF THE SCOTTISH GOVERNMENT

The Scottish Government is responsible for making and carrying out policies on the devolved powers. Depending on the share of seats after each election, it can either be a **coalition**, **minority** or **majority**.

First Minister Nicola Sturgeon's first Cabi
(21 November 2014)

DON'T FORGET 

The nature of the Scottish electoral system (AMS) is such that a coalition is more likely in Scotland than it is the UK Parliament.

THE CABINET

The Cabinet is the central decision-making body of the Scottish Government. It is made up of the First Minister and other senior ministers, called **Cabinet Secretaries**, who are each responsible for the work of a government department. It usually meets weekly, while parliament is in session, at Bute House, Charlotte Square, Edinburgh.

The First Minister can propose whomever they like to be in their Cabinet, based on their expertise in that subject area. These members must be approved by a vote of the Scottish Parliament. If the Scottish Government is a majority government (like the SNP government from 2011–2016), then the ministers will all be members of the same party. For example, John Swinney (SNP, Perthshire North) was appointed Deputy First Minister and Cabinet Secretary for Finance, Constitution and Economy in First Minister Nicola Sturgeon's first cabinet in November 2014. He has been Cabinet Secretary for Finance since the SNP came into power in 2007. Before being elected for the first time, Mr Swinney worked for five years as a business and economic development consultant.

Jeanne Freeman MSP

If the government is a coalition government (like the Labour–Liberal Democrat governments of 1999–2003 and 2003–2007), then the Cabinet will be made up of members of both parties. In 2005, Tavish Scott (Liberal Democrat, Shetland) was appointed Minister for Transport under Labour First Minister Jack McConnell. After a Cabinet re-shuffle in May 2016, there were 12 cabinet ministers including Derek McKay, Cabinet Secretary for Finance, Economy and Fair Work, Jeane Freeman, Cabinet Secretary for Health and Sport and Humza Yousaf, Cabinet Secretary for Justice. All 12 cabinet ministers are SNP MSPs although the SNP fell just short of an overall majority.

Junior ministers

The First Minister also appoints junior ministers, who are responsible for specific policy areas. For example, Maree Todd MSP (SNP, Highlands and Islands), was appointed Minister for Children and Young People in 2018.

Maree Todd MSP

POWERS OF THE SCOTTISH GOVERNMENT

The main power of the Scottish Government is to propose legislation, called **Executive Bills**. Under a coalition, both (or all) parties in government have to agree to policy before it can be introduced. This may be problematic as it may involve compromises to be made between the coalition partners' differing manifestos policies on the area, or trade-offs to be made as regards a different policy area. For example, the Liberal Democrats agreed to join a coalition with Labour in 2003 only if a proportional representation (PR) system was adopted for local council elections, and so we now use the Single Transferable Vote (STV) for local elections.

In a minority government, the government must rely on the power of persuasion to convince other parties to vote with it. In March 2018, the Scottish Parliament voted in favour of the UK Withdrawal from the European Union (Legal Continuity) Bill. The bill, which had undergone more than 20 hours of debate and scrutiny across three weeks, was finally backed by MSPs by a margin of 95 votes to 32. The Scottish Conservatives were the only party to wholly oppose the bill, with Labour and the Greens backing it and the Lib Dems split. When elected with a majority in 2011, the SNP did not have these restrictions.

contd

In coming up with policy, Cabinet Secretaries and junior ministers are each supported by staff in the relevant Scottish Government **directorate** (department in charge of a particular policy area). The members of these **directorates** are not party-affiliated; and so their expertise is not lost if one party loses a Scottish General Election. There are more than 5 000 civil servants who work for the Scottish Government overall.

ONLINE

Check out Nicola Sturgeon's 2016 victory speech at www.brightredbooks.net

Collective responsibility

Cabinet may be invited to consider a matter which the Cabinet Secretary wishes to have advice on. If two (or more) Cabinet Secretaries disagree about a decision, they must not bring the issue to Cabinet until all other options (including meetings between those who disagree) have been tried. The Scottish Government operates on the basis of **collective responsibility**. This means that once a decision has been made by the government (either meeting together or by the Cabinet Secretary on their own), all members of the government have to support this decision. To protect this, the minutes (written record) of Cabinet meetings are kept secret on a 'need to know' basis.

Acts of the Scottish Parliament by Session

Session/Type of Government	Executive Bills	Member's Bills	Private Bills	Committee Bills	Total
2003–2007 (Coalition)	53 (80%)	3 (5%)	9 (14%)	1 (2%)	66
2007–2011 (Minority)	42 (80%)	7 (13%)	2 (4%)	2 (4%)	53
2011–2016 (Majority)	81 (94%)	3 (7%)	5 (6%)	0 (0%)	86
2016–2018 (Minority) *(Incomplete Session)*	19 (90%)		2 (10%)	0 (0%)	21

CHECKS ON THE GOVERNMENT

There are many ways in which parliament can scrutinise the Scottish Government.

Motions of no confidence

Any MSP can let the Presiding Officer know that the Scottish Government (as a group) or an individual Cabinet Secretary or junior minister is no longer trusted to carry out their role and can call for a **motion of no confidence**. If this is supported by at least 25 MSPs, the motion is given time in the parliament chamber, usually at least two days later. However, provided the government (which is bound by collective responsibility) has a majority in parliament, or can convince other members, it is likely that the vote will not pass. In May 2014, the Labour group of MSPs called for a vote of no confidence in Health Secretary Alex Neil, over his role in controversial changes to mental health services in his constituency. The vote was defeated 57–67, but Mr Neil was moved from Health to Social Justice, Communities and Pensioners' Rights in Nicola Sturgeon's first Cabinet.

Question Time

General Question Time and Portfolio Question Time are opportunities for MSPs to question Cabinet Secretaries and junior ministers about decisions they have made or matters which are under their department's remit. MSPs can scrutinise the performance of the Cabinet Secretary or minister's department (or the official themselves). In June 2018, Cabinet Secretary for Health and Sport Shona Robison (Dundee City East) resigned after three and a half years in the post. At the end of her period in office, Ms Robison had come under pressure following a series of issues at the health board in her own constituency, NHS Tayside. In the Scottish Parliament, Labour's Anas Sarwar (Glasgow) put a number of questions to her and also made more than a dozen calls for her to quit the cabinet. MSPs later held a debate focusing mainly on her future, at which the SNP accepted the wording of a Conservative motion concluding that "failing sustained and immediate action, the Cabinet Secretary for Health and Sport should be held accountable for the ongoing problems" at NHS Tayside.

MSPs can also highlight perceived failings of (members of) the Cabinet during First Minister's Question Time. In Alex Salmond's last FMQs as First Minister, Jackie Baillie (Labour, Dumbarton) asked: 'Given their record of failure, which members of the First Minister's Cabinet would he recommend should keep their jobs when his deputy takes over?'

DON'T FORGET

The success of a government depends on its effective delivery of policy, and unity.

ONLINE TEST

Head to www.brightredbooks.net and test yourself on your knowledge of the role of the Scottish Government.

THINGS TO DO AND THINK ABOUT

1 Using the quote from Jackie Baillie as an internet search term, find out:
   a which members of Alex Salmond's Cabinet she criticised directly.
   b what happened to each of these when Nicola Sturgeon announced her first Cabinet.

2 Evaluate the effectiveness of parliamentary representatives in holding the Scottish Government to account. (12)

LOCAL GOVERNMENT IN SCOTLAND

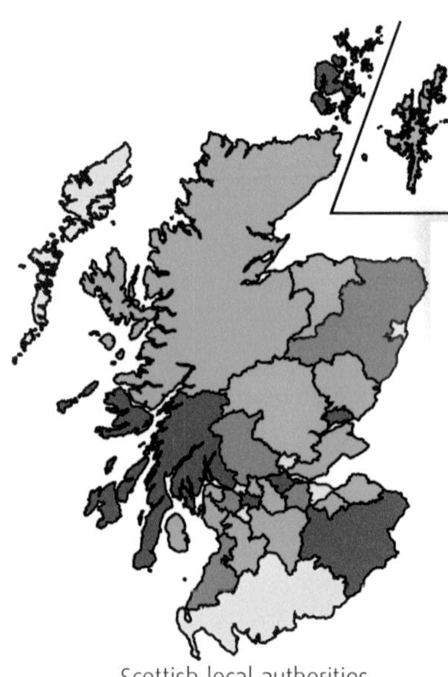

Scottish local authorities
Each local authority is governed by a local council, elected using the Single Transferable Vote system. There are 1 227 local councillors in Scotland.

Local government in Scotland provides a range of services in a local area. Scotland is divided into 32 local authorities, ranging in size from 26 square miles in Dundee to 12 437 square miles in the Highlands, and from about 20 000 people in the Orkney Islands to over 600 000 in Glasgow.

LOCAL COUNCIL FUNDING

Most local councils get the majority (around 85%) of their money in a **General Revenue Grant** from the Scottish Government. The rest of their money comes from:

- Grants are sometimes given by the Scottish Government for **capital expenditure** (for expensive projects, like new schools or bridges).
- **Non-domestic rates** are local taxes on businesses. Local authorities with large industries tend to get a higher share from this.
- **Council Tax** is paid on each residential property (house or flat), roughly based on its value.

Comparison of council funding (2018–19 Budgets)

Funding source	City of Edinburgh	Highland Council
General revenue grant	£365.5m (37%)	£443.8m (78%)
Non-domestic rates	£340.5m (34.4%)	£0m (0%)
Council Tax	£283.1m (28.6%)	£119.6m (22%)

As the Scottish Government provides so much of local authorities' budgets, the Scottish Government can often effectively force its will onto local councils.

COSLA

The **Convention of Scottish Local Authorities** (COSLA) is an organisation which local councils can join in order to allow efficient cooperation, and to gain representation in discussions with the Scottish Government, and for nation-wide pay agreements with trade unions.

The **Concordat** was an agreement between the Scottish Government and COSLA made in 2007, 'based on mutual respect and partnership', covering a range of funding and servicing issues.

In 2015, four Labour-run local authorities (Aberdeen City Council, Glasgow City Council, Renfrewshire Council and South Lanarkshire Council) left COSLA to form a new organisation, the Scottish Local Government Partnership. They believed at that time that COSLA was not representing them effectively in negotiations with the Scottish Government, especially in terms of their funding allocation. They also complained COSLA's decision-making structures were flawed.

One council, Inverclyde, also announced its intention to leave COSLA in 2015, but reversed its decision six months later after COSLA altered its constitution to highlight the fact that there is no hierarchy between members. COSLA funding is divided up according to an area's wealth, its population demographics, and how rural or urban the population is: a very complicated formula. Some Labour councils (like Inverclyde) felt this was unfair. However, in view of these changes, all councils rejoined COSLA in 2017.

COOPERATION WITH THE SCOTTISH GOVERNMENT

Scottish Futures Trust

The SNP Government set up the Scottish Futures Trust (SFT) in 2008 in order to oversee capital spending (big building projects) by the government, government agencies, and councils. By finding ways of avoiding some of the high costs of private development, including expensive consultants' fees, these organisations have been able to save considerably more money than the £4m per year it costs to run SFT. The new Boroughmuir High School in Edinburgh (opened in 2016) is partly funded through the Scottish

contd

Government's £1.25bn 'Scotland's Schools for the Future' Programme, managed by SFT.

There has, however, been criticism of some of the delays some SFT projects have had. The new Royal Hospital for Sick Children in Edinburgh was supposed to be open by the end of 2012, but it did not open until March 2021 giving rise to calls for a review of the Scottish Futures Trust in terms of its transparency and long-term sustainability.

Tackling the 'Bedroom Tax'

When the UK Government announced it was to scrap the spare room subsidy in 2013, a moved dubbed the **'bedroom tax'** by critics, COSLA was quick to raise concerns. COSLA President David O'Neill (Labour, North Ayrshire) said: 'The huge damage it will do to our communities is not something that COSLA can support, and nor should others.'

The Scottish Government fought very hard to limit the damaging effects of this policy. In May 2014, Nicola Sturgeon announced that due to Scottish Government action, 'there will be no need for anyone to fall into rent arrears, or face eviction, as a result of the "bedroom tax"'. After negotiations between the Scottish and UK Governments, the power to set the cap on Discretionary Housing Payments was devolved to Scotland. Jackie Baillie (Labour, Dumbarton) had previously introduced a bill on the matter, and criticised the Scottish Government for what she saw as a delayed response.

CONFLICT WITH THE SCOTTISH GOVERNMENT

Council Tax

Under the Concordat, Council Tax levels have been frozen at 2007–08 levels. In December 2014, then Finance Secretary John Swinney pledged to give local authorities almost £10.85bn to run services for the next year, in exchange for maintaining the Council Tax freeze. However, stopping councils from generating extra funding by raising Council Tax has meant that councils had to make more cuts than they might have done otherwise. Aberdeen City Council finance convener Willie Young said: 'There must also be respect for local government because people voted us in to look after local services and make our own decisions on Council Tax. This policy represents centralisation at its worst.'

In 2016 the Scottish Government announced it was to end the Council Tax freeze the following year. Whilst the move was welcomed by councils – they were given the option of vary the tax by up to 3% - it also sparked an almighty political row between COSLA and the Scottish Government over local taxpayers' money being spent on a Scottish Government priority as the Scottish Government had originally planned for the extra cash raised to be spent on schools. However, with COSLA claiming the principle of local accountability was being undermined, the Scottish Government eventually backed down.

Nevertheless, the argument over local government funding rumbles on with COSLA continuing to argue that the Scottish Government is cutting direct financial support. The Scottish Government, on the other hand, argue that the total amount for local services is rising as there is extra direct funding which councils receive for services such as the attainment fund for schools or investment in health and social care partnerships.

Tourist Tax

In 2018, some councils in Scotland, including Edinburgh, announced they would like to introduce a tax on tourists. The new tourist tax or "transient visitor tax", it has been claimed, would raise extra revenue for councils and give them more control over their finances. Possible tax options could include a daily charge on each hotel room or a one-off charge as happens in many cities across the world.

The Scottish Government, on the other hand, said it had no plans for such a scheme, although as part of its Local Governance Review, it would welcome further discussions about revenue raising powers. COSLA, however, is pushing the Scottish Government to devolve more powers to local authorities so that councils can reduce their dependence on government for cash.

THINGS TO DO AND THINK ABOUT

1. Look for details of any interaction between your local council and the Scottish Government.
2. Find an example of an SFT project in your local council.
3. Essay practice: "Local government and the Scottish Government only ever come into conflict." Discuss. (20)

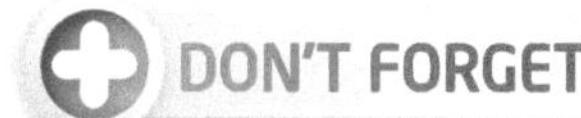

DON'T FORGET

Some councils have introduced new charges for services they provide to increase council revenues. For example, Dundee City Council has introduced a Garden Waste Charge of £35 per year.

One controversial charging proposal is the option for councils to introduce a Workplace Parking Levy (WPL). If introduced, it would see employers pay an annual levy or charge for every parking space they provide for employees.

DON'T FORGET

Local councils are **accountable** for the money they spend and the quality of services they provide.

ONLINE

Learn more about local government in Scotland by following the link at www.brightredbooks.net

ONLINE TEST

Head to www.brightredbooks.net and test your knowledge of Scottish local councils.

VOTING SYSTEMS: FIRST PAST THE POST (FPTP)

England	533
Scotland	59
Wales	40
Northern Ireland	18

Constituencies in the UK Parliament

OVERVIEW

The **First Past The Post** (**FPTP**) voting system is used to elect Members of the UK Parliament.

There are 650 seats in the UK Parliament (**constituencies**) which each elect one MP. Constituencies are roughly based on population size, with an average number of voters (**electorate**) of approximately 69 700. (England 72 200, Scotland 67 200, Northern Ireland 68 300, Wales 56 000.)

The winning candidate in each seat requires only a **plurality** (more than any other, but not a majority) to win the seat. The party which wins more seats than any other is invited by the Queen to form the government.

Every constituency must hold an election in the UK General Election, which takes place every five years (under normal circumstances) under the Fixed-term Parliaments Act 2011. In 2017 and 2019, MPs voted to dissolve Parliament early as they can if two-thirds support.

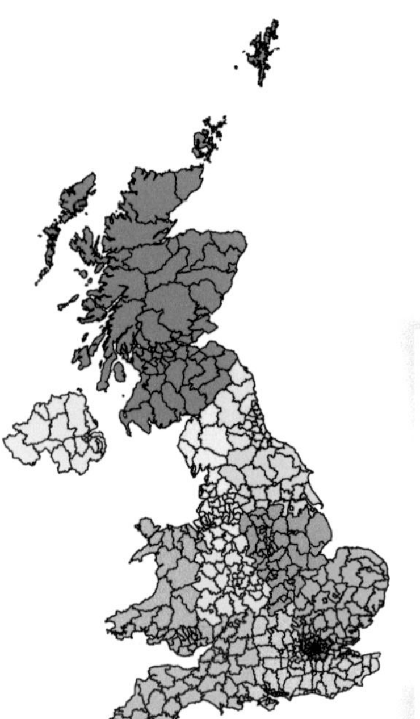

UK Parliament constituency map

BY-ELECTIONS

If a seat becomes vacant between general elections, a **by-election** must be held. The seat may become vacant due to the MP dying in office, resigning, becoming a member of the House of Lords, or in some other way becoming ineligible as an MP. By-elections can often be seen as a **protest vote**, when the electorate have a chance to voice their discontent with the government, without actually questioning the balance of power in the country.

ADVANTAGES OF FIRST PAST THE POST

Simplicity

In order to vote, voters simply mark the candidate they would like to win in the box next to their name, ideally with a cross (X). This is simpler than some other voting systems, such as those used in Scottish elections.

Additionally, each party will only put forward one candidate per seat, so voters need not do a great deal of research into the viewpoints of individual candidates; they can vote to express their party preference. An SNP supporter in Dundee West in 2019 would know Chris Law was likely to share most of the same political beliefs without having to know him personally.

Candidate	Party	Votes	% vote
Chris Law	SNP	22,355	53.8
Jim Malone	Labour	10,096	24.3
Tess White	Conservative	5,149	12.4
Daniel Coleman	Liberal Democrat	2,468	5.9
Stuart Wailton	Brexit Party	1,271	3.1
Quinta Arrey	Christian People's Alliance	240	0.6
Majority		**12,259**	**29.5**
Turnout		**41,579**	**64.5**

2019 General Election Result, Dundee West

Close Constituency – MP link

It is the job of each MP to represent all their **constituents**, including those who do not vote for them. That means that each MP is directly accountable to their constituents, so constituents must clearly know who to contact with their concerns. In Dundee West supporters of any party know that if they want an issue raised in the UK Parliament it is Chris Law whom they need to contact.

Strong, stable government

As each seat is winner-takes-all, the UK General Election almost always ends up with either a Conservative or Labour Party majority. The 7-month minority Labour Government of February–October 1974 was the only time there was not a majority government between 1945 and 2010.

Majority government means that the winning party has a clear **mandate** (authority to govern), and the other parties and the public could feel they are entitled to carry out their **manifesto** promises. Even the House of Lords will not vote against manifesto promises

contd

from a majority government, under the **Salisbury Convention**. Such parliaments are likely to pass a lot of legislation, and have clear policies and direction. However, as winning parties almost always have a majority of seats on a minority of votes, it may be seen as undemocratic as these policies, which are essentially unopposed in the parliament, were voted for by less than half of all voters. Note: In 2010 and again in 2017, unusually, no one party secured an overall majority. As a result, in 2010 the Conservatives entered into a coalition government with the Liberal Democrats. In 2017, the Conservatives agreed a confidence and supply agreement with Northern Ireland's Democratic Unionist Party (DUP). In each case, the Conservatives, with the support of the other parties, were able to form an effective government.

Party	Seats	Votes	% votes
Conservative	365	13,966,451	43.6
Labour	203	10,295,912	32.2
SNP	48	1,242,380	3.9
Liberal Democrat	11	3,696,419	11.5
Green Party	1	865,707	2.7

UK General Election Results 2019 (selected parties)

DISADVANTAGES OF FIRST PAST THE POST

Safe seats

Most of the UK General Election seats are described as **safe** (the seat is usually won by the same party in most elections). Some seats are so predictable that the Electoral Reform Society (ERS) was able to predict the winner in 316 of the 650 seats in the 2019 General Election. This was also the case in 2015 and 2017 when the ERS predicted the result in over half of the seats.

Another disadvantage of safe seats is that voters are more likely to be taken for granted by the political parties if they live in a safe seat. For example, post 2019 General Election analysis by the ERS showed that people in safe seats received far fewer election leaflets or other pieces of communication through their door compared to those voters in marginal seats. Overall, just 79 seats changed hands in the 2019 General Election which represents only 12% of all UK seats.

Disproportionality

As FPTP rewards the winning of seats, and not overall votes, there can be a huge disparity between the overall share of votes a party wins across the country, and the share of seats won. In the 2019 General Election, the Conservatives secured 43.6% of the vote but returned 56.2% of the MPs. In fact, no political party has won a majority of the vote in recent elections although in most years FPTP returns a majority government.

Disproportionality also punishes smaller parties, by rewarding the concentration of votes in fewer constituencies. This is because smaller parties tend to finish second in a lot of constituencies, while the Conservatives and Labour tend to win the seat. The Liberal Democrats in 2019 received 11.5% of the votes but only 1.7% of the MPs. Based on analysis from 649 seats, ERS analysis shows that, despite receiving over 864,743 votes, only one Green MP was returned to parliament; meanwhile, it requires 25,882 to elect each SNP MP. Brexit Party voters have also failed to see their votes transfer into party representation in Westminster, with 642,303 votes failing to elect a single MP.

In Scotland, the 2019 General Election results were also highly disproportionate. The SNP gained 45% of the vote but secured a huge 81.4% of the seats. On the other hand, Labour secured 18.6% of the vote but returned only 1.7% of the seats (one seat only – Edinburgh South). The Liberal Democrats, who had around half the share of the vote of Labour (9.5%) managed to claim four seats and the Conservatives, who benefited disproportionately outside of Scotland from FPTP only won 10.2% of the seats from a 25.1% share of the vote.

Wasted votes

As a **plurality** of votes is required to win a seat, the vast majority of votes in each constituency do not contribute to the result. This could either be votes for losing candidates, or votes for the winning candidate over the number of votes required to win. Across the UK, the figure for wasted votes in 2019 has been calculated as 45% by the Electoral Reform Society.

THINGS TO DO AND THINK ABOUT

1 Study the 2017 General Election results. Note the details of the overall result in the UK and Scotland as well as the closest constituencies to where you live.

At the 2019 General Election the most marginal seat in Scotland was Caithness, Sutherland and Easter Ross won by the Liberal Democrats with 204 votes. By contrast, the safest seat in Scotland was Falkirk won by the SNP by a majority of 14,948 votes.

ONLINE

For more details of the Guardian newspapers analysis on the visits of the party leaders to different constituencies in the run up to the 2017 General Election visit www.brightredbooks.net

ONLINE

For a closer analysis of the 2017 General Election result visit www.brightredbooks.net

ONLINE

Follow the link to the Electoral Reform Society at www.brightredbooks.net

VIDEO LINK

For more on the events of the 2017 General Election, check out the clip at www.brightredbooks.net

ONLINE TEST

Head to www.brightredbooks.net and test yourself on the FPTP voting system.

VOTING SYSTEMS: THE ADDITIONAL MEMBER SYSTEM (AMS)

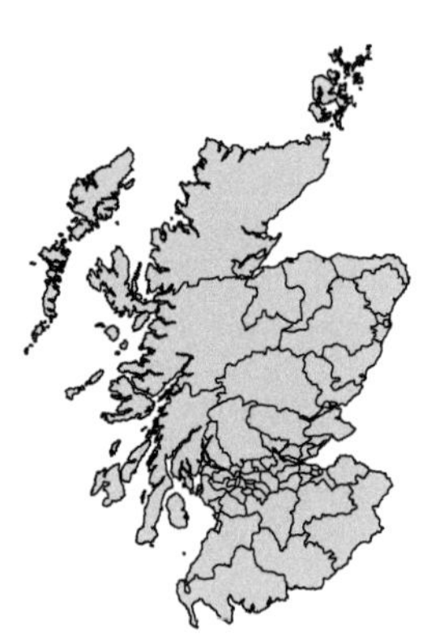

Scottish Parliament constituencies

The Additional Member System (AMS) is used to elect Members of the Scottish Parliament (MSPs). It is a **hybrid** or **mixed system**, because it uses a mixture of First Past The Post (FPTP) and a type of Proportional Representation (PR) list.

SCOTTISH PARLIAMENT CONSTITUENCIES

There are 73 Scottish Parliament constituencies, which each elect one MSP using FPTP. This means that to win each seat, the winning candidate only needs to receive one more vote than the person coming second. Just as in UK General Elections, FPTP elections in each constituency result in a **disproportionate** share of seats nationally.

SCOTTISH PARLIAMENT REGIONS

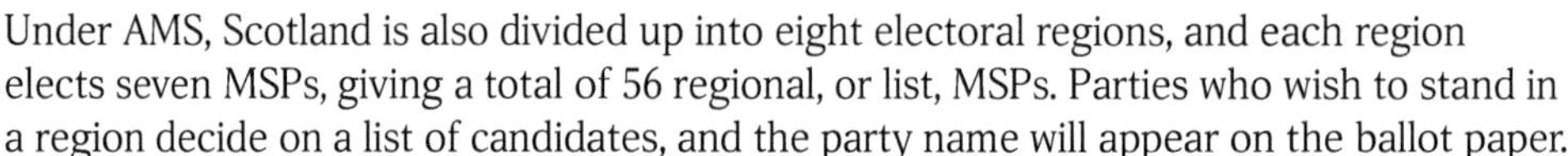

Under AMS, Scotland is also divided up into eight electoral regions, and each region elects seven MSPs, giving a total of 56 regional, or list, MSPs. Parties who wish to stand in a region decide on a list of candidates, and the party name will appear on the ballot paper.

To vote, voters mark their **preferred party** (not candidate) on the ballot paper. The order of the candidates on the list is decided by the parties themselves, and so voters have no choice in the order they are placed. Parties usually place their most important or influential candidates high up a regional list, as well as having them stand as a constituency candidate, in order to maximise their chances of being elected.

The party list element of AMS uses the **D'Hondt** formula to distribute the 56 regional seats between the parties, to give as **proportional** an overall result as possible. This works by running various rounds of counting, in which the votes for each party in that region are divided by the number of elected MSPs the party has already had elected, plus one.

Scottish Parliament regions

$$\frac{\text{votes}}{\text{seats} + 1}$$

The D'Hondt Formula

	Constituencies		Regions		Overall	
Party	**% vote**	**% seats**	**% vote**	**% seats**	**Seats**	**% seats**
SNP	47.7	84.9	40.3	3.6	64	49.6%
Conservative	21.9	6.8	23.3	46.4	31	24%
Labour	21.6	2.7	17.9	35.7	22	17%
Scottish Green	1.3	0	8.1	14.3	8	6.2
Liberal Democrat	6.9	5.5	5.1	0	4	3.1%
Others	0.6	0	5.1	0	0	0%

Scottish Parliament Election results 2021

As can be seen from the 2021 results, the under-representation of both the Scottish Conservative Party and the Scottish Labour Party after the constituency vote was balanced out by the allocation of additional list MSPs on the regional vote to make overall party representation more proportional.

BY-ELECTIONS

When a constituency seat becomes vacant between Scottish Parliament Elections, a by-election must be held. In a by-election in June 2017, Rachael Hamilton retained the constituency of Ettrick, Roxburgh and Berwickshire by-election for the Conservatives after John Lamont had resigned to stand in the 2017 UK General Election.

There is no such system in place for a regional MSP resigning from their party. In June 2017 Ross Thomson (Conservative North East Scotland) resigned his seat in the Scottish Parliament. His place was taken by another Conservative, Tom Mason.

contd

ADVANTAGES OF THE ADDITIONAL MEMBER SYSTEM

Proportionality

Using AMS means that all parties feel they have a realistic chance of gaining MSPs and that their vote share is represented in parliament. However, the system was disproportional enough to allow the SNP a majority of MSPs on a minority of the vote in 2011.

Constituency link

Constituency MSPs, elected by FPTP, ensure that each constituent knows that they have one specific MSP whose job it is to represent their area, including those who did not vote for them. Furthermore, it could be argued that the list MSPs, who are likely to be from a range of parties, allow constituents a greatly increased chance of being able to contact someone who represents both their area and the party they support, and a choice of people to contact after each election.

On the other hand, as list MSPs have not been voted in as individual candidates, some people believe they are 'second-class' MSPs, who nobody knows enough about to turn to anyway, and are therefore not as accountable as constituency MSPs.

Coalition/minority government

As AMS is broadly proportional, it is likely that the result of each election will be a coalition or minority government. In the Scottish Parliament there were Labour–Liberal Democrat coalition governments from 1999–2003 and 2003–2007, and an SNP minority government from 2007–2011 and 2016–present. This means that government decisions and Acts passed must be the result of consultation between at least two parties, and so will reflect more of the country's views than those of a majority government elected on a minority of votes.

However, while mathematically unlikely, the SNP managed to gain a majority government in 2011, despite getting a plurality of the vote (45%). This means that the SNP can carry forward their policies largely unopposed with a strong **mandate**, having been elected under a broadly proportional system. Others also argue that coalitions and minority governments are slow and inefficient ways of running a country.

ONLINE

Different electoral systems produce different results. Follow the link at www.brightredpublishing.net

Constituency	
Joe Fitzpatrick	SNP
North East Scotland Region	
Jenny Marra	Labour
Lewis MacDonald	Labour
Tom Mason	Conservative
Peter Chapman	Conservative
Bill Bowman	Conservative
Liam Kerr	Conservative
Mike Rumbles	Liberal Democrat

MSPs representing Dundee West (October 2018)

DISADVANTAGES OF THE ADDITIONAL MEMBER SYSTEM

Parties are more powerful than voters

It could be argued that parties are placed in a very powerful position, as the order of candidates is decided by political parties, and voters have no way of deciding between them. This means that candidates may campaign with their main priority being keeping the party leadership happy, rather than appealing to the voters' wishes.

Some may argue that parties perform a useful function by choosing the party lists. It could be argued that this allows them to put forward the best people for election, so voters don't have to get to know up to seven candidates from each party, before each election.

List MSPs

A number of questions have been raised about the legitimacy and importance of the regional list MSPs. Firstly, parties can place candidates as FPTP candidates and first on a region's list. Voters could feel like an unpopular candidate for a popular party should not have the right to be elected at the second chance. Secondly, they may be spread so thinly across a geographically huge area (like Highlands and Islands) that they cannot hope to effectively represent their diverse region. Finally, the lack of by-elections questions the legitimacy of some list MSPs.

The newly-formed Scottish Parliament chose AMS, above all other systems, when setting up the first elections in 1999.

ONLINE

Learn more about the Additional Member System at www.brightredbooks.net

Head to www.brightredbooks.net and test yourself on the AMS voting system.

THINGS TO DO AND THINK ABOUT

1 Essay practice: Analyse the view that the Additional Member System (AMS) leads to better representation than First Past the Post (FPTP). (12)

VOTING SYSTEMS: SINGLE TRANSFERABLE VOTE AND THE PARTY LIST

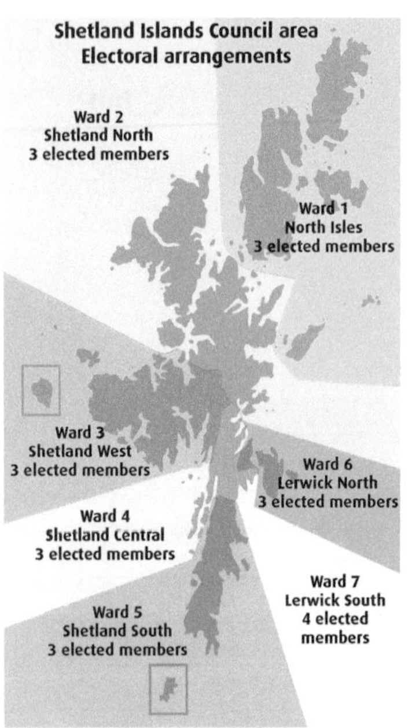

Shetland Council Wards

City of Edinburgh Council Wards

SINGLE TRANSFERABLE VOTE

The Single Transferable Vote (STV) has been used for Scottish local council elections since 2007. It was a 2003 Scottish Election manifesto policy of the Liberal Democrats, and the Lib Dems were not prepared to enter into a coalition government with Labour unless it was implemented: a deal-breaker. Up until this point, Labour had dominated Scottish local councils through the First Past the Post system.

STV is a form of proportional representation. This means that the share of representatives for each party elected in an election should closely reflect the share of votes for that party.

Scotland's 32 local authorities elect 1 227 councillors, who are elected in electoral areas called **multi-member wards**. Each **ward** elects three or four councillors. Urban, densely-populated areas have more wards than rural areas.

Voting

To vote, voters rank-order candidates in order of preference by numbering them ('1' being the first choice, '2' being next favourite, and so on). Parties often put forward multiple candidates, as they may well win more than one seat in each ward.

In order to be elected, a candidate must meet a **quota** (specific share) of votes. Once all the votes have been counted and a candidate is elected (has met the quota), any votes that candidate receives over the amount required are called **surplus votes**, and are '**re-allocated**' (redistributed) to the next preference candidates.

If the seats are not filled by the re-allocation of surplus votes, then the candidate with the fewest votes by that stage is eliminated, and their next-preference votes are re-allocated. This means nearly all votes will contribute to the result at some stage.

STV Quota formula

$$\text{Quota} = \frac{\text{Share of votes}}{\text{Number of seats available} + 1}$$

Name of Candidate	Party	Result
Mhairi Hunter	SNP	Elected (Stage 6)
Soryia Siddique	Labour	Elected (Stage 6)
Alexander Belic	SNP	Elected (Stage 7)
James Scanlon	Labour	Elected (Stage 10)
Cass MacGregor	Scottish Green	Unsuccessful (Stage 10)
Qasim Hanif	SNP	Excluded (Stage 5)
Gordon Fraser	Conservative	Excluded (Stage 4)
Lorraine Duncan	UKIP	Excluded (Stage 3)
Chris Young	Liberal Democrats	Excluded (Stage 2)
Mark Fiddy	Independent	Excluded (Stage 1)

Glasgow City Council Election results 2017: Ward 8 Southside Central – 4 seats

Advantages of Single Transferable Vote

STV gives voters far more choice than FPTP or AMS. Voters can choose not just between candidates from different parties, but in many wards can choose between candidates within a party. In 2017, there was an average of 7.3 candidates standing in each ward, compared to 3.4 in the 2003 local council election, when FPTP was used. It can be time-consuming, however, and voters may not know many candidates or have many strong preferences. In 2017, only 28.6% of ballot papers contained a fourth preference vote.

STV gives voters a real chance to have a say in the result of the election. As three or four candidates are elected in each ward, there is a strong possibility that most people's first preference candidate is elected at some stage. In 2017, around 75% of voters gave their first preference vote to a successful candidate. In the 2003 FPTP election, only 52.3% of voters voted for a successful candidate.

Year	2003	2017
Voting system	FPTP	STV
Candidates	27.7%	30.5%
Councillors	21.8%	29%

Female candidates and councillors in Scottish local elections

STV, in theory, should benefit ethnic minority and female candidates. As parties can nominate more than one candidate per ward, there is a potential electoral advantage in presenting a diverse range of candidates, as different candidates may appeal to different sections of the electorate. In the 2017 election for Glasgow's Southside Central Ward, Labour had one white male and one female ethnic minority candidate elected, and the SNP had one male candidate and one female candidate elected.

contd

Disadvantages of STV

Critics of STV claim that it is a confusing system. In 2017, 1.95% of votes were rejected, compared to 0.77% in the 1999 FPTP local council election. The most common reason for ballots being rejected (50%) is that voters indicated more than one first preference.

As each ward must elect at least three councillors, there can be extremely large wards in rural areas with a low population. In wards like Highland Council's Ward 6: Wester Ross, Strathpeffer and Lochalsh, constituents may rarely see their councillors at all.

Party	% 1st Preferences	% Seats	Councils controlled
Conservative	25.3%	22.5%	0
Green	4.1%	1.6%	0
Labour	20.2%	21.4%	0
Liberal Democrat	6.9%	5.5%	0
SNP	32.3%	35.1%	0
Independent	10.4%	14.1%	3
Others	0.7%	0.1%	0

2017 Scottish Local Council Election Results Summary

THE PARTY LIST SYSTEM

The Party List system is a proportional representation voting system, which is used to decide the regional list vote as part of the Additional Member System (AMS) in Scottish Parliament elections. It is also used to decide the regional list vote as part of the Additional Member System (AMS) used for elections to the Scottish Parliament. Under this system, the UK is divided up into 12 electoral regions, one of which is Scotland. It is called the Party List system as political parties, not candidates, appear on the ballot paper.

Voting

In Party List elections, voters simply place an 'X' next to their preferred party. Seats are allocated to the parties using the D'Hondt formula (again just like the regional list used in AMS), resulting in a broadly proportional result overall.

Advantages of the Party List

The Party List's biggest advantage is its proportionality. The share of seats each party wins is very close to the share of votes it receives nationally. However, in each region of the UK the result may be quite disproportional, such as UKIP (compared to the Greens) in Scotland.

The second advantage of the Party List system is that large, multi-member regions allow parties, potentially, the opportunity to promote under-represented groups (like ethnic minorities or women). In the 2014 elections, almost 40% of the UK's MEPs elected were women (compared to 29% of MPs), and 10% of MEPs elected were from an ethnic minority (compared to 6.6% of MPs).

Another advantage of the Party List system is that there are relatively few wasted votes. As seats are allocated through the D'Hondt system, people can vote for their preferred party knowing that party has a realistic chance of being elected.

Finally, the Party Lists system, with its large multi-member regions, saw that the vast majority of voters were represented by at least one MEP from the party they voted for. In Scotland in the 2014 election, supporters of the SNP, Labour, the Conservatives and UKIP (82% of Scottish voters) were represented by at least one MEP.

Disadvantages of the Party List

As the order of the candidates on each party's list is chosen by the party, not by voter preference, the voters have a very limited choice in who represents them. UKIP voters may have preferred Kevin Newton, who was second on their party list, but instead their votes elected David Coburn.

Secondly, in such large multi-member regions, the electorate may feel that there is a very weak **constituency link**; that their MEP was too far-removed to represent them and their interests. Scotland's five million citizens had only six MEPs to represent them.

THINGS TO DO AND THINK ABOUT

1 Essay practice: To what extent does the Single Transferable Vote (STV) electoral system provide for fairer and better representation than any other electoral system? (20)

FACT

In 2017, there were 3 **uncontested wards** (wards where there was only one candidate standing), compared to 61 **uncontested wards** in the 2003 FPTP election.

Ward	People per sq. km	Area (sq. km)
Wester Ross, Strathpeffer and Lochalsh (Highland Council)	2.4	4,948
Meadows/ Morningside (City of Edinburgh Council)	48.2	691

DON'T FORGET

There is no perfect voting system: if there was, every election would use it! Each voting system has its advantages and disadvantages.

ONLINE

The Closed Party List system is explained at www.brightredbooks.net

ONLINE TEST

Head to www.brightredbooks.net and test yourself on the STV and Party List voting system.

Party	% Votes	MEPs (%)
UKIP	27%	24 (33%)
Labour	25%	20 (27%)
Conservative	24%	19 (26%)
Green	8%	3 (4%)
SNP	2%	2 (3%)
Liberal Democrat	7%	1 (1%)
Sinn Fein*	-	1 (1%)
DUP*	-	1 (1%)
Plaid Cymru	1%	1 (1%)
Ulster Unionists*	-	1 (1%)
Others	6%	0

2014 European Parliament Elections: UK (*Northern Irish parties, elected using STV)

VOTING INFLUENCES: SOCIOLOGICAL FACTORS

There are a number of factors which seem to affect a person's likelihood of supporting one party over another. Factors about that person's characteristics, such as social class or age, are called **sociological** influences.

	Voting Percentage (%)				
	Con.	Lab.	Lib Dem	SNP	Other
All	45	33	12	-	10
Gender					
Male	46	31	12	4	7
Female	45	35	11	4	6
Age					
18-24	21	56	11	6	6
25-29	23	54	12	4	7
30-39	30	46	14	5	5
40-49	41	35	13	5	6
50-59	49	28	12	4	7
60-69	57	22	11	3	7
70+	67	14	11	2	6
Social class					
AB	42	32	15	4	7
C1	43	34	12	4	7
C2	49	31	9	4	7
DE	47	34	8	4	7
Men by class					
AB	47	29	15	-	9
C1	47	31	12	-	10
C2	48	30	8	-	14
DE	43	37	8	-	12
Women by class					
AB	42	31	17	-	10
C1	44	33	13	-	10
C2	46	33	9	-	12
DE	39	40	9	-	12
Ethnicity					
White	48	29	12	-	11
BME	20	64	12	-	4

2019 UK General Election: Voting by Group (Ipsos-MORI)

SOCIAL CLASS

Social class refers to the socio-economic section of society a person belongs to. There are a number of ways of measuring this, but the most commonly used in voting behaviour is the Social Grade System, based on the National Readership Survey (NRS).

Social class and voting

One would expect that people vote for the political party which represents their personal economic interests. This is called **class partisanship**.

As its name suggests, Labour could be expected to speak up for the interests of people with average or lower earnings, those in least affluent classes (social classes D and E). One would therefore expect their vote among the lower social classes to be high. Similarly, as the party more associated with above average incomes and wealth, one would expect the Conservative vote among the upper and middle classes (social classes A and B) to be high. In Scottish Parliament Elections, the SNP's collectivist policies (like free prescriptions and university tuition) have been popular with those in the least affluent classes.

Class dealignment

The link between social class and voting has been on the decline in the last few decades. As working and industrial patterns have changed in the UK, the traditional split between professional middle and less affluent working classes (ABC1 and C2DE) have been blurred. Party policies from both Labour and the Conservatives have reflected this, with policies from both designed to appeal to a wider range of voters. As such, between the October 1974 and 2017 UK General Elections, the Conservative vote in social classes ABC1 has decreased from 56% to 43%, and the Labour vote in DE has decreased from 57% to 34%.

GEOGRAPHICAL VOTING PATTERNS

Clearly linked to social class are geographical patterns of voting. Wealthy constituencies tend to vote Conservative, while less affluent areas tend to vote Labour. Conservative seats are concentrated in the wealthy south-east of England and in rural constituencies, while Labour votes are in the less affluent large cities in the north of England and Scotland (traditionally), until the 2015 General Election when SNP became the dominant party.

However, there are some more affluent constituencies which elect Labour MPs. Dulwich and West Norwood, a diverse London constituency with an average income of £36 691, elected Helen Hayes with 69.6% of the vote in 2017.

In the 2016 Scottish Parliament Elections, there were similar geographical patterns of voting. Most of the Conservatives' constituency seats came from rural areas of relative affluence, such as the seats along the border with England or in North East Scotland. On the other hand, two of Labour's three constituency MSPs represent areas that are more urban and have lower average income such as Edinburgh Southern or Dumbarton.

GENDER

In recent years there has been evidence of a marginal increase in the number of women voting for Labour compared to men e.g. 35% of women voted Labour to 31% of men in the 2019 General Election. However, overall, more women (and men) voted Conservative (44%) to Labour (35%). Instead, other factors, such as the age of voters, proved to be more of a deciding factor in influencing voters. Nonetheless gender cannot be ignored completely as a factor influencing voting behaviour. Why?

First, women are more likely to be employed in the public sector than men and public spending cuts associated with the Conservatives' policy of austerity has hit women harder. Also, a greater number of women are in part-time, low paid employment and Labour's more explicit support for raising the National Minimum Wage/National Living Wage or extending workers' rights has, therefore, greater appeal to women. After the 2019 General Election there were 104 female Labour MPs (51%) to 98 male MPs. Altogether, in total, women make up a total of 220 MPs (34%), the highest percentage to date.

Secondly, the Labour Party appears to be more in tune with women's priorities. In the 2017 General Election, women's top vote decider was the NHS. The NHS is also, overwhelmingly, a Labour priority with 41% of the electorate believing a Labour government would be best to manage the NHS (YouGov June 2017). Further, the 2017 Labour Party manifesto contained a pledge to appoint a specific commissioner to tackle violence against women, an issue that was also important to a great many women. After the 2019 General Election there were 104 female Labour MPs (51%) to 98 male MPs. Altogether, in total, women make up a total of 220 MPs (34%), the highest percentage to date.

Finally, some political commentators have argued that Labour has worked harder than the Conservatives to secure the election of women through the use of all-women shortlists for the selection of candidates. In 2017, there were 119 female Labour MPs from 262 Labour MPs altogether (45%), compared to just 65 Conservative women MPs from 317 Conservative MPs altogether (21%).

In Scotland, gender is far less of a factor affecting voting behaviour than support for issues such as Scottish independence. Having said that, the SNP have also moved to introduce all-women shortlists as well as legislation that will be of direct help to women.

AGE

Younger voters tend to vote for more collectivist parties, which favour government providing for people through welfare and social provision. In UK General Elections, Labour and the Liberal Democrats, or the SNP in Scotland, achieve a higher share of the youth vote, and see their vote decline as the age of voter increases. For example, YouGov found 56% of 18-24 year-olds voted Labour in the 2019 General Election to 21% for the Conservatives.

Conversely, the Conservatives see their vote increase considerably as the age of the voter increases. This is likely to be because of a combination of its focus on traditional values on issues like family, and low-tax policies (such as raising the threshold for inheritance tax) being attractive to older voters who are more likely to have savings. In the 2019 General Election YouGov found 67% of people aged 70+ voted Conservative.

In elections to the Scottish Parliament there is a similar trend in terms of voting behaviour and age to that of UK elections. YouGov found in a poll taken 2-4 May 2016, that 35% of voters aged 65+ intended voting Conservative compared to 33% and 22% for the SNP and Labour respectively. In terms of voters aged 16-24 years, the SNP and Labour could count on 41% and 27% of the vote with the Conservatives securing just 15% of this vote.

ETHNICITY

In the UK, ethnic minority groups are more likely to have a lower income than white people. Voting among ethnic minorities, therefore, tends to favour the Labour Party, with its tradition of collectivist policies to help those in need. The Conservatives, on the other hand, tend to do much worse among ethnic minorities than among white voters.

Party	Conservative	Labour	Liberal Democrat	Other
White	48%	29%	12%	11%
All BME	20%	64%	12%	4%

UK General Election 2019 White and Black Minority Ethnic Voting in Percentage (%) Source: Ipsos MORI

Note: For exam purposes it is important to remember that the factors which influence voting behaviour are inter-connected. Age and social class play a part in influencing voters along with gender, the media, ethnicity, the image of the party leader and of course, individual party policies.

DON'T FORGET

All the figures here suggest a likelihood to vote a certain way: not a guarantee.

ONLINE

Follow the link at www.brightredbooks.net to find out more data and test yourself on voting influences.

THINGS TO DO AND THINK ABOUT

1 Essay practice: Evaluate the importance of social class as a factor affecting voting behaviour. You may refer to Scottish and/or UK election results in your answer. (12)

VOTING INFLUENCES: RATIONAL CHOICE

DON'T FORGET 

Rational choice theories of voting suggest that voters are swayed by not just one, but a range of factors.

ONLINE 

Check out the link at www.brightredbooks.net to see which party's policies you agree with.

UNDECIDED VOTERS

While many believe that the key voting influences are sociological i.e. determined by the type of society a person grows up or lives in, there are others who believe that modern voters are more discerning than that and that the political parties have to work harder to convince individuals to vote for them. People who are not clearly aligned to one party are called **undecided** or **floating voters**.

In the 2019 General Election, YouGov found that the Conservatives managed to retain 85% of their voters from 2017 but 15% switched away to other parties. Labour retained 72% of their vote from 2017 with 28% switching to other parties. The SNP did best of all parties with only 13% of their 2017 vote switching away. For floating voters, it is conscious decisions about which party best represents a voter's interests or wishes that is the main determinant of voting outcomes. These are called **rational choice** theories of voting.

WHICH ISSUES MATTER?

For a number of years, research has been carried out to determine which issues matter most to voters. In late April 2017, just before the 2017 General Election, a poll of 30,000 by the British Election Study found that Brexit was the dominant issue in the minds of voters and that the Conservatives were the better party to manage the UK's exit from the EU. After the 2019 General Election, YouGov research described Brexit as continuing to be the dominant issue influencing voters with 55% of Remainers voting Labour and 65% of Leavers voting Conservative.

In Scotland the picture is different from England and Wales as the biggest issue for some Scottish voters is independence. At the 2019 General Election, the SNP increased their share of the vote by 8.1% to 45% of the electorate. They also won 48 of the 59 seats north of the border. As well as the issue of Scottish independence, the SNP stood on a platform of remaining within the EU which reflected the 2016 EU referendum vote where Scotland voted 68% to 32% to remain. At the same time both the Conservatives and Labour lost seats (–7 and –6) and votes (–3.5% and –8.5%) as a result of their parties' European stance of pro Brexit and a second referendum on retaining EU membership respectively.

LEADERSHIP

Opinion polls suggest that there are a number of leadership qualities which people look for in a potential Prime Minister including competence, ability to relate to the electorate, strength of character and honesty. Just before the 2019 General Election (December), YouGov reported that neither Boris Johnson or Jeremy Corbyn were rated highly among voters with Johnson rating a –5 score for whether he was judged a good or bad leader (36% good to 41% bad). However, Johnson's rating remained hugely superior to Corbyn with the public rating him –41% (16% good to 57% bad), one of the lowest scores for a leader of a party prior to an election in history. The main reasons to explain both men's relative unpopularity were down to the public's perception that neither was a good role model or kept their promises. However, Corbyn's ambivalent stance on Brexit, his perceived failure to properly apologise for antisemitism within his Party and his past support for Irish republicanism were also thought to have cost Labour votes. Johnson, on the other hand, was viewed as more charismatic and in touch with popular opinion.

ONLINE

For more information on the issues which influenced voters in the 2017 General Election visit www.brightredpublishing.net

Alongside leadership, party manifesto promises also affect voter choice. In 2019, the Conservatives', manifesto message was simple and often repeated i.e. "Get Brexit done". This pledge plus a small number of promises to have more nurses and police officers and build new hospitals, appeared popular with voters. Labour, on the other hand, was thought to have too many manifesto pledges – free care for the elderly, reducing the voting age, free broadband and free university tuition fees, etc – that, on reflection, appeared impossible to deliver or too costly in the long term. In Scotland, the SNP

contd

manifesto promising support for a second Scottish independence referendum and rejecting Brexit was viewed as hugely important in the SNP's success in 2019.

A successful election campaign is also thought to influence voters in the period before an election. Before the announcement of the 2017 General Election, opinion polls suggested the Conservatives would be returned to power with a comfortable majority. However, research for the BBC found that the Labour election campaign swung 54% of those who made their mind up within the last three days of the election to Labour. This compares with the Conservative campaign which attracted only 19% of the "switchers" over the last three days of the campaign. Arguably, this late shift towards Labour cost the Conservatives their parliamentary majority.

In 2019, the Conservatives appeared to have learned from their 2017 election mistakes. As well as a clear message on Brexit, the Conservatives also successfully projected themselves as led by someone who was not part of the problems of the past but instead would get the country moving and deliver the types of policies supported by most of the voters e.g. more police, more nurses and more money for schools.

TV leaders' debates

Televised TV election debates with different party leaders are a regular feature of Scottish and UK elections. Although there is disagreement as to the importance of these debates as a factor affecting voting behaviour, a study by Leeds University entitled "Democracy and Demand", found TV debates were "reaching sections of the population least likely to be touched by the rest of the campaign". The study claimed TV debates often influenced first-time voters, younger voters and those who claimed they were not interested in politics. Further, the study claimed that among undecided voters, they were cited ahead of TV news, interviews, newspapers and social media for helping people make up their minds. At the 2019 General Election, there were numerous TV debates across the UK/TV channels. Some of these debates saw party leaders from all the main parties represented, others were regional e.g. only the party leaders in Scotland and others again, just Johnson and Corbyn going head-to-head. The largest audience was an ITV debate with Johnson-Corbyn going head-to-head which attracted 7.34m viewers. Overall, political analysts were split on who "won" with opinion polls changing little after any of the debates.

TACTICAL VOTING

The two-party system in UK General Elections encourages opponents of one of the big two parties, Labour and Conservative, to vote for another party to keep their most disliked party out. Instead of voting for their favourite party, they vote for another party who will defeat their least favourite. At the 2019 General Election, several newspapers, including The Guardian, published a list of 50 parliamentary seats where voting tactically would result in the Conservatives losing the election. In most of these constituencies anti-Conservative voters were urged to vote Labour or Liberal Democrat to keep the Conservative candidate from winning.

As things turned out, the Conservatives were returned with a huge majority (80 seats) winning in constituencies, that included many traditional Labour seats (so called "Labour heartlands"), which hadn't returned a Conservative MP in decades. In its post-election analysis, the Guardian concluded that the results of its campaign to oppose the Conservatives and stop Brexit "were not great". Of the 50 seats it had identified where tactical voting could prevent Conservative election success, only 13 were won by non-Conservatives – four in England (two Labour and two Lib Dem) and nine in Scotland (all won by the SNP). Unlike 2017, where tactical voting had played a part in preventing Theresa May's Conservative Party from winning an overall majority, tactical voting was less of a factor affecting voting behaviour.

FACT

The Electoral Reform Society found that up to a record 30% of the UK electorate were considering voting tactically at the 2019 General Election.

ONLINE

Find out about twin-track or split-ticket voting on www.brightredbooks.net

FACT

Under Boundary Commission proposals, the number of parliamentary constituencies at the next planned UK General Election (May 2022) will fall from 650 to 600. In Scotland the number of constituencies is planned to fall from 59 to 53.

ONLINE TEST

Head to www.brightredbooks.net and test yourself on voting influences.

THINGS TO DO AND THINK ABOUT

1 Summarise the reasons for the Conservatives landslide election win in December 2019. In your answer make reference to floating voters, election issues, leadership and tactical voting.

VOTING INFLUENCES: THE MEDIA

The media in all its forms is a huge part of everyday life. It helps to keep us informed about what is happening in terms of decisions being made, and also the actions of those in power. In the run-up to elections, there are a number of ways in which the media may have influenced voters.

VIDEO LINK

Check out the Party Election Broadcasts at www.brightredbooks.net

VIDEO LINK

Watch the BBC's 2019 UK General Election Debate at www.brightredbooks.net

ONLINE

Follow the link to view PMQs for 05/02/20 at www.brightredbooks.net

FACT

The Corbyn-Johnson head-to-head debate was watched by 6.7m people which is around 0.5m to 1m less than any episode of Coronation Street.

ONLINE

See what newspapers had on their front pages the day before the UK General Election of 2019 by visiting www.brightredbooks.net

ONLINE

Learn more about how social media might have had an effect on the 2019 UK General Election at www.brightredbooks.net

PARTY ELECTION BROADCASTS (PEBS)

Party Election Broadcasts (PEBs) are TV (or radio) broadcasts produced by political parties, in which they put forward their point of view, or criticise opposition parties. Party broadcasts allow political parties to portray their messages to the public. Their message is not altered or interpreted by journalists or outside influences.

TV LEADERS' DEBATES

TV election debates are relatively new to UK elections although they are now widely expected as part of an election campaign. The first time the leaders of the main parties debated live on TV was just before the 2010 UK General Election. For Scottish Parliamentary elections the first TV debate was in 2011.

Since 2010, the format of TV debates has developed to include interviews or questions to a party leader or leaders from an invited audience, to debates involving the party leaders or representatives in different parties of the country. For example, BBC Scotland hosted a TV debate with the Scottish leaders of the main parties in Edinburgh in the run-up to the 2019 UK General Election.

The extent to which TV debates influence voters is not easy to quantify. Research in 2017 published by the Electoral Reform Society (ERS) found 56% of voters believed leaders' debates were important in helping them make their decision. Also, the vast majority of people said party leaders should be taking part in head-to-head live debates; something which Theresa May did not do. The research from the ERS went further and found that of the 4m people who watched the BBC's Question Time leaders' special (not a head-to-head but individual party leaders questioned by an invited audience), one third of a representative cross-section of viewers (extrapolated to 1.4m people) stated the debate influenced their vote. These figures matter when research shows the Conservatives could have won an overall majority in 2017 with just 533 extra votes in the nine most marginal constituencies, while a working majority could have been achieved on just 75 additional votes in the right places. The ERS research concludes by stating, "TV debates have become incredibly important for general elections in the UK and it's time to make such debates a core and established part of 21st century campaigning in the UK – with party leaders expected to take part. For the 2019 General Election TV leaders' debates, there was no consensus as to whether Boris Johnson or Jeremy Corbyn benefited most from going head-to-head. Further, where all the leaders or a leading party spokesperson took part in a debate e.g. ITV's election debate on 1 December, commentators again disagreed as to "who won". However, even relatively small changes in electoral support can have a significant effect on the result and this may explain why party election campaign teams are quick to claim their side as the "winner".

NEWSPAPERS

Unlike the broadcast media (TV and radio), newspapers can be (and are) very open about their support for a party. In their choice of headlines, use of pictures, stories and editorial comment, newspapers clearly aim to influence their readership. Wealthy owners, such as Rupert Murdoch who is Chairman and CEO of News Corporation who own The Sun, saw his interest as best served by supporting the Conservative Party in the General Elections of 2017 and 2019. Therefore, it was no surprise that The Sun strongly backed the Conservatives on both occasions.

Newspapers and election campaigns

In 2017, most national newspapers supported the Conservative Party. The Sun newspaper, which has the

contd

highest daily circulation figures, was particularly critical of Jeremy Corbyn and Labour urging its readers not to "chuck Britain in the Cor-bin" on its final front page before the country went to vote. The Daily Mail, the second highest selling daily newspaper, was more subtle in its support for the Conservatives by asking its readers to remember "your country needs you" and to back Theresa May. In 2019, the political stance of the country's best-selling newspapers remained unchanged. The Sun urged its voters to support Boris Johnson and to "save Brexit". The Daily Mail led with a call to "back Boris".

So do newspapers influence their readers? Although people buy newspapers for different reasons other than politics, there is some evidence that the "drip-drip" effect of repeated political information for or against a party or its leader can affect voting behaviour. YouGov reported after the 2017 General Election that most of the readers of the Conservative-backing Daily Mail, Daily Telegraph, Express, Sun and Times voted Conservative. Also, YouGov reported that 60% of voters said they got their information from newspapers and television (primarily the BBC) with the Guardian and Daily Mail being the most popular newspapers for political news with their readers. After the 2019 General Election, the Guardian reported that Jeremy Corbyn partly blamed the Sun and Daily Mail for Labour's defeat. However, as political analysts try to explain the results, it seems clear that the way people consume their news – glancing quickly at headlines as opposed to reading a whole article or via memes and images on social media such as Facebook – is changing, making it harder to judge the influence of any type of media, including newspapers. on voting behaviour.

Overall newspaper readership is falling (although online readership has increased) and individual readers tend to buy a newspaper that chimes with their political views as opposed to being changed themselves by the politics of their paper. It is also true that newspapers have been known to switch their support from one party to another as they would prefer to "back a winner" in an election. Finally, YouGov found that despite the Sun's strong endorsement of the Conservatives in 2017, 30% of the paper's readers still backed Labour in the election.

OPINION POLLS

Opinion polls are surveys in which members of the public are asked to state who they will vote for in an upcoming election. It could be argued that seeing a very clear predicted result in opinion polls could put off voters, who think their vote won't matter to the overall outcome. For this reason in many countries outside the UK, including Brazil, Canada and Norway, there is a ban of some sort on opinion polls in the period of the election campaign.

Although opinion polls are sometimes very inaccurate, every opinion poll taken before polling day in the 2017 UK General Election suggested that the Conservatives were ahead in the polls and were going to win. However, in the final weeks of the campaign the opinion polls were criticised for being 'all over the place and for failing to take account of an increase in turnout among younger voters who were more likely to vote Labour'. Arguably, this is another reason why the Conservatives lost their overall majority. In the six months before the 2019 General Election with Boris Johnson as PM, the opinion polls did consistently record a healthy lead for the Conservatives indicating a sizeable Conservative majority at the election. This time it would appear the polls were a very good indicator of voting behaviour.

THE INTERNET AND SOCIAL MEDIA

All the major parties and almost all candidates take to social media, including Twitter and Facebook, to publicise their activities on the campaign trail. Undoubtedly, social media is increasing as a factor affecting voting behaviour, especially among young voters.

In the 2016 Scottish Parliament Election Campaign, the SNP again had the most successful social media campaign. In the UK General Election of 2017 evidence suggests Labour did best online. In recent years Nicola Sturgeon and Jeremy Corbyn have both taken part in live webchats with the popular website for parents Mumsnet.

Improvements in technology now allow parties to target specific groups of voters more accurately. Data from Who Targets Me? showed that in 2017 parties had attempted to reach specific constituencies with tailored messages. For example, the Conservatives issued adverts to Facebook users in constituencies with nuclear industries – such as Derby and Chester - with a message that Corbyn and Labour "would put nuclear jobs at risk".

However, in elections up to now, there isn't sufficient evidence that suggests social media is a big influence on voting behaviour. Instead YouGov found in the 2017 General Election voters were more likely to say the likes of television (42%) and newspapers (32%) had more of an influence than social media (26%). Then again, among younger voters aged between 18-24 years, YouGov found 50% thought social media influenced them with their choice of party in the election.

THINGS TO DO AND THINK ABOUT

1 Essay practice: To what extent does the media influence voting behaviour?

POLITICAL INFORMATION AND PARTICIPATION: THE MEDIA

FUNCTIONS OF THE MEDIA

The media performs two key functions in a democracy: providing the public with political information, and giving people an opportunity to participate in politics by having their say. In order to make informed choices about political opinions, many people rely on a free media to give them the information they desire.

During election campaigns, the media really comes to the fore, but the media still has a role to play at other points in the electoral cycle with the internet (younger voters) and TV (older voters) proving to be the most common way people access political news.

	All	16-24	65+
Television	79	57	94
Internet (any device)	64	82	38
Radio	44	24	54
Newspapers (printed)	40	21	60

Use of main platforms for news by demographic group in percentage (%) 2018 (Source: Ofcom)

HIGHLIGHTING FAILINGS OF POLITICIANS

The media keeps a very close eye on representatives. Through investigative reporting in particular, failings or misdemeanours of those in positions of power can be highlighted to the general public. For example, the Daily Telegraph reported in April 2018 that Jeremy Hunt, then Secretary of State for Health, breached anti-money laundering legislation by failing to declare his 50% interest in a property firm. Hunt later rectified the error stating his was an "honest administrative mistake".

POLITICAL TV PROGRAMMES

As television coverage of political issues is important to the public's political education, TV is closely regulated in law. TV news editors and reporters must aim to allow a range of political views to be heard, conduct interviews in an even-handed and balanced way and give people of different political persuasion an equal opportunity to reply. In surveys, around three-quarters of people claim they watch the news at some point in the month with the BBC the most watched channel for news. According to Statista, in the second quarter of 2018, BBC news programmes were viewed by 17.05m people.

One of the longest running political programmes on TV is the BBC's Question Time. Question Time, usually aired on a Thursday evening and lasting 60 minutes, features a panel of guests drawn from a range of political parties as well as other public figures who answer pre-selected questions put to them by members of an pre-selected, balanced audience. The average viewing figure for Question Time is about 2.7m.

One aim of Question Time is to give an opportunity to members of the public to directly ask questions to the panel. It also allows the panel members to cross-examine each other. However, there has been criticism of the make of up Question Time panels. For example, some politicians have featured far more often than others e.g. former UKIP leader Nigel Farage (33 appearances by May 2019) compared to Green Party leader Caroline Lucas who appeared considerably fewer times. In Question Time's defence the programme (and by extension the BBC) has faced criticism from many groups including Labour, Conservatives and SNP politicians which could mean, ironically, it is not biased after all.

ONLINE

Check out the Question Time Twitter feed which has over 541,000 followers at @ bbcquestiontime

VIDEO LINK

Watch the BBC's Andrew Marr question PM Boris Johnson in December 2019 at www.brightredbooks.net Do you think he performed well? Explain your answer.

ONLINE

Go to BBC iPlayer and watch a recent episode of Question Time www.brightredbooks.net

COVERAGE OF ISSUES AND PARTY POLICIES

Newspapers are permitted to display bias, in a way that the broadcast media are not allowed to. In the reporting of political policies and legislation, newspapers' bias will be evident. For example, Conservative policies are likely to be well-received by the *Daily Express*, but opposed by the *Daily Mirror*. On the other hand, Labour policies usually have the support of *The Guardian* newspaper whilst the *Daily Telegraph* will more likely criticise Labour.

VOICE OF THE PEOPLE?

It could be argued that the media provides an opportunity for the public to present their opinions to the government, one of relatively few ways of doing so between elections. The *Daily Mail* believed it was speaking for the British public when it began campaigns to "Turn the Tide On Plastic", a campaign which aims to banish plastic bags and reduce plastic bottle and coffee cup use which are blighting the country and poisoning the oceans. Also, the "Save Britain's high streets" campaign which aims to stem the loss of shops from high streets from what the Daily Mail claims are crippling business rates (July 2018) costing 50,000 retail jobs throughout the UK in the first half of 2018. In terms of success, the Mail would claim its campaign against plastic use has seen Prime Minister Theresa May unveil proposals for a levy on all disposable packaging as part of her war on plastic. They may also claim success in helping to reduce store closures in high streets as in Sept. 2018 Labour announced an "emergency five-point plan" to save Britain's high streets.

TO WHAT EXTENT IS THE MEDIA IMPORTANT IN THE POLITICAL PROCESS?

One reason why many people think the role of the media is becoming increasingly important in the political process is the increase in undecided voters. As people are becoming less likely to closely associate themselves with one political party, and more likely to change their votes during an election campaign, the media can provide them with the up-to-the-minute information which will allow them to form political opinions.

As well as an increase in undecided voters, political news is now far easier to access and more readily available than it has ever been before. From 24-hour news stations to non-stop updates on mobiles via Twitter and Facebook, voters now have faster and easier access to politics – most likely on their mobile - than at any time in the past.

Finally, the sheer amount of money spent by political parties on media engagement illustrates how important the media is to them. At the 2017 General Election, according to figures from the Electoral Commission, the Conservatives spent £18.5m on their campaign, against £11m of spending by Labour, £6.8m by the Liberal Democrats and £1.6m for the SNP. The Electoral Commission data also showed the increasing role of social media in campaigning with the Conservatives spending about £2.1m on Facebook advertising against £500,000 and £244,000 for Labour and the Liberal Democrats respectively.

Despite the prominent role played by the media, there is some distrust of the media. In 2018, according to media organisation Campaign, only 61% of people trusted traditional media (TV and newspapers) as a source of news information. For online media such as Buzzfeed and Huffington Post, this figure fell to 45% and for social media to only 24%. Overall, only around 32% of people said they trusted the media in general with one third believing the media to be biased.

Over half of Britons (53%) also worry about being exposed to fake news on social media, and 64% per cent cannot distinguish between proper journalism and fake news. This may be one reason to explain why voters today have been described as "news-skimmers" i.e. voters take note of what's going on politically, but they are not really persuaded by what they read, hear or see.

Another reason why the media's role in politics may be overstated is the fact that media is consumed much more selectively now than ever. There are many newspapers, TV channels, and online media to choose from, so people are able to shop around until they find a paper, TV show or social media page which reaffirms political beliefs they also have. This suggests that instead of 70% of readers of *The Telegraph* voting Conservative, the reverse is true – a significant number of Conservative voters choose to buy *The Telegraph* because it mirrors their view.

FACT

In a 2018 survey by Ofcom, it was found that one in seven adults claim to use all four of the main platforms for news, while one in ten use only the TV or only the internet for news. The Ofcom survey also found a greater proportion of adults claim to use social media for news nowadays than other internet sources.

British Election Study data indicates that in 2019 just 16% of Britons felt a very strong party identification. At the General Election in 2017, 33% said they switched their vote from 2015. Ipsos Mori reported that this figure could be as high as 40% in 2019.

YouGov found in the run up to the 2019 GE 13% of voters were undecided (19% of female voters, 7% of male voters, 16% Social Class C2/D/E and 12% ABC1).

Brexit had a huge impact on the 2019 General Election. In the period before the election, voters were much clearer on their position on Brexit than they were on their choice of political party.

DON'T FORGET

A free press is an important part of a democracy.

THINGS TO DO AND THINK ABOUT

1 Essay practice: Evaluate the importance of the media on voting behaviour. (12)

ONLINE TEST

Head to www.brightredbooks.net and test yourself on political information and participation.

POLITICAL INFORMATION AND PARTICIPATION: PRESSURE GROUPS

Party/Pressure Group	Membership September 2018
Conservatives	124 000
Labour	540 000
Liberal Democrat	99 200
SNP	125 500
RSPB	1.1m
National Trust	3.4m

Membership of selected political parties and pressure groups

WHAT ARE PRESSURE GROUPS?

Pressure groups are organisations of like-minded individuals who share concerns about a certain issue. By joining together, pressure groups are much more likely to influence the decisions which the government makes than individuals would be alone.

Pressure groups give individuals the chance to regularly participate in politics, between elections. While membership of political parties was decreasing before the Scottish Independence Referendum, the membership of pressure groups has been growing steadily for a number of years.

INSIDER PRESSURE GROUPS

Insider pressure groups are organisations which work closely and formally with political parties and governments. Governments often rely on them for their expertise and advice in policy discussions. They will hold meetings and negotiations with government ministers and their departments, and provide expert witnesses for committee inquiries.

For many years health campaign groups such as Alcohol Focus Scotland (AFS) have been concerned with the impact of alcohol on Scottish society. AFS estimates that alcohol misuse costs Scotland billions of pounds per year (£3.6bn, 2017). As an insider pressure group with an agenda that is in tune with that of the SNP Scottish government, representatives from AFS, through regular meetings with ministers, have helped inform government policy on alcohol for over a decade. For example, through pressure from AFS and other groups, legislation was passed introducing Minimum Unit Pricing (MUP) for alcohol. However, due to a number of legal challenges the Scottish Government were prevented from implementing the legislation until May 2018. In 2017, AFS produced a report which made a number of recommendations for further action on alcohol. The then Health Minister Shona Robison said she welcomed the report and the Scottish government would consider the report's recommendations.

OUTSIDER PRESSURE GROUPS

Outsider pressure groups do not usually have the same privileged access to decision- makers as insider pressure groups. Without this access, they have to resort to more direct or extreme measures to get their point of view across.

Lobbying is the process of gaining access to government ministers, to try to convince them of a particular point of view. Types of lobbying include organising and presenting petitions, providing information or research to back up a case for change or inviting an MP/MSP or member of the House of Lords to a meeting or event where they can find out more about an issue.

In both the Scottish and UK parliaments, there are a great many lobbyists working on behalf of different pressure groups. Lobbyists are firms or individuals which are paid to try and influence government decisions. They are often former politicians or ex-civil servants who have developed personal contacts with those in power. Alternatively, individuals, firms, charities and other groups can lobby on their own, without paying professional lobbyists. However, in recent years there have been concerns that lobbyists are too influential in the political process and that this could lead to corruption and therefore undermine democracy. By way of response, both the Scottish and UK Parliaments have clear rules to regulate lobbying. In the UK Parliament all MPs, including ministers, are subject to a code of conduct when it comes to their outside interests. They must register their financial interests, including any payments received for employment outside Parliament. Taking payment for any form of parliamentary business such as asking questions to a minister is strictly forbidden. In 2016, the Scottish Parliament passed a bill regulating lobbying (The Lobbying Scotland Act 2016) to ensure transparency between MSPs and lobbying contacts.

Denied a formal meeting, pressure groups often petition the government. The Scottish Parliament's Public Petitions Committee considers every petition it receives, while the UK Government considers every petition receiving 100 000+ signatures. More than 156,000 people signed a UK Parliament e-petition calling for the then PM Theresa May to ensure that a range of individuals from different backgrounds should sit on the inquiry panel examining the fire that engulfed Grenfell Tower in June

contd

2017. Tragically, 72 people lost their lives in the London fire. By way of response, the UK Parliament's Petitions Committee considered the petition before writing, twice, to the PM for a response. The e-petition was also debated in the UK Parliament. In May 2018, the PM agreed to extend the inquiry panel in phase two of its work.

In order to gain media attention and therefore highlight their cause to as many people as possible, pressure groups can organise marches, demonstrations and protests. In October 2018, as many as 700,000 people attended a march in London to demand a UK-wide "people's vote" on the final terms of any Brexit deal. This demonstration was the second largest protest in the UK this century after the Stop the War demonstration in 2003. The organisers hoped that the huge number of protestors marching would attract significant media publicity and put further pressure on the UK government to respond to their demand. However, Theresa May stated on more than one occasion that there would be no such public vote.

A more extreme measure which pressure groups can take is **direct action** or civil disobedience. This is any action which directly impedes or stops the protested action being carried out. In September 2018, three Greenpeace activists were jailed for causing a public nuisance during protests at a fracking site in North-West England. The men had climbed atop lorries used in the fracking process, preventing the company involved undertaking drilling. The protest lasted around 100 hours, gaining widespread media coverage.

PRESSURE GROUP SUCCESS

There are a number of factors which affect whether a pressure group can be seen as successful. The first factor of pressure group success is whether or not their aim is achievable and politically supported. Patrick Harvie MSP was at the Faslane blockade, and urged for a 'Yes' vote in the referendum in order to remove Trident from Scotland: 'If Scotland decides next year to take control of its own defence policy, we will be able to consign Trident to history and make Scotland a force for peace in the world.'

However, after the people of Scotland returned a 'No' vote to Scottish independence in 2014, those who continue to oppose Trident hope that after a future UK election, the SNP may be in a position in the UK Parliament to form a coalition government and that the price of their support would be the removal of Trident from Scotland. Arguably, if this were ever to happen, this would be a huge success for the Scrap Trident Coalition.

Secondly, the resources that a pressure group has available is a key factor in their success. Pressure groups with large memberships (The Royal Society for the Protection of Birds (RSPB) has over a million members) are likely to be able to influence the government as they can claim to speak to a large proportion of the UK population. Many pressure groups have many more members than political parties.

Thirdly, pressure groups with wealthy donors, celebrity endorsements or volunteers who are particularly skilled in things like social media or PR (public relations) are likely to be able to get their message out to a wide audience. For example, celebrities such as singer Alexandra Burke, entrepreneur Sir Richard Branson and former Beatle Sir Paul McCartney, have all make donations to Greenpeace in recent years. This support, it can be argued, has helped Greenpeace campaign on a number of fronts in the UK e.g. mounting legal challenges to fracking.

Of course, insider status is the most likely method by which a pressure group may secure its aims. However, as political interaction between decision makers and insider pressure groups often goes on out of sight of the media, it is not always easy to measure the extent of influence which an insider group may exert.

VIDEO LINK

Find out more about the Grenfell Tower Inquiry at www.brightredbooks.net

ONLINE

Find out more about Greenpeace's campaign to prevent fracking at www.brightredbooks.net

DON'T FORGET

Pressure groups give members of the public an opportunity to have their opinions represented between elections.

ONLINE TEST

Head to www.brightredbooks.net and test yourself on political information and participation.

THINGS TO DO AND THINK ABOUT

1 Essay practice: To what extent are groups outside parliament effective in influencing decision-making in government? You may refer to groups in Scotland, the United Kingdom or both in your answer. (20)

SOCIAL INEQUALITY IN THE UK

WHAT IS POVERTY?

POVERTY: AN OVERVIEW

UK official poverty levels are measured by the Department of Work and Pensions using their **Households Below the Average Income** (HBAI) annual report. This information is based on the 20 000 UK households that take part in the Family Resources Survey. The most recent HBAI figures were released in March 2018 based on statistics relating to 2017–18.

- **Household** – One person living alone or a group of people (not necessarily related) living at the same address who share cooking facilities and share a living room, sitting room, or dining area. A household will consist of one or more benefit units/families.
- **Family or Benefit Unit** – A single adult or a couple living as married and any dependent children.

ONLINE 

For more data on poverty in the UK, head to www.brightredbooks.net

FACT 

In 2017-18, 22% of people in the UK had a relative low income AHC and 17% had a low relative low income BHC (source ONS/DWP).

RELATIVE POVERTY

Professor Peter Townsend, the leading authority of the last 50 years on UK poverty, defines poverty as when someone's 'resources are so seriously below those commanded by the average individual or family that they are, in effect, excluded from ordinary living patterns, customs and activities'. Therefore, income poverty thresholds depend on the social norms of the society in which someone lives and on the incomes of the ordinary people in that society. Social norms change over time and as society becomes richer, the levels of income and resources that are considered to be adequate rise. Unless the poorest can keep up with growth in average incomes, they will become more excluded from the opportunities that the rest of society enjoys.

Poverty is measured by net household income, adjusted for size and after housing costs have been deducted. The gap between the cost of essentials to live and real wages continues to widen, meaning less expendable income.

Poverty thresholds for different family sizes, AHC 2017–18

	Single Parent	Two Parent
One Child	£205	£315
Two Children	£255	£365
Three Children	£310	£420

Based on average weekly income after benefits, taxes and housing costs. Source DWP

The latest published poverty statistics are from 2017/18, but for many children and working age-adults with low household incomes, the tightening of incomes has been ongoing since 2008/09 due to a variety of factors including wage stagnation or even wage freezes during this period. These issues have clearly increased the numbers of people affected by poverty and how far household incomes are below the poverty line.

Welfare reforms have also resulted in fewer people being eligible for benefits available, smaller increases in benefits and sanctions for those who fail to comply with tougher conditions to receive these benefits. The UK Government's welfare policies will be discussed and analysed in more detail later in the chapter, but most have affected those with low or near-low incomes. Almost all of the welfare reforms have affected both working and non-working families, but the scale and depth of impacts vary greatly. Many families have been affected by more than one benefit change, so the reality is that current poverty levels in 2020 may be different.

Relative low income households (AHC) millions (m) and percentage (%),2007/08–2017/18

	2007/08	2017/18
All People	12.7m/22%	14m/22%
Children	4m/30%	4.1m/30%

VIDEO LINK 

Find out more about the different ways that poverty is affecting families today. Learn more at www.brightredbooks.net

VIDEO LINK 

Foodbanks are becoming more important for working families, struggling to meet their basic needs. Learn more at www.brightredbooks.net

FACT 

14.3 million people were in poverty 2017-18 (AHC) which is an increase of 1.3 million since 2011-12 although average incomes have risen from £402 in 2011-12 to £437 in 2017-18 (Source: ONS/DWP).

SOCIAL EXCLUSION

The term **social exclusion** refers to the alienation or disenfranchisement of certain people within society. It highlights the fact that the issue of social exclusion relates to low income and to other factors relating to severe and chronic disadvantage, and that these are closely connected. Participation in society can be measured in terms of social relationships, membership of organisations, trust in other people, ownership of possessions and purchase of services. All are lower among people with low incomes.

In today's society, people can be socially excluded in a variety of ways, such as **digital exclusion**, meaning a lack of access to ICT and the internet. Statistics have shown that people in poverty are less likely to have access to ICT and the internet either at home or on a portable electronic device, which has proved to have a **negative impact** on **educational attainment** and **self-esteem**.

DON'T FORGET

Material deprivation, social exclusion and poverty are all very closely linked. It is important to have a wider definition of poverty than one simply based on income alone, particularly when referring to children. For example, living standards can also provide a measurement of poverty.

GROUPS AT RISK OF POVERTY AND SOCIAL EXCLUSION

There are certain groups in society that are more at risk of poverty and social exclusion than others, such as women and ethnic minorities. The reasons for this are discussed later.

Children and young people

Children are often born into poverty, which is outwith their control, but they are often the ones hit hardest by the impact of poverty and social exclusion. Children can find themselves stuck in a **poverty cycle** that can impact the rest of their lives. A 2016 study by UNICEF found that the UK was ranked bottom out of 37 countries for healthy eating for children from the poorest households compared to those in better-off households. A poor diet in childhood can affect a child's ability to learn and contribute to lower educational attainment. It can also increase the risks of obesity and diabetes later in life. Childhood economic deprivation increases the likelihood of being socially excluded as an adult and is the strongest predictor of emotional problems, poor educational attainment and engagement in deviant behaviour in adolescence.

The UK and Scottish Governments have tried to tackle child poverty in a variety of ways, which will be discussed in more detail later in this chapter, but the Child Poverty Act 2010 has set clear targets for dealing with the significant problem of child poverty to be met by 2020.

Meanwhile, in 2016 the UK Government replaced this Act with the Welfare Reform Act which revised (some would say reduced) the targets on reducing poverty and the measure of poverty based on family income.

However, in 2017, Holyrood passed Scotland's first child poverty bill, which reintroduced the targets revised by the UK government a year earlier. The four goals, which include reducing relative poverty from 26% to 10% of children and absolute poverty from 21% to 5% of children, must be met by 2030.

FACT

The Welfare Reform Act (2016) will now measure:

- the proportion of children living in workless households as well as long-term workless households
- the educational attainment of all pupils and the most disadvantaged pupils at age 16

The government will also develop a range of other measures and indicators of root causes of poverty, including family breakdown, debt and addiction, setting these out in a children's life chances strategy.

The elderly

According to a 2017–18 report by Joseph Rowntree Foundation, around 16% to 17% of people aged 65 and over in the UK were living in poverty, compared with around 22% of the total population. There are many factors involved in elderly poverty, but it is likely that those who found themselves on a low income throughout their lives may become entirely reliant on government support in their retirement. This may be in the form of a **state pension**. In 2020, the basic state pension was £129.20 per week for a single person (old pension) or £168.60 per week for a single person if you are entitled to the new state pension.

THINGS TO DO AND THINK ABOUT

1 To get an idea of what some young people who are socially excluded or living in poverty may experience think about your daily routine and create a table of Needs and Wants. Needs are things that you use almost daily that you think you couldn't survive without. Wants are luxuries or items which you could manage without. Are all your 'needs' really needs? Would a young person in poverty be likely to make the same lists? If not, why not?
2 Explain the poverty cycle and why it continues.
3 Why do you think the need for foodbanks is on the rise for working families?

ONLINE TEST

Test yourself on this topic online at www.brightredbooks.net

ECONOMIC INEQUALITIES

According to the Equality Trust, people in more equal societies live longer, have better mental health and have better chances of a good education regardless of their background. Community life is stronger where the income gap is narrower, children do better at school and they are less likely to become teenage parents. When inequality is reduced people trust each other more, there is less violence and rates of imprisonment are lower.

There is evidence to show that British society is socially and economically very unequal and that the gap between rich and poor continues to grow. The Gini coefficient is a way to measure income or wealth in a society. The higher the number, the greater the inequality. In 2019, the ONS recorded a UK income inequality Gini coefficient of 32.4% or 0.325 (up slightly from 2018), which makes the UK more unequal than most other similar developed countries.

Selected countries Gini coefficient income inequality 2020 (source: World Population Review): Australia 30.3%; Canada 32.1%; France 29.3%; Germany 27%; Italy 31.9%; Netherlands 30.3%; Norway 26.8%; Sweden 24.9%; UK 32.5%; US 45%.

VIDEO LINK

Watch a video on income inequality in the UK at www.brightredbooks.net

SOCIAL CLASS

Traditionally, social class has been defined by the Office of National Statistics (ONS) based on employment conditions and pay.

Social class	Category	Type of employment
Higher managerial occupations	1	**1.1** Company directors, police Inspectors, bank managers, senior civil servants, military officers **1.2** Doctors, barristers, solicitors, clergy, librarians, teachers
Lower managerial	2	Nurses and midwives, journalists, actors, prison officers, police and soldiers
Intermediate	3	Clerks, secretaries, driving instructors, computer operators
Small employers	4	Publicans, farmers, play group leaders, window cleaners, painters and decorators
Lower supervisory and craft	5	Printers, plumbers, butchers, bus inspectors, TV engineers, train drivers
Semi-routine occupations	6	Shop assistants, traffic wardens, cooks, bus drivers, hairdressers, postal workers
Routine occupations	7	Waiters, road sweepers, cleaners, couriers, building labourers, refuse collectors
Never worked	8	Long-term unemployed and non-workers.

Terms like upper, middle and working class are rarely used in official statistics as they are so difficult to define. However, category 1.1 in the ONS classifications could be described as **upper middle class**, 1.2, and 2 could be described as **middle class** and 3–7 as **working class**. Category 8 has also been referred to as an **underclass**. This group are difficult to measure as they may work but are not officially registered as doing so. They may not pay taxes and/or National Insurance and could be uneducated and unskilled, relying heavily on the State as a source of income. The UK Government terms families within this category as 'troubled' and the children within this group are often neglected and tend to adopt the behaviours of their parents, meaning the underclass perpetuates itself.

FACT

According to the UK Government, troubled families cost the taxpayer £9 billion every year.

THE GREAT BRITISH CLASS SURVEY 2013

In 2013, 161 000 people participated in the Great British Class Survey. The results showed that people in the UK could now fit into seven social classes. This reflects a shift in the traditional view of social class as no longer can class be measured simply on the basis of occupation, wealth and education. This survey took into account three measures of capital:

- economic capital (income, savings, house value)
- social capital (the number and status of people they know)
- cultural capital (the extent and nature of their cultural interests and activities).

contd

Category	Definition
Elite	The most privileged group in the UK with the highest levels of all three capitals.
Established middle class	They make up around 25% of the UK population and score highly on all three capitals.
Technical middle class	A small group which is prosperous but scores low for social and cultural capital. They are distinguished by their social isolation and cultural apathy.
New affluent workers	A young class group which is socially and culturally active, with middling levels of economic capital.
Traditional working class	Its members have reasonably high house values and make up around 14% of the UK population.
Emergent service workers	A new, young, urban group which is relatively poor but has high social and cultural capital.
Precariat	The poorest, most deprived class, scoring low for social and cultural capital.

The British Social Attitudes Survey 2013 showed that 66% of people polled believed that a person's social class affects their opportunities.

ONLINE

Work out which bracket you fall into by following the link to 'The Great British Class calculator' at www.brightredbooks.net

DON'T FORGET

The fact that several methods of categorising social class exist reflects how difficult it is to measure and people may move among different categories throughout their lifetimes.

MEASURING ECONOMIC INEQUALITIES

There are three main types of economic inequality:

- income
- pay
- wealth.

Income inequality

Income is all the money received on an individual or household basis from employment (wages, salaries, bonuses etc.), investments, interest on savings, stocks and shares, state **benefits**, pensions and rent. Income inequality, therefore, refers to the unequal distribution of income within a group.

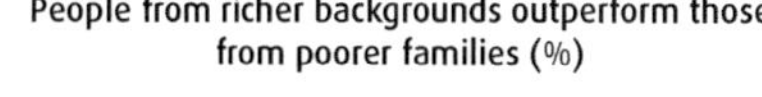

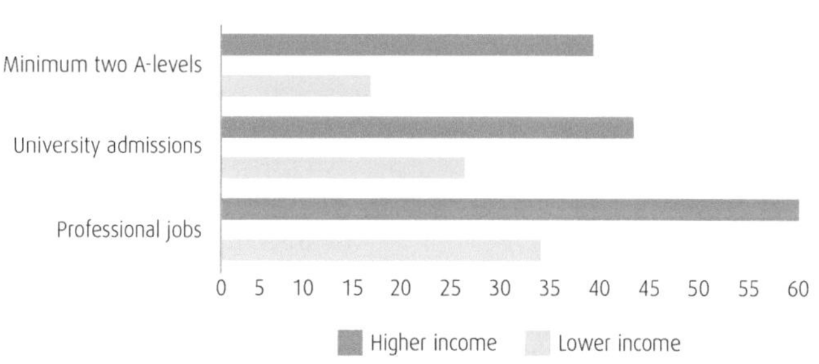

Pay inequality

Pay refers to payment from employment only. Pay inequality describes the difference between people's pay within one company or across the UK. Issues such as gender and race can affect pay inequality.

Wealth inequality

Wealth refers to the total amount of assets of an individual or household, so wealth inequality refers to the unequal distribution of assets in a group of people.

In 2018, the left wing think tank The Institute for Public Policy Research (IPPR) reported that there was rising inequality across the UK in terms of income, geography, gender, ethnicity and age. The IPPR found that the UK was the fifth most unequal country in Europe, stating more than a fifth of the population live on incomes below the poverty line after housing costs are taken into account, even though most of these households are in work. Nearly one in three children live in poverty and the use of food banks is rising. Further, there was a sixfold difference between the income of the top 20% of households and those of the bottom 20%. Wealth inequality is much worse, with 44% of the UK's wealth owned by just 10% of the population, five times the total wealth held by the poorest half.

Social Mobility

Social mobility is the term used to describe the movement of individuals, families, households or other categories of people between social classes. In its 2019 State of the Nation report, the Social Mobility Commission stated that inequality in the UK was "entrenched from birth" and that this position had remained stagnant in the previous five years. At all levels, people from wealthier backgrounds outperform those from poor backgrounds.

ONLINE

For information on economic inequality, follow the links at www.brightredbooks.net

ONLINE TEST

Take the 'economic inequalities' test at www.brightredbooks.net to revise your knowledge of this.

THINGS TO DO AND THINK ABOUT

1 Think about your own household. According to the traditional model, which social class category do you think your household falls in to? Explain why you came to this conclusion.

Now use the link to the Great British Class Calculator and answer the questions to determine your new social class. Analyse your result and compare it to your chosen category using the traditional model.

CAUSES OF ECONOMIC INEQUALITIES

FACT

Many parents, who have sufficient income, buy an expensive house in the catchment area of the schools with the best exam results. Increases in university fees in England may also put young people from low-income families off going to university.
To find out about some of the problems of living on Universal Credit go to www.brightredbooks.net.

UNEMPLOYMENT AND WORKLESSNESS

A person is classed as **unemployed** if they are out of work, but are actively looking for work and available to start work within a fortnight. **Worklessness** is when an individual cannot work due to commitments such as looking after children or being a carer, or perhaps due to health reasons. Therefore they are out of work, but not actively seeking employment.

Most people rely on employment as a source of income, but not everyone who wants to work is in employment. **Unemployment figures** are based on a survey carried out by the Office for National Statistics (ONS) using information from the Department of Work and Pensions (DWP). They show the average number of people unemployed over a three-month period and a new survey is done every month. A separate survey known as the Claimant Count measures the numbers claiming Jobseekers Allowance (JSA) plus the number of Universal Credit (UC) claimants who are required to look for work. This has been the case since Universal Credit was introduced in 2013. Gradually, Jobseekers Allowance is being phased out and replaced by Universal Credit around the UK. Unemployment figures and claimant count are different as not everyone who is unemployed is entitled to or claims JSA or UC. Employment figures vary across the UK which is sometimes known as the North-South divide.

Percentage of people in employment on a zero-hours contract

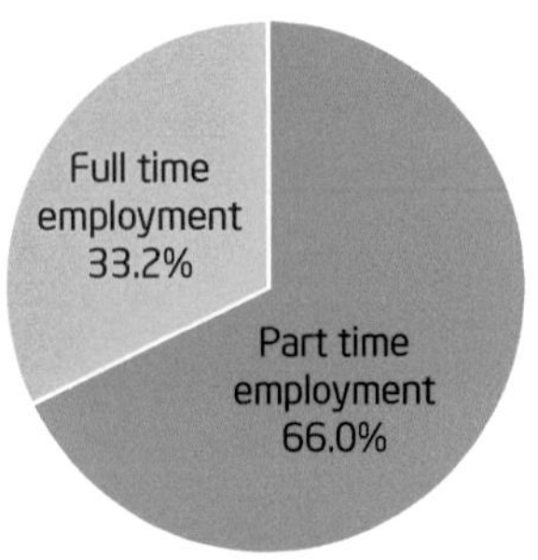

Percentage of people in employment not on a zero-hours contract

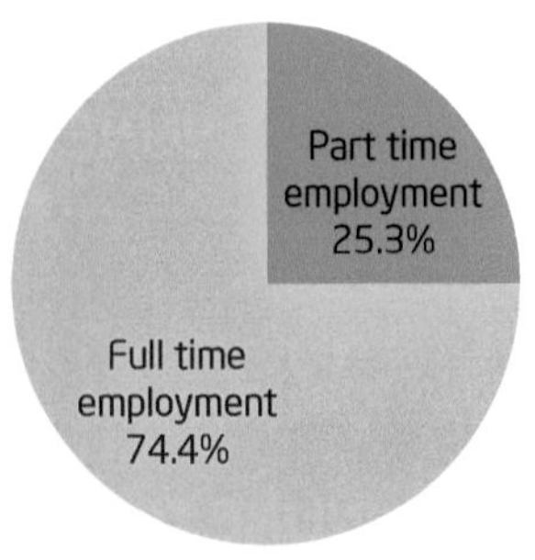

Source: Office for National Statistics - Contracts that do not guarantee a minimum number of hours: April 2018

ZERO-HOURS CONTRACTS

Zero-hours contracts allow employers to hire staff with no guarantee of work, which means employees work only when they are needed by employers, often at short notice. Their pay depends on how often they work. Some zero-hours contracts oblige workers to take the shifts they are offered, but others do not. As of December 2019 there were 974,000 people in the UK on zero-hours contracts, which represented about 3% of the UK workforce. One in five zero-hours workers say they are penalised if they are not available for work and almost half of zero-hours workers say they receive no notice or find out at the beginning of an expected shift that work has been cancelled. In 2018, Alasdair Thomson, from Inverness, won a legal case against his employers. He argued successfully that due to his zero hours contract his shifts were cancelled at the last minute on a number of occasions leaving him unable to find other work to replace his lost wages.

High street examples of employers who use zero-hours contracts include cinema chain Cineworld and Sports Direct which, following public criticism for its use of zero hours contracts, now offers workers the option of either fixed or zero hours contracts. However, it should be noted that hotels and restaurants and, surprisingly, health and social work employ more workers on zero hours contracts than the retail sector. These contracts can make planning and the management of finances very difficult and can lead to people falling into poverty despite being in employment. Employers say zero-hours contracts allow them to take on staff in response to fluctuating demand for their services, in sectors such as tourism and hospitality. Employers also say that many workers appreciate the flexibility a zero-hours contract gives them. The ONS found that one-third of workers on zero-hours contracts want extra hours. That compares with 9% of staff who work on other types of contract. Many workers are in full-time education and so may be unsuited to less flexible work - they account for 18% of the zero-hours cohort, or 172,000 people.

The Gig Economy

The "gig economy" is a phrase used to describe a type of working where people are increasingly on short-term contracts or work freelance, as opposed to permanent jobs. In June 2019, the Guardian reported that the gig economy was booming with around 4.7m people (9.6% of all workers; two-thirds aged 16-34 years) in the UK working in precarious employment. To support gig economy workers, the UK government has promised to boost worker rights, however, progress has been slow leaving many workers exploited and victim to low pay and insecure work.

LOW PAY: THE WORKING POOR

Despite the **National Minimum Wage** and the **National Living Wage**, many employees still find themselves struggling to end meet as wages do not keep up with prices. In 2017, around one-fifth (5.5 million) of British workers were paid less than the recommended amount required to cover workers basic needs. In work poverty affects women employees (25%) more than male employees (16%). Part-time workers are also proportionally worse off with 3.1m part-time workers earning less than the living wage compared to 2.4m full-time workers. Some employment can be low paid and cyclical where some workers may find themselves experiencing periods of unemployment rather than long-term unemployment. This is often referred to as **low pay, no pay**. In April 2020, the National Living Wage was increased to £8.72 per hour for people over 25, whilst the National Minimum Wage was increased to £8.20 per hour for people aged 21-24. However, for younger workers such as those aged 16-18, the National Minimum Wage remains low. In April 2020, it increased by 20p to £4.55 per hour which, many critics would argue is too low for a young person who may be married, with children and in their own home to live on.

The majority of people in poverty are from working households. Research by the Social Mobility Commission in 2017 found that 25% of workers were stuck on a low salary with little prospect of improvement. Most new jobs are in low paid industries and often provide little prospects for progression or incentives to work more hours. Some workers will actually have to pay back some of the benefits received due to their low pay if they work overtime. This can be as much as 76p deducted from every £1 of overtime earnings and is known as **claw back**. The cost of childcare has increased by 48% between 2008 and 2016 for parents in England with a one-year old child. This is not in line with earnings since average wages have risen by only 12% therefore some families may find they end up paying more in childcare than they earn due to the type of work available to them.

FACT

The Child Poverty Action Group reported in 2018 that low-earning parents working full-time are still unable to earn enough to provide their family with a basic, no-frills lifestyle. A single parent on the National Living Wage is £74 a week short of the minimum income needed and a couple with two children would be £49 a week short of the income needed, the charity said. A report for the Joseph Rowntree Foundation found that while paid employment reduces the risk of poverty, about 56% of people living in poverty in 2018 were in a household where at least one person had a job, compared with 39% 20 years ago and seven in 10 children in poverty are now in a working family.

RECESSION, AUSTERITY AND GOVERNMENT POLICY

Irresponsible lending by many banks led to a global recession in 2008 and governments cut back on public spending. Many businesses were forced to cease trading and unemployment started to rise sharply. When the global financial crisis hit, the UK unemployment rate was a little over 5% or 1.6 million. Towards the end of 2009, with the UK coming out of its severest recession since the 1950s, it was 2.5 million, or 8%. In December 2019, unemployment has now fallen below its pre-recession levels of unemployment at 1.29 million or 3.8%, its lowest level since the mid-1970s.

However, the impact of the recession has been felt throughout this period and, continues to be felt today. The impact on welfare has been significant as the government tries to cut back on public spending to cover debts and losses and there has been an increase in means testing and, tougher conditions applied to those who are claiming and receiving benefits. This, along with other Government spending cuts are known as austerity measures.

FACT

According to the British Social Attitudes Survey 2018, 70% of those polled support wage top-ups for single parents and 58% support top-ups for couples with children.

ONLINE

Head to www.brightredbooks.net for further reading, videos and tests on this topic.

UK Government Policy	Description
Welfare Reform Act 2012: The Welfare Benefit Cap	A limit on the total amount of certain benefits that most people aged 16-64 can get. The state retirement age rose to 66 by 2016 for men and 2020 for women. Will eventually rise to 68 by 2044 for both men and women.
Welfare Reform Act 2012 (The 'Bedroom Tax')	The amount of Housing Benefit claimants can receive is reduced if they are deemed to have too much living space in the property they are renting from local government.
Welfare Reform Act 2012: Universal Credit (Note: Still not fully rolled out across the UK)	A new benefit to replace six existing benefits with a single monthly payment if someone is out of work or on a low income. The six benefits are: Jobseeker's Allowance; Working Tax Credit; Employment and Support Allowance; Child Tax Credit Income Support; Housing Benefit.
The Welfare Reform Act 2016	New National Living Wage by 2016. Benefits cap reduced from £26,000 per household in London and £20,000 in the rest of the country. Four year freeze in working age benefits. Two-child limit placed on Universal Credit and Child Tax Credit for claims made after April 2017.

Other changes include the introduction of the Personal Independence Payment, which replaced Disability Living Allowance for those with long-term disabilities and/or illnesses and the introduction of the Work Capability Assessment (WCA). These assessments have resulted in many people with serious illnesses and/or disabilities being classed as fit for work.

THINGS TO DO AND THINK ABOUT

1 Explain why some people may choose not to work due to current government policy.

TACKLING ECONOMIC INEQUALITIES

COLLECTIVIST AND INDIVIDUALIST APPROACHES

The **collectivist approach** means that society is responsible for all its citizens. The State (government, local authorities) has an obligation to provide services such as health and education for all. **Individualists** on the other hand, argue that it is up to each person to look after their own health and welfare and that of their family, and believe that when the state provides too much, some people give up on their own responsibilities. Individualists say collectivism leads to an expensive, inefficient **nanny state** and may prefer private providers of health, education and insurance, believing that competition between service providers saves money and is more efficient. They believe collectivism creates a **dependency culture**, but collectivists disagree stating that the founding principles of the **welfare state** are collectivist, and believing that the state should provide for its citizens through taxation.

Traditionally Labour has been viewed as collectivist with the Conservatives as individualist. In recent years, Labour has attempted to re-establish its collectivist ideology under current leader Jeremy Corbyn. Meanwhile, the Conservatives have clearly developed their own version of an individualist approach since becoming the Government in 2010. Former Chancellor George Osborne talked about how the benefits system penalised those who worked and rewarded those who did not; the 'strivers vs. skivers' as he called it. This tough approach to the benefits system continued under former Conservative PM Theresa May despite her initially adopting a softer tone, referring to her aim to help those who were, 'just about managing'.

However, it would appear that public attitudes towards benefits are slightly shifting away from that of George Osborne and Theresa May. In the 2018 British Social Attitudes Survey, only 20% supported higher benefits for the unemployed, however, this represented the highest support since 2002. As well as this, 56% believe that cutting benefits would do damage to people's lives, a 14% increase since 2010.

DON'T FORGET 

The UK living wage, promoted by the Living Wage Foundation, in 2020 is £9.30 and £10.75 in London. In 2018, there are 1262 accredited living wage employers in Scotland, including Heart of Midlothian Football Club, AG Barr (makers of Irn Bru) and Councils including Dundee City and North Lanarkshire.

THE SCOTTISH PERSPECTIVE

The SNP Government supports universal benefits and a collectivist approach to the welfare state, including policies such as free university tuition fees. But with cuts being imposed on the Scottish budget, opposition parties question the longevity of these policies. Decision-making in Scotland can influence the rest of the UK too.

Following the 2016 Scotland Act, additional welfare powers have been devolved to the Scottish Parliament. Eleven benefits are being wholly transferred, including Disability Living Allowance and Personal Independence Payments, along with the opportunity to top up existing benefits such as Universal Credit and Employment Support Allowance and also create new ones. As well as these new powers, the Scottish Government has paid to cover the losses incurred by people affected by the 'Bedroom Tax' since 2012 and also established a Scottish Welfare Fund to replace the Discretionary Social Fund which was scrapped by the UK Government. By 2021, a new service: Social Security Scotland will be set up to administer these new powers over benefits.

FACT 

Work and Families Act 2006 – This sets out statutory rights for leave and pay in connection with the birth and/or adoption of children.
Equality Act 2010 – This law makes it illegal for anyone to be discriminated against on the basis of gender, race, age, disability, sexuality, especially in employment.

THE WELFARE STATE

In 1942, the Beveridge Report was published highlighting the 'five giants standing in the way of social progress.' These five giants were Want, Squalor, Ignorance, Disease and Idleness. The report specifically focused on Want which, today, we refer to as poverty. Beveridge believed that it was the government's responsibility to tackle these 'giants' and that a welfare state should be introduced to do so. The founding principles of the **welfare state** were that it should be collectivist (state funded), universal (free at the point of need), comprehensive (available for everyone) and equal (services provided to the same standard regardless of region). This 'from the cradle to the grave', Labour Government welfare state provided a National Health Service, housing, education and employment

contd

ONLINE 

Head to www.brightredbooks.net for further reading on this topic.

programmes and benefits, all paid for via taxation and National Insurance in order to tackle poverty and its consequences. Things have changed since the 1940s!

FACT

Educational Maintenance Allowance is £30 per week paid every two weeks.

ONLINE

For more on sanctions, head to www.brightredbooks.net.

BENEFITS

The Department of Work and Pensions (DWP) administers a range of benefits to tackle economic inequalities. Many of them are means-tested, so the amount of each benefit can vary per person/household.

Child Benefit (No longer universal)	Paid to parents earning less than £50 000 per year for each child they have. 2020 Child Benefit rates were £20.70 per week for the eldest or only child and £13.70 for each additional child.
The Claimant Commitment (Jobseekers Allowance)	Temporary payment paid to those actively seeking employment. Financial penalties imposed on those who break the terms of their commitment to seek employment.
Income Support	Top-up payment for those on a low income.
Personal Independence Payment (Replaced Disability Living Allowance)	Paid to those who cannot work due to a disability or long term illness.
Working Tax Credits	Paid to those on a low income based on their hours of work per week.
Child Tax Credits	Paid to those on a low income who have children.
Housing Benefit	Payment towards housing costs for those on low or no incomes.
Universal Credit	A single benefit payment which is paid directly to recipients each month. Universal Credit is gradually being rolled out around the UK and replaces the six other benefits above.

Benefit sanctions are penalties imposed on claimants who do not meet conditions such as attending job centre meetings or failing to show enough effort to find work. For example, claimants can lose 100% of their Universal Credit payment. The DWP believes sanctions are reasonable and are only used in a minority of cases. However, the UK Parliament's Work and Pensions Committee stated in late 2018 that sanctions were "pointlessly cruel" and appeared to disproportionately affect certain vulnerable groups such as single parents and carers.

WORK AND HEALTH PROGRAMME

The Work and Health Programme (WHP) was launched in 2017. It provides specialised employment support for people with disabilities and long-term unemployed people. It is available, on a voluntary basis, to those with health conditions or disabilities. It also provides support to those who have been unemployed for over two years and is compulsory for this group. The WHP replaced the Work Programme and Work Choice schemes. Funding for the WHP will be at least £130 million a year by 2019/20. This includes funding to be devolved to Scotland.

THE SCOTTISH GOVERNMENT

The SNP Government works alongside private businesses and a range of agencies to tackle Scotland's youth unemployment problem as part of the **More Choices, More Chances** initiative.

Modern apprenticeships are programmes run by Skills Development Scotland providing individuals with the opportunity to secure industry-recognised qualifications while earning a wage.
Educational Maintenance Allowance (EMA) is paid to Scottish students between the ages of 16 and 19 undertaking a range of educational opportunities. There are various eligibility criteria such as family income, numbers of dependent children, age and residency. EMA is also provided in Northern Ireland and Wales, but not in England.

Curriculum for Excellence is the overall development of the school curriculum in Scotland. To improve educational attainment there are now reduced primary 1 class sizes and financial education is provided in secondary schools, as well as Skills for Work courses. Free school meals are provided for all primary 1–3 pupils. The Pupil Equity Funding is allocated directly to schools and targeted at closing the poverty related attainment gap between P1 and S3. This funding is to be spent at the discretion of the school. Additional resources have also been provided through the Scottish Attainment Challenge. The Scottish Attainment Challenge is about achieving equity in education. It focuses on improvement in literacy, numeracy and health and wellbeing in the poorest areas of Scotland.

THINGS TO DO AND THINK ABOUT

1. Analyse the view that individuals should be responsible for their own health and wellbeing. (12)
2. To what extent have government policies been successful in reducing poverty in Scotland and/or the UK? (20)

ECONOMIC INEQUALITIES IN GENDER AND RACE

ONLINE

Learn more about this at www.brightredbooks.net

ONLINE

Go to www.brightredbooks.net to find out more about the gender pay gap.

FACT

In the UK, 20% of women are in poverty compared to 18% of men. That's 5.2 million women to 4.7 million men.

FACT

The #MeToo movement originally highlighted the impact of sexual abuse in the film industry but has now spread to almost all industries. Is has also shown the extent of male domination in the film industry where women made up only 16.4% of film directors in 2017 and just 4.57% of film directors since records began.

FACT

In 2018, 62% of those earning less than the real Living Wage were women. 26% of all working women in the UK don't earn a wage they can live on.
In 2019, Eurostat found that 71% of women in the UK were employed, which is higher than many other developed countries e.g. the USA (66%) but behind Iceland (81%) and Switzerland (76%).

EVIDENCE OF ECONOMIC INEQUALITIES IN GENDER

Despite the fact that women make up 52% of the UK population, various reports including the Sex and Power 2020 (in Scotland), ONS and the Resolution Foundation found that Britain is still a country run largely by men. For example, 47% of the UK's workforce are women, but there remains an 17.3% median hourly **gender pay gap** and imbalanced representation at senior management and board level. However, women are still much more likely to be low paid - 22% of working women are low paid (3.4million), compared to 14% of men (2.1million). In 2017, the World Economic Forum ranked the United Kingdom 15th out of 144 countries when measuring the gender pay gap. The UK was ranked 26th in 2014 but was ranked 9th back in 2006.

Women are paid just £380,000 on average over their lifetimes compared with £643,000 for men, £260,000 less, according to an ONS report in 2019.

The Sex and Power in Scotland Report 2020 highlighted, again, the under-representation of women across many areas of Scottish society. Following up from a similar report in 2017, the 2020 report stated that women had only achieved marginal gains in some sectors over three years whilst going backwards in others. Of 39 areas researched, only 5 had achieved 50% women. One area of genuine improvement was within the Scottish Government with 50% of Cabinet Secretaries and members of the Scottish Parliament Corporate Body are now women.

CAUSES OF ECONOMIC INEQUALITIES IN GENDER

Cause of gender inequality	Description
Interrupted employment/education/training	Women often have to take time out of their careers or education to have and care for children. This can negatively impact their opportunities, experience and progress.
Presenteeism	Women often struggle to balance career and family making it difficult to exist in corporate culture where male executives spend time together outside of the workplace and outwith normal working hours. Women may even be viewed with suspicion if they do try to compete!
Stereotyping/discrimination/sexism	There are still some misconceptions that women are incapable of certain tasks or that a male would do the task better. Women may miss out on work or promotion due to assumptions related to domestic responsibilities. This is often called the **glass ceiling**.
Childcare/lone parenthood/part-time work	Women often take on the role of primary care giver for children meaning they are responsible for the costs involved. This can also impact their employment and educational opportunities. 9 out of 10 lone parents are women. This is often referred to as the **motherhood penalty**. 73% of all part-time workers are women, which affects their income significantly.
Gender segregation	Certain jobs remain 'female' while others remain 'male'. 'Female' jobs are predominantly within the 5 'C's of caring, cleaning, cashiering, catering and clerical. These are often low-paid and/or temporary jobs. Nearly two-thirds of women work in these roles.
Welfare dependency	Lone parenthood and part-time employment often lead women to become reliant on benefits.
Life expectancy	Women tend to live longer than men which can lead to increased female poverty levels in old age. Low income throughout their lifetimes may result in low pension contributions.
Lack of female role models and intimidation	Male-dominated work places can be threatening and there are few women in positions of authority or power to look up to.

EVIDENCE OF ECONOMIC INEQUALITIES IN RACE

In 2017, a study by the Guardian newspaper, in conjunction with Operation Black Vote, found that only 36 (3.4%) of the UK's most influential 1000+ people came from Black Asian and Minority Ethnic Groups (BAME). This list is a mixture of the UK's most influential political, financial, judicial, cultural and security figures including people like London Mayor Sadiq Khan and former Home Secretary Sajid Javid. This is despite almost 13% of the UK's population coming from a BAME background. Even more worryingly,

contd

only 7 (0.7%) of these influential people were BAME women. In some sectors – the police, military, supreme court and security services as well as top consultancies and law firms – there were no non-whites represented in influential positions.

People from BAME group are more likely to be in poverty than white British people. In 2016, just over half of Bangladeshis (51%), around 46% of Pakistanis and 40% of Black/African/Caribbean/Black British people were living in poverty compared to 19% of people in White ethnic groups. Research by KPMG found that for every £1 earned by someone from a White ethnic group in the UK, a worker from an ethnic minority group only earns 66 pence.

Unemployment and BAME

2018 data from the UK Government found 4% of White people were unemployed compared with 7% of people from all other ethnic groups combined. Black people had the highest unemployment rate out of all the ethnic groups at 9%.

Income and BAME

After housing costs were deducted and dividing the UK population into fifths, White British households had the largest percentage of households in the highest income quintile (21%), and the smallest percentage in the lowest income quintile (17%). Bangladeshi households had the smallest percentage of households in the highest income quintile (4%), and the largest percentage in the lowest income quintile (44%). The ethnic groups with the largest percentage of households in the 2 lowest quintiles were Pakistani (76%), Bangladeshi (74%) and Black (62%). By comparison, 37% of White British households fell into the 2 lowest income quintiles.

Following the murder of black teenager Stephen Lawrence in 1993, the **MacPherson Report** highlighted the **institutional racism** within the Metropolitan police. This term refers to racism that is so ingrained within an organisation that it affects daily decision-making and produces regular inequality. Anger over the shooting of mixed-race suspect Mark Duggan led to the London Riots in 2011. These riots then spread to other towns and cities across England. Poverty, affluence, class, geography and opportunity were all found to be drivers of the riots and an estimate from the Ministry of Justice (MoJ) showed that of those arrested in London, 46% were black or of mixed heritage and 7% were from an Asian or mixed Asian background.

CAUSES OF ECONOMIC INEQUALITIES IN RACE

Cause of race inequality	Description
Stereotyping/discrimination/racism	There are still some misconceptions that people from BME groups are incapable of certain tasks or that whites would do the task better. Ignorance and hatred may cause some BMEs to miss out on opportunities.
Welfare dependency/lone parenthood	Many BMEs find themselves reliant on state benefits and therefore on a low income. There are also high rates of lone parenthood within black African and black Caribbean communities.
Language barriers	Some first-generation immigrants may not speak English as a first language which can limit opportunities.
Educational attainment/skills transfer	Qualifications and certification gained outside the UK may not be recognised in the UK.
Culture and tradition	Many Pakistani and Bangladeshi women are expected to stop education, training or work to have children or look after family members. Some jobs that require uniforms may limit cultural dress.
Lack of role models	There are few BMEs in positions of power or authority to aspire to be like. There were once again 2 ethnic minority MSPs elected in the 2016 Scottish Parliament election.
Low pay/unemployment	Black men and Pakistani and Bangladeshi women consistently have the lowest employment rates in the UK.

THINGS TO DO AND THINK ABOUT

1 Explain the causes of gender inequalities in the UK.

2 Essay practice: To what extent are women and people from ethnic minority groups equal in society. Your essay may refer to Scotland and/or the UK examples. (20)

Women often bear the brunt of domestic responsibilities too. For example, they spend an average of 26 hours per week on care and household activities, compared with only 16 hours for men.

Some women have become very successful and are now independently wealthy as a result. Baroness Michelle Mone OBE, for example, founded the very successful Ultimo Company and is now a member of the House of Lords.

ONLINE

New revelations relating to the Met Police and the MacPherson Report can be found at www.brightredbooks.net

Rishi Sunak, Chancellor of the Exchequer

ONLINE

Read the report at www.brightredbooks.net for more on this.

ONLINE TEST

Test yourself on this topic at www.brightredbooks.net

TACKLING ECONOMIC INEQUALITIES IN GENDER AND RACE

TACKLING ECONOMIC INEQUALITIES

The UK Parliament introduced the Equality Act in 2010 which merged existing legislation such as the Equal Pay Act 1970, the Sex Discrimination Act 1975 and the Race Relations Act 1976 to make it illegal to discriminate on the basis of:

- gender
- pregnancy
- age
- gender reassignment
- race
- religion or belief
- disability
- sexual orientation.

The Scottish Government introduced the **public sector equality duty** to encourage Scottish local authorities to remove discrimination and harassment, encourage equal opportunities and promote positive relations between different groups.

The **Equality and Human Rights Commission** (EHRC) has a mandate by the UK Parliament to identify and tackle areas where there is still unfair discrimination or where human rights are not being respected.

Positive Action is a UK-wide policy that aims to reduce inequalities and improve opportunities for women and ethnic minorities in the workplace by encouraging employers to have an equal and balanced workforce.

ONLINE 

For more on the National Advisory Council on Women and Girls, go to www.brightredbooks.net

FACT 

The 1999 Scottish Parliament election returned 48 women to the chamber out of 129 MSPs. By the 2016 election that number had fallen to 45.

DON'T FORGET 

Despite various legislation, there is evidence to suggest that up to 54 000 women are sacked each year simply for being pregnant, and each year an estimated 100 000 mothers said they had experienced harassment or negative comments related to pregnancy or flexible working at work.

FACT 

Women-only shortlists for political representation are permitted until September 2030

GENDER

- MSN UK have introduced flexible working hours for all staff and Apple have an equal opportunities policy. The Scottish Parliament follows standard working hours and provides childcare facilities.
- The **2017 Flexible Working Survey** by Pow Wow Now found Women (34%) are more likely to ask for flexible working over a pay rise compared to men (26%). However, 6% more men than women are offered flexible working.
- The **Fawcett Society** campaigns for women's equality and rights and puts pressure on the government to reduce gender inequalities in the UK.
- The UK Government's **Gender Pay Gap Service** highlights several actions which are most effective in reducing the gender pay gap. These include including multiple women on shortlists for jobs, using skills based tasks in recruitment rather than interviews, encouraging workers to negotiate their salaries, being open about pay and promotion processes and appointing diversity managers or task forces.
- **Think, Act, Report** is a voluntary initiative introduced by the UK Government in 2013 to help improve gender equality in the workforce. There are hundreds of companies and thousands of employees signed up. A recent initiative introduced in November 2014 encourages flexible working to support parents.
- An alliance of women's organisations and the Scottish Parliament launched the Scotland's Women Stand initiative in June 2019. The initiative aims to tackle the gender imbalance in Scottish politics.
- The National Advisory Council on Women and Girls exists to advise the First Minister on what's needed to tackle gender inequality in Scotland.

Despite these actions, until all employers introduce standard working hours, men, in general, will find it easier to attend training courses, network after hours and so on, and therefore climb the career ladder.

RACE

- The independent **McGregor-Smith Review** 2017 outlined 26 recommendations on areas such as raising transparency and celebrating success, to help increase black and ethnic minorities' participation and progression in the workplace. It concluded that if Black, Asian and Minority Ethnic (BAME) talent was fully utilised, the economy could receive a £24bn boost each year.
- The recommendations of the McGregor-Smith Review have been followed up by the UK Government in the **Race at Work Survey** 2018 to find what steps employers have taken to remove barriers to workplace progression for ethnic minorities.
- 21 UK universities have signed up to the Equality Challenge Unit's **Race Charter Mark**. Institutions taking part must work to improve the representation, progression and success of minority ethnic staff and students, and submit an action plan for future progress.
- **Operation Black Vote** aims to ensure greater racial justice and equality throughout the UK.
- **Business in the Community** has a racial equality campaign called **Race for Opportunity** which calls for a government review of racial barriers in the workplace and works to ensure ethnic minorities progress into management positions at the same pace as the general working population.
- The **Joseph Rowntree Foundation** publishes information relating to poverty within social groups in the UK and encourages political debate based on their findings.
- **Age UK** is a charity which works to highlight the specific needs of elderly minority ethnic groups and women.

The UK Ministry of Justice published an update in February 2020 setting out a comprehensive set of proposals to tackle racial and ethnic disparity in the Criminal Justice System in England and Wales. This report came three years after the Lammy Review (2017) which highlighted an over-representation of people from ethnic minority backgrounds in the Criminal Justice System.

PROGRESS?

- Whilst there remains only two BAME MSPs in the Scottish Parliament, Humza Yousaf has now been appointed Justice Secretary in the Scottish Government, the first BAME Scottish Cabinet Secretary.
- In March 2020, seven out of the 12 members of the Scottish Cabinet are women. The Scottish Government, including junior ministers, will be fully gender balanced at 13 men and 13 women.
- The UK female employment rate reached a record high of 72.4% in December 2019. The male employment rate was 80.6%. 9.31 million women were working full-time, while 6.30 million were working part-time.
- The 2019 UK General Election returned the highest number and proportion of female MPs ever recorded: 220 (34%) of 650 MPs were women, up from 208 in 2017 (+12). This continues the trend of increasing female representation in Parliament. At 34%, the UK is in 39th position in the proportion of women in the lower (or only) house of parliament. In 2020, 36% of the MSPs were women with Nicola Sturgeon as First Minister. However, this is marginally less than the 37% of women who were MSPs in the first Scottish Parliament in 1999.

THINGS TO DO AND THINK ABOUT

1 Complete spider diagrams to highlight policies introduced to reduce **gender** and **race** inequalities in Scotland and the UK.

2 Evaluate the effectiveness of government policies to tackle gender or race inequalities. In your answer you may refer to Scottish and/or UK policies. (12)

FACT

In late 2017, Glasgow City Council confirmed it would settle a long-running equal pay dispute with 6000 female workers who claim they were paid £3 an hour less than male counterparts over many years. Overall, £750 million has been spent in Scotland settling equal pay disputes. However, around 27,000 claims remain active.

ONLINE

Head to www.brightredbooks.net for further reading and more information on ethnicity.

FACT

The Scottish Parliament has also elected only four MSPs from ethnic minority background in the past two decades.

ONLINE TEST

Test your knowledge of this topic at www.brightredbooks.net

HEALTH INEQUALITIES: EVIDENCE AND POLICY

WHAT ARE HEALTH INEQUALITIES?

There is a great deal of evidence to show that some groups of people are more likely to enjoy better health and have longer life expectancy than others i.e. everyone's health is not equal. Four ways in which health inequalities can be demonstrated (in terms of life expectancy/healthy life expectancy or mortality/morbidity) are by: geographic location within the UK, Scotland and also within or between areas e.g. Dundee/Tayside; social class i.e. between wealthiest and poorest; gender between males and females; ethnicity between different ethnic groups.

There have been many studies carried out both by government and other bodies, which set out the causes of health inequalities, evidence of these inequalities and how they persist over time. Unfortunately, Scotland continues to have a poorer health record than the rest of the United Kingdom. However, health inequalities remain a problem everywhere.

ONLINE

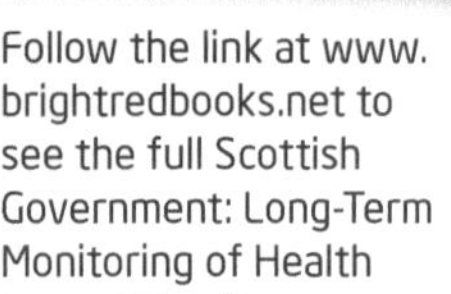

Follow the link at www.brightredbooks.net to see the full Scottish Government: Long-Term Monitoring of Health Inequalities (January 2020 report).

EVIDENCE

Scottish Government: Long-Term Monitoring of Health Inequalities

The Scottish Government regularly produces a report on a range of health indicators in Scotland, the latest of which was in January 2020 and is based on evidence up to 2018. The key findings and evidence were:

- Inequalities in heart attack hospital admissions. In 2018, the admission rate in Scotland's most deprived areas was more than twice that of those living in the least deprived (132.4 cases per 100 000 compared to 55.1 per 100 000).
- Inequalities in premature mortality. In 2018, the premature mortality rate in the most deprived areas was 820.0 per 100 000, four times higher than the rate in the least deprived areas (210.6 per 100 000).
- Inequalities in Coronary Heart Disease (CHD) deaths. In 2018, the CHD mortality rate was more than four times greater in Scotland's most deprived areas compared to the least deprived (219.8 compared to 54.0 deaths per 100 000 population).
- Levels of absolute inequality for cancer deaths have fluctuated but in 2018 cancer mortality rates (aged 45-74) have consistently been twice as high in the most deprived areas compared to least deprived areas.
- Inequalities in alcohol-related hospital admissions. In 2018, alcohol-related admissions were 4 times higher in the most deprived areas of Scotland compared to the least (426.8 compared to 98.6 cases per 100 000).

FACT

Healthy Life Expectancy (HLE) is the number of years a person spends in 'good health'. Women living in the 10% least deprived areas can expect to spend 23 more years in good health than those in the 10% most deprived areas. For men, the difference in healthy life expectancy is 22.5 years.

LIFE EXPECTANCY

Data published by the National Records for Scotland (NRS) in 2019 show a boy born in 2018 in one of the 10% most deprived areas of Scotland will live for 13 years less than a boy from the most affluent areas. Girls born between 2015 and 2017 in the 10% most deprived areas in Scotland can expect to live 9.6 years less than those who live in the 10% least deprived areas.

In 2019, the NRS reported that Scotland's life expectancy was the lowest in the UK. Girls born in Scotland between 2015 and 2017 could expect to live until they are 81.1 years. Life expectancy for boys born in the same period is 77 years. In England, life expectancy for girls was two years higher, and for boys it was 2.5 years higher. Girls born in Wales and Northern Ireland could expect to live until they were 82.3 years old. For boys the figures were similar - 78.3 years in Wales and 78.4 years in Northern Ireland.

DON'T FORGET

Mortality means people dying whilst morbidity means people suffering ill health. Men have higher mortality rates whilst women have higher morbidity rates.

contd

Overall, life expectancy in Scotland has been increasing over the long term but recent estimates indicate that it has stopped improving. The largest causes of the stall in life expectancy are the slowing of improvements seen in the reduction of deaths from heart disease and increases in drug related deaths. Of most concern, the NRS report also stated that Scots' life expectancy had fallen for first time in 35 years.

HEALTH INEQUALITIES DASHBOARD, MAY 2019

The **Health Inequalities Dashboard** provides information to monitor progress on reducing inequalities within England. The annual report by the UK Government presents information on a range of areas and has been found to show that health inequalities in England are similar to those in Scotland:

- for both males and females, the gap in life expectancy between the most and least deprived areas of England has significantly widened between the years 2011 to 2013 and 2015 to 2017 to 9.4 years for males and 7.4 years for females
- the gap in healthy life expectancy was around 19 years in 2015 to 2017
- inequalities in health have narrowed within England for several indicators, including children living in low-income families, young people not in employment, education or training, and the employment gap between those with a long-term health condition and the overall employment rate
- within England, inequality has narrowed for alcohol-related hospital admissions and self-reported wellbeing - however, babies in the most deprived areas are twice as likely as those in the least deprived to be born with low birth weight and this inequality has not changed since the baseline
- there are wide inequalities in the prevalence of overweight children by deprivation and ethnicity
- although premature mortality rates from cancer and cardiovascular disease have decreased in recent years in England, the relative inequality gap has widened, with rates in the most deprived areas twice as high for cancer and 4 times higher for cardiovascular disease than the least deprived areas.

The National Performance Framework

In 2020, the Scottish Government published the National Performance Framework (NPF). The aim of the NPF is to: create a more successful country; give opportunities to all people living in Scotland; increase the wellbeing of people living in Scotland; create sustainable and inclusive growth; reduce inequalities and give equal importance to economic, environmental and social progress. For the Scottish Government, wellbeing is seen as important as economic growth i.e. people's quality of life should matter as well as increasing Scotland's GDP.

POLICY

Equally Well: ministerial task force on health inequalities (Reviewed 2014)

Equally Well is the Scottish Government's plan to tackle health inequalities in Scotland, outlining the roles of local and national government, NHS Scotland and the **third (voluntary) sector**. It recognises that health varies according to people's age, disability, gender, race, religion or belief, sexual orientation and other individual factors, and that health improves with socio-economic status.

The Early Years Framework

The Scottish Government recognises that what happens to children in their earliest years is key to outcomes in adult life. This view is based on a wide range of research evidence from education, health, justice and economic experts.

THINGS TO DO AND THINK ABOUT

1 What evidence is there of health inequalities in Scotland and in the rest of the UK? In your answer make reference to death rates from different causes and life expectancy.

ONLINE

Read more about Equally Well by following the link at www.brightredbooks.net

ONLINE

For more information on health inequalities in England and the obesity crisis in the UK go to www.brightredbooks.net.

ONLINE

Head to www.brightredbooks.net to find more information on Scotland's National Performance Framework and how Scotland is performing against it. "

FACT

Scotland has fallen five places from 16th to joint 21st in the 2020 update Scottish Trends Index of Social and Economic Wellbeing.

ONLINE

To hear First Minister Nicola Sturgeon explain more on the Scottish Government's approach to improving Scotland including reducing inequalities go to www.brightredbooks.net.

DON'T FORGET

Reducing health inequalities has been a priority for successive governments in Scotland but most indicators show that inequalities are not reducing.

ONLINE TEST

Head to www.brightredbooks.net and revise this topic by taking the online test.

CAUSES OF HEALTH INEQUALITIES

Health inequalities are the unjust and avoidable differences in people's health across the population and between specific population groups. Numerous studies have shown that poverty, marginalisation in society, and failures in the past by government to prioritise a reduction in health inequalities are the fundamental reasons why health inequalities persist today.

SOCIOECONOMIC STATUS

A person's social status is, by far, the biggest factor impacting on their health. Living in poverty at any age damages both physical and mental health. Low income, poor housing, discrimination and access to health services all significantly reduce life expectancy and increase mortality and morbidity rates.

For anyone from an affluent background, understanding the grinding impact of poverty on individuals is extremely difficult. Damp housing, overcrowding, having to skip meals or choose between turning the heating on in winter or eating, etc. is unbelievably stressful and stress wears people down. The constant worry over bills or providing for children, especially when it comes to birthdays, Christmas and holidays all take a heavy toll on health. Poverty, without question, inexorably destroys health.

The biology of poverty

"The biology of poverty" is a phrase linked closely to Scotland's former Chief Medical Officer Harry Burns. More than two decades ago, Professor Burns, as he is now, stated the relentless cycle of children being born into poverty and remaining there all their lives was blighting Scotland's future and must be broken. His work at the time drew connections between social deprivation and chronic ill health, especially for those who experience poverty and adversity early in life.

GEOGRAPHY

Where someone lives within Scotland also plays a part in securing good health and is closely linked to socioeconomic status. For example, in 2018, there was a big gap in life expectancy between the most and least deprived areas of the country. The life expectancy gap in Scotland in 2018, at its widest, is roughly 13 years for males and around 10 years for females. Part of the explanation for geographic health inequalities is the way in which deprivation within a community adds to the pressure on the most deprived people, i.e. the poorest members of society often live in the most deprived communities, which are often characterised by poorer housing, fewer green spaces, greater noise, higher crime levels and fewer affordable, accessible community facilities.

There is also a **north-south divide** health inequalities gap across the UK. For example, the ONS found in 2017, life expectancy for a male born in Scotland was 77 years (females 81.1 years), England 79.6 years (83.1), Wales 78.3 years (82.2) and Northern Ireland 78.5 years (82.3). Again, these statistics are linked to levels of deprivation throughout the UK but they also hide significant differences in health within each part of the UK.

LIFESTYLE CHOICES

A wealth of evidence proves poverty is the single most important factor impacting on health. However, individual lifestyle choices - smoking, alcohol consumption, drug misuse, exercise and diet - also play a part in exacerbating health inequalities.

There is also clear evidence to show that many of the people living in the most deprived communities make poorer lifestyles choices. One reason to explain these poorer choices is that many people in deprived communities look to alleviate the problems poverty creates by seeking out the "feelgood factor". What this means is that some of those from the most deprived communities smoke, drink alcohol or overeat as a way of making themselves feel better in the short-term. However, long-term, repeated poor lifestyle choices eventually impact on health.

Smoking

In Scotland, around 13000 people die every year from smoking-related diseases. Smoking is a major cause of cancer, heart disease and stroke. There are an estimated 1.1m smokers in this country. Within the population, 28% of men and 25% of women smoke. However, in deprived communities 42.1% of adults aged between 16-64 smoke. Children whose parents smoke are 1.5 times more likely to develop asthma.

contd

Alcohol

Excess consumption of alcohol plays a part in poor health in Scotland. The NRS reported that in 2018 there were 1 136 alcohol-specific deaths in 2018 (where alcohol was the underlying cause of death) - an increase of 16 (1.4%) more than in the previous year. 1 in 4 people (24%) drink at hazardous or harmful levels (defined as drinking more than 14 units per week). Drinking more than 14 units a week was reported by 32% of men and 16% of women.

Alcohol Focus Scotland reported that alcohol harm costs Scotland £3.6 billion a year in health, social care, crime, productive capacity and wider costs. Alcohol costs the health service in Scotland £267 million a year. Finally, alcohol-related mortality rates for those living in the most deprived areas are six times the rate for those in the least deprived areas. The rate of alcohol-related hospital admissions for those living in the most deprived areas is almost nine times the rate for those in the least deprived areas.

Drug misuse

Figures taken from NHS Health Scotland show, in 2016/17, that there were an estimated 57300 individuals with problem drug use in Scotland - almost 1 in 60 of our population aged between 15 and 64. There were 1 187 drug-related deaths in 2018, 253 (27%) more than in 2017. This is the largest number ever recorded and was 613 (107%) more than in 2008, which was 574. The extent of loss of life to drug-related deaths, particularly among those aged 35 to 55 years, is now a substantial contributor to the worsening life expectancy trends in Scotland. Drug misuse is the sixth leading cause of early death in Scotland and the overall burden is 17 times higher in the most deprived areas compared to the least deprived. It is estimated that the total economic and social cost of drug misuse exceeds £3.5bn per year.

Obesity

In 2016, 65% of adults were overweight including 29% obese. For children, 29% were at risk of becoming overweight (including obesity) with 14% at risk of becoming obese according to NHS Health Scotland. Obesity in Scotland shows a strong link with inequalities. Lower socio-economic status is associated with higher levels of obesity. The risk of obesity in children is lowest for those living in more affluent areas. Around 32% of adults living in the most deprived areas are obese, compared with 20% of those living in the least deprived areas. Women and children in the most deprived areas are particularly affected by more extreme obesity. It is estimated the cost to the economy of obesity in Scotland is anywhere between £0.9 billion and £4.6 billion.

OTHER FACTORS: GENDER, RACE AND AGE

Three other factors which also play a part in bringing about inequalities in health are gender, race and age. However, these factors are also interrelated as, again, they are closely linked to socioeconomic status.

Gender: women are likely to outlive men in Scotland. In 2017, the average life expectancy at birth was 81.2 years for females and 77.1 years for males. Reasons to explain this difference are many but include behaviours, i.e. men's greater involvement in risk taking activities and women's better lifestyle choices, i.e. lower illicit drug use, as well as biological and environmental factors. On the other hand, women tend to experience greater rates of morbidity which can be partly explained by women's greater willingness to report illness but also environmental factors such as lower incomes or greater caring roles or biological factors such as childbearing.

Race: statistics from the NHS suggest there are significant health inequalities between ethnic groups in Scotland. For example, most ethnic groups in Scotland reported better health than people who identify as white Scottish. Also, mortality in Scotland is higher in the majority ethnic (white) population than in the black and minority ethnic population. However, there is greater prevalence of sickle cell disease in African origin groups and of cardiovascular conditions and diabetes in South Asian origin populations.

Age: as people get older their health deteriorates with elderly people the greatest users of health services. Conditions such as dementia, which affects 90,000 people in Scotland, is most common in older people but can affect younger people too.

ONLINE

Follow the link at www.brightredbooks.net to find out more about health inequalities in Glasgow and how NHS Scotland is working to reduce health inequalities in Glasgow.

ONLINE

To find out the experience of children growing up in poverty watch Poor Kids: at www.brightredbooks.net."

ONLINE

For more on the impact of poverty on children, review the Educational Institute of Scotland's (EIS) Face up to Child Poverty booklet at www.brightredbooks.net.

FACT

Suicide is three times greater for males in Scotland than females.

DON'T FORGET

Health is a devolved matter in Scotland.

ONLINE TEST

Test yourself on the causes of health inequalities at www.brightredbooks.net

THINGS TO DO AND THINK ABOUT

1 Essay practice: Analyse the different lifestyle choices that can result in poor health. (12)

TACKLING HEALTH INEQUALITIES

SCOTTISH GOVERNMENT AND NHS HEALTH SCOTLAND – THE BIG PICTURE

To reduce health inequalities, the Scottish Government and NHS Scotland need to act across a range of areas, with policies to tackle economic and social inequalities alongside actions with a specific focus on disadvantaged groups and deprived areas. Both the Scottish Government and NHS Scotland need to shift the focus from meeting the cost of dealing with health or social problems after they have developed to prevention and early intervention. Key messages for both are:

- Implement policies that bring about a fairer share of income, power and wealth through legislation, regulation and taxation.
- Ensure fair and equitable access to good quality housing, education, health and other public services for all.
- Ensure all public services are planned and delivered in proportion to where need is greatest.

Examples of action to undo the fundamental causes of health inequalities

- Introduce a minimum income for healthy living.
- Ensure the welfare system provides sufficient income for healthy living and reduces stigma for recipients through universal provision in proportion to need (proportionate universalism). See the Scottish Government's Fairer Action Plan 2016.
- A more progressive individual and corporate taxation. For example, the Scottish Government raising more from income tax from higher earners e.g. 46% rate for those earning over £150 000 per year.
- Active labour market policies (e.g. hiring subsidies/self-employment incentives, apprenticeship schemes) and holistic support (e.g. subsidised childcare, workplace adjustments for those with health problems) to create good jobs and help people get and sustain work. For example, the Scottish Government is funding up to 600 hours of free childcare or roughly 16 hours per week in term time for all three and four-year-olds and a quarter of two-year-olds at a cost of £1.5bn.

Examples of action to prevent harmful environmental influences on health inequalities

- Ensure local service availability and high quality green and open spaces, including space for play.
- Raise the price of harmful commodities like tobacco (see graphic) and alcohol (Minimum Unit Pricing; 50p per unit) through taxation and further restrict unhealthy food and alcohol advertising.
- Protection from adverse work conditions (greater job flexibility, enhanced job control, support for those returning to work and to enhance job retention).
- Provision of high-quality early childhood education and adult learning.

Examples of action to mitigate the effects of health inequalities on individuals

- Link services for vulnerable or high-risk individuals (e.g. income maximisation welfare advice for low income families linked to healthcare).
- Provide specialist outreach and targeted services for particularly high-risk individuals (e.g. looked after children and homeless).
- Ensure that services are provided in locations and ways which are likely to reduce inequalities in access (i.e. link to public transport routes; avoid discrimination by language).

contd

ONLINE 

Learn more about this by following the link at www.brightredbooks.net

FACT 

In 2020, 80.6 per cent of Scottish workers – approx. 1.95m people - earn at least the real Living Wage of £9 per hour, but the Scottish Government want to see a 1 per cent rise by 2022.

FACT 

Well Woman and Well Man Clinics offer free advice and support related to gender-specific health issues such as cervical smears for women and prostate checks for men.

SPECIFIC EXAMPLES OF SCOTTISH POLICIES TO REDUCE HEALTH INEQUALITIES

Since the National Health Service (Scotland) Act 1947 came into effect in July 1948, the NHS has provided comprehensive, universal and free health care for all. Health is a **devolved matter**, meaning the Scottish Government is in control of health policy.

Smoking, Health and Social Care (Scotland) Act 2005

It has been illegal in Scotland to smoke in the majority of enclosed public places since 2006. England followed suit shortly after in 2007.

The Schools (Health Promotion and Nutrition) (Scotland) Act 2007

A number of initiatives are aimed specifically at schools and school children. The Schools (Health Promotion and Nutrition) (Scotland) Act combines the work of initiatives such as **Health Promoting Schools** and **Hungry for Success** in Scottish schools. The Nutritional Requirements for Food and Drink in Schools (Scotland) Regulations 2008 set health standards for school meals. **Health and Wellbeing Outcomes** are embedded within the Curriculum for Excellence alongside specific health-promoting programmes such as: supervised tooth brushing in primary schools; substance misuse education; **Let's make schools more active** initiative increasing PE allocations; **Active Schools** programmes; sex and relationships education (SRE); HPV vaccinations for girls aged 12–13; The Children and Young People (Scotland) Act 2014 – Getting it Right for Every Child, Named Person etc.

Tobacco and Primary Medical Services (Scotland) Act 2010

People must be at least 18 years old to buy tobacco products. Tobacco products cannot be openly displayed in larger shops, and cannot be sold in vending machines. Packs of ten cigarettes and flavours such as menthol will be phased out in accordance with EU policy by 2020. Meanwhile, the UK Government introduced legislation in 2015 and 2016 forcing all tobacco products to be sold in plain green packaging by 2017.

The Alcohol (Minimum Pricing) (Scotland) Act 2012

The aim of the Alcohol (Minimum Pricing) Act is to set at a minimum price of 50p per unit of alcohol in an attempt to improve health in Scotland. The Chief Medical Officer has stated that when it is fully implemented, alcohol-related deaths would fall by about 60 in the first year and 318 by year ten of the policy, and hospital admissions would fall by 1600 in year one, and by 6500 per year by year ten of the policy.

Free prescriptions were introduced in Scotland in 2011 and free eye tests are available for all in Scotland. The UK Government also introduced a ban on **new psychoactive substances** or so-called legal highs in 2016. Police now have the power to shut down "headshops" - stores which sell drug paraphernalia - and online dealers in the UK.

NHS: A Fairer, Healthier Scotland

This report sets out NHS Scotland's five-year strategy for 2017-2022 to provide fairer health improvement. It highlights how the health of the people of Scotland is improving but that improvements have not been equal across the population. The five strategic priorities are: fairer and healthier policy; children, young people and families; a fair and inclusive economy; healthy and sustainable places; transforming public services.

FUTURE POLICIES?

The Scottish Government has agreed to introduce to extend **free personal care** for everyone who needs it regardless of age by 2019. 9000 people will benefit from the policy. New rules are now in place restricting TV adverts for food which are high in fat, salt and sugar. These must not be shown at times where children aged under 16 are the target audience.

THINGS TO DO AND THINK ABOUT

1 Describe the Scottish government's approach to tackling health inequalities.

ONLINE

Explore more health services offered by the Scottish Government by following the link at www.brightredbooks.net

DON'T FORGET

Laws and health provisions can vary in different parts of the UK as a result of devolution.

ONLINE

Learn more about this by following the link at www.brightredbooks.net

FACT

E-cigarettes have become more common. An estimated 2.9m people vape in the UK. Smoking numbers have fallen but there are worries about the long-term use of e-cigarettes. New rules on the sale of e-cigarettes, including banning sales to under-18s and establishing a register of shops selling the devices, came into effect in 2016.

ONLINE TEST

Take the test on tackling health inequalities at www.brightredbooks.net

ONLINE

Head to www.brightredbooks.net for an explanation of how to answer these essay questions.

CRIME AND THE LAW IN SCOTLAND

THE ROLE OF LAW: RIGHTS AND RESPONSIBILITIES

THE ROLE OF LAW: AN OVERVIEW

For society to function in a civilised manner, there have to be boundaries on acceptable behaviour. Rules and laws are developed in order to create structure in society, and to reduce confusion and social and political disorder which might arise from a lack of governmental and societal control.

VIDEO LINK 

Watch the clip at www.brightredbooks.net for more on this!

Rules apply to groups of people, situations or organisations, so they can vary. For example, there may be rules at home and at school about how to behave, as well as on the football pitch. People are encouraged to follow the agreed rules and breaking them can have consequences such as being grounded, sent to detention or sent off the pitch.

DON'T FORGET 

In the UK, laws are made and reviewed by the UK Parliament and by the Scottish Parliament as a result of devolution.

Laws apply to a whole country. Laws provide a solution when someone takes unfair advantage of another person. They protect property and allow a person to know the consequences of their behaviour before they act, thus acting as a deterrent. They allow the removal from society of those who are dangerous and protect every person's rights.

LEGAL RIGHTS AND RESPONSIBILITIES

FACT 

The Psychoactive Substances Act (2016) made a number of new psychoactive substances illegal. These so-called legal highs had previously been sold online or in shops known as headshops.

As soon as they are born, people are entitled to have or do certain things. These are known as **rights**. With every right comes a corresponding **responsibility**. The table shows some of the general rights and responsibilities. If responsibilities are not adhered to, then rights may be taken away.

Right	Responsibility
Vote	Make an informed choice and use your vote
Free speech	Do not abuse or offend others
Protest and assembly	Do not damage people or property
Freedom of the press	Not to defame or slander

The **United Nations Convention on the Rights of the Child** (UNCRC) is an international human rights treaty that grants all children and young people (aged 17 and under) a comprehensive set of rights.

In most cases, parents have responsibility for their children until the child is 16 years old. There are, however, occasions where the courts will take action and make decisions that ensure the wellbeing of a child, such as when parents fail to take responsibility.

In Scotland, the policy of **Getting it Right for Every Child** (GIRFEC), which focuses on the rights of children, is based on the UNCRC.

AGE LIMITS IN SCOTLAND

As we get older, the law gives us more responsibility for our own lives.

Buy tobacco products	18
Buy alcohol	18
Have your own bank account	From birth
Adopt a child	21
Make a will	12
Give blood	17
Buy fireworks	18
Stand as an MP or Councillor	18
Vote in UK General Election	18
Vote in Scottish elections	16
Leave school	16
Get a tattoo	18
Get married	16
Get a job	14 (limited hours) 16 (full-time)
Age of consent	16
Get a piercing (with consent)	16
Be prosecuted for a crime	12

FACT

The 2014 Scottish Independence Referendum gave 16- and 17-year olds the right to vote in the referendum. The legal age to vote in Scottish Parliament elections and Scottish Local Council elections has now been lowered to 16. However, the UK Government has resisted requests for a similar reduction for UK General Elections.

ONLINE

For more information about drugs, head to www.brightredbooks.net

LAWS IN SCOTLAND

Devolution allows the Scottish Government to make and amend laws on a range of devolved matters, including health and crime.

Tobacco and Primary Medical Services Act 2010	Tobacco products cannot be openly displayed in large shops or sold in vending machines. People must be 18 to purchase tobacco products.
The Road Traffic Act 1988 (Prescribed Limit) (Scotland) Regulations 2014	Series of laws relating to driving: ● limit of 50mg of alcohol per 100ml of blood for drivers ● speed limits on public roads ● all occupants of a car must wear seatbelts ● drivers cannot use hand held devices while driving.
Alcohol and Minimum Pricing Act 2012	Since 1 May 2018 each unit of alcohol costs at least 50p.
Smoking Prohibition (Children in Motor Vehicles) (Scotland) Act 2016	Made it an offence to smoke in a motor vehicle with anyone aged under 18 present to limit exposure to second-hand smoke.
Domestic Abuse (Scotland) Act 2018	Creates a specific offence of "abusive behaviour in relation to a partner or ex-partner". This includes psychological abuse such as coercive and controlling behaviour as well as violence and intimidation.

UK Drug Classification 2018

Class A	Cocaine, Heroin, Ecstacy
Class B	Cannabis, Ketamine, Speed, synthetic cannabinoids (e.g. Black Mamba), synthetic cathinones (e.g. Mephedrone)
Class C	Anabolic Steroids, GHB, Khat

FACT

Ketamine was reclassified in June 2014 from a Class C to a Class B drug. Cannabis was briefly classified as a Class C, but is currently a Class B drug.

ONLINE TEST

Test yourself on this topic at www.brightredbooks.net

THINGS TO DO AND THINK ABOUT

1 Create a table of at least three arguments for and three arguments against the voting age being lowered to 16.

2 Describe the current government classification of drugs and new psychoactive substances. Use the website https://www.talktofrank.com/ for more information. Is drug classification an effective method of stopping drug use?

3 Should cannabis be legalised? Provide arguments for and against.

4 Describe current Scottish government policy relating to alcohol.

THE ROLE OF LAW: THE LEGAL SYSTEM IN SCOTLAND

Law has a role is every aspect of society from registering the birth of a child to dealing with property after death.

There are many different areas of law:

- **civil law** covers private matters between individuals
- **criminal law** covers crime or offences (minor acts of law breaking)
- **employment law** covers the relationships between employers and employees
- **family law** covers family-related matters.

CIVIL LAW

Civil law covers private matters between individuals. Although there are many different types of cases dealt with under civil law, examples would include:

- defamation of character
- legal disputes relating to property ownership
- disagreement in relation to a divorce.

FACT

There were 81,200 civil law cases initiated in 2017-18. This was an increase of 10% from 2016-17, which was the lowest figure since 2008-09.

CRIMINAL LAW

Criminal law refers to any acts that are offences or crimes, such as exceeding the speed limit while driving, burglary or murder. The age of criminal responsibility in England and Wales is 10 years old, but because of devolution it is different in Scotland. Following a successful change in the law in the Scottish Parliament in 2019, the age of criminal responsibility in Scotland is now 12 years old, matching the age of criminal prosecution. This bill was introduced by the Scottish Government and had the support of the Scottish Children's Reporter Administration, the Scottish Children and Young Person's Commissioner and organisations such as CYCJ and Children 1st

> Early Years Minister Maree Todd said: "All children deserve the best possible start in life and this legislation marks a key milestone in Scotland's journey to ensure children are respected and valued. "We know the actions of children who harm others are often a symptom of trauma in their own lives and that accruing a criminal record actually drives more offending."
>
> *Source: BBC News 2018*

ONLINE

Read more about this at www.brightredbooks.net

The Scottish **Children's Reporter Administration** (SCRA) deals with any criminal cases relating to children in Scotland and the **Crown Office and Procurator Fiscal Service** (COPFS) deals with adult cases.

THE CROWN OFFICE AND PROCURATOR FISCAL SERVICE

The Crown Office and Procurator Fiscal Service is Scotland's criminal prosecution service and is an important part of the justice system. The Crown Office is headed by the **Lord Advocate** and the **Solicitor General** for Scotland. They receive reports from the police and other agencies related to criminal acts and decide what action to take, which may be **prosecution.**

Prosecution involves the legal proceedings against the person or persons accused of a crime. COPFS also investigate deaths that need further explanation and allegations of criminal conduct against police officers.

FACT

In 2018-19, the COPFS received 170 575 criminal reports (from the police and other specialist reporting agencies), a decrease of 4% compared with 2017-18 (177 801).

TYPES OF CRIME

The **Scottish Crime and Justice Survey** (SCJS) surveys peoples' experiences of crime in Scotland annually. The survey findings show that young males are the most likely social group to be both victims and offenders, and that the crime rate is higher in areas of social deprivation, particularly in Glasgow with 717 crimes committed in 2018–19 per 10 000 of the population. The information published by the SCJS does not necessarily reflect official statistics.

These figures are not a true reflection of crime rates as many crimes go unreported. For example, 61% of violent crimes went unreported in 2017–18.

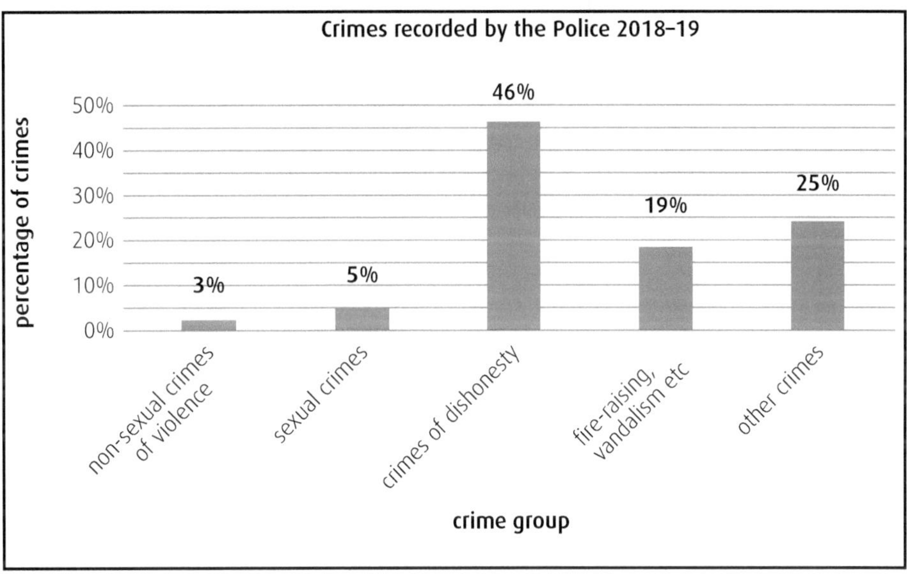

Source: Recorded Crime in Scotland 2018–19

According to official Scottish Government statistics, recorded crime is at its lowest level since the mid-1970s. But Niven Rennie of the Violence Reduction Unit (VRU) maintains the level of crime in society is not reflected in the figures. "We're still at the stage where we see more victims of violence coming to A&E than we do to the police," Rennie said. "We know the statistics are as accurate as they can be, but there's a lot of crime going unreported."

Source: The Scotsman Sept, 2018

THINGS TO DO AND THINK ABOUT

1 Evaluate the current Scottish legal age of responsibility. Explain your answer in detail and if you believe it should change, what should it be?

2 Both civil and criminal laws have to be regularly updated. Why might this be? Provide examples in your answer. (Hint – think about new technology.)

3 Describe the different reasons there may be for a crime not being reported.

4 Explain why both Recorded Crime in Scotland and the Scottish Crime Survey (SCJS) are used to show and evaluate levels of crime in Scotland.

ONLINE TEST

Head to www.brightredbooks.net to test yourself on this topic.

THEORIES AND CAUSES OF CRIME

To tackle and prevent crime, it is important to examine why crimes are committed. There are a number of social and individual theories. Social theories (also referred to as collectivist theories) suggest that crimes are committed due to the community a person lives in and is exposed to, which influences their behaviour. It suggests that the behaviour of others and societal structures create criminals. Individual theorists believe in a more innate biological cause; however, others argue that for some people, committing a crime is simply a choice. The overall discussion is known as the **nature vs nurture** debate.

DON'T FORGET

The nature vs. nurture debate continues today. Recent research by Robert Plomin in his book 'Blueprint: How DNA Makes Us Who We Are' argues that 50% of our behaviour is determined by our genetics and that these traits are hereditary. However, he argues that whilst the other 50% is environmental, much of this is either determined by your parents' actions (based on their genes) or, is random and happens by accident rather than being 'nurtured'.

FACT

Joanna Dennehy is the first woman in the UK to be sentenced to a full life term by a judge. She was found guilty of brutally murdering three men in the space of ten days in March 2013 and the attempted murder of two dog walkers whilst on the run from the police. Despite coming from a stable and comfortable home background, Dennehy has been diagnosed with several psychopathic and anti-social disorders and showed no remorse for her crimes.

THE THEORIES

The born criminal

Cesare Lombroso was an Italian physician who noted that some physical features such as receding hairlines, forehead wrinkles, broad noses and fleshy lips were shared among criminals. He associated these characteristics with primitive man and labelled this condition **atavism** – the born criminal. Lombroso said the born criminal was pre-destined for criminal behaviour due to their physical configuration. His theories have been discredited but provided a starting point for research into innate biological reasons for crime.

Eysenck's personality theory of offending

Psychologist Hans Eysenck used a series of personality tests to measure the connection between personality and crime. He viewed offending as natural and even rational, on the assumption that human beings were hedonistic, sought pleasure, and avoided pain. He assumed that delinquent acts such as theft, violence, and vandalism were essentially pleasurable or beneficial to the offender.

Strain theory

Most people aspire to similar levels of success and material wealth, but not everyone has the same opportunities or access to employment which can deliver the lifestyle they want. Some people will try to achieve such success through criminal activities.

Labelling theory

The labelling theory suggests that the very act of calling someone a criminal will determine their behaviour and make them more likely to act in a criminal way. Society is less accepting of criminals in terms of social opportunities and employment, so labelling someone a criminal may lead to more criminal behaviour. There are two consequences of labelling – the creation of stigma and the modification of self-image.

In 1973, criminologist William Chambliss conducted a study into the labelling theory where he followed two groups of high school males for two years. Both groups were regularly involved in deviant behaviour and committed crimes, but only one group appeared to face any punishment. He found that because one group came from respectable families, were high achievers and politely spoken, people labelled them as 'good' whereas the other group, who came from poorer family backgrounds and underachieved in comparison, were labelled as 'bad' and faced punishment for their behaviour. This labelling resulted in different consequences for the same behaviour for each group.

Social control theory

Travis Hirschi's social control theory suggests that society places controls on the behaviour of individuals which prevent them committing crime. The controls are imposed through institutions such as schools, workplaces, churches and families.

Social learning theory

Albert Bandura's social learning theory suggests that people learn criminal behaviour – the motivation and the skills – from people they associate with and the behaviour they observe.

contd

Rational choice theory

Theorists such as Daniel Kahneman believe that people take rational decisions about committing crime by comparing the potential risks of being caught and punished against the benefits of the crime.

Social disorganisation theory

The environment in which a person lives can have an influence on the choices a person makes. In particular, areas of deprivation with poor social structures are more likely to have high crime rates.

FACT

Mark Duggan was shot and killed by police on 4 August 2011 in London. The police thought he was armed and planning an attack. This event sparked a series of riots across several English cities, causing an estimated £200 million worth of property damage. Five people died, there were at least 16 injured as well as around 3000 arrests for crimes related to violence, criminal damage and theft. Poverty, affluence, class, geography and opportunity were all found to be drivers of the riots.

CAUSES OF CRIME

It is difficult to state simply one cause of crime. There is usually a combination of factors.

Poverty and social exclusion

Large cities and urban areas tend to have higher crime rates than more rural areas. Many of these areas are considered deprived and Glasgow City Council has more areas of deprivation than any other local authority in Scotland, and has the highest crime rate of all council areas.

In some areas a lack of facilities, especially for young people, can lead to boredom, which can lead to crime.

Drugs and alcohol

In 2017–18, 83 people were accused of homicide (murder) in Scotland. 35% were reported to have been drunk and/or under the influence of drugs at the time. This figure is significantly lower than previous years. Between 2009–10 to 2018–19, 46% of all accused were reported to have been under the influence of alcohol and/or drugs at the time of the homicide.

Greed

Not all crimes are committed by those in poverty. Some crimes are committed by those from affluent backgrounds who want more money and think they can get away with it. This is known as **white collar crime**, and includes crimes such as fraud and tax evasion. For example, in 2017, Mark Conway, an IT Officer with Dundee City Council, was found guilty of defrauding the council of £1,065,085 between August 2009 and May 2016.

Lack of positive role models and poor family background

Some people may come from poor family backgrounds and have no positive role models in their lives. In some areas, the people who are viewed as successful and influential are those who deal drugs or run gangs.

VIDEO LINK

Watch 'The Peer Pressure Experiment' at www.brightredbooks.net

THINGS TO DO AND THINK ABOUT

1 What is the difference between collectivist and individual theories of crime? List the above theories under the appropriate headings 'Individualist Theories' and 'Collectivist Theories'. Briefly summarise each theory.
2 Watch the 'Peer Pressure Experiment' on YouTube. How would you react?
3 Carry out your own research into the 2011 riots.
  What were the main causes of the 2011 riots? What theories of crime could be attributed to the riots?
4 Essay practice: To what extent is poverty the main cause of crime? (20)

ONLINE

Read more about Chambliss at www.brightredbooks.net

ONLINE

Read more about the English riots at www.brightredbooks.net

THE IMPACT OF CRIME

DON'T FORGET

Crime can make everyone in society a victim in the sense that government spending on crime increases, insurance premiums rise, laws get tighter and police presence increases.

DON'T FORGET

It is not just the individual victims of crime that suffer, their family and friends can too.

ONLINE

Read the results of the crime and justice survey at www.brightredbooks.net

PERSONAL IMPACT

Crime can have a physical, social, emotional and economic impact on individuals. The extent of the impact can vary according to a number of factors such as the type of crime, if the offender was known to the victim and the support the victim receives.

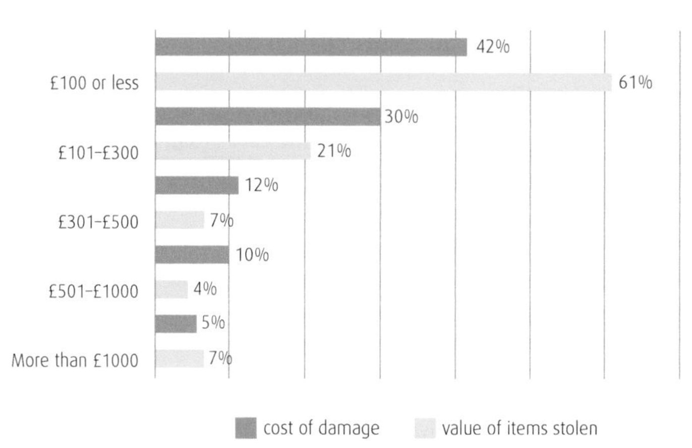

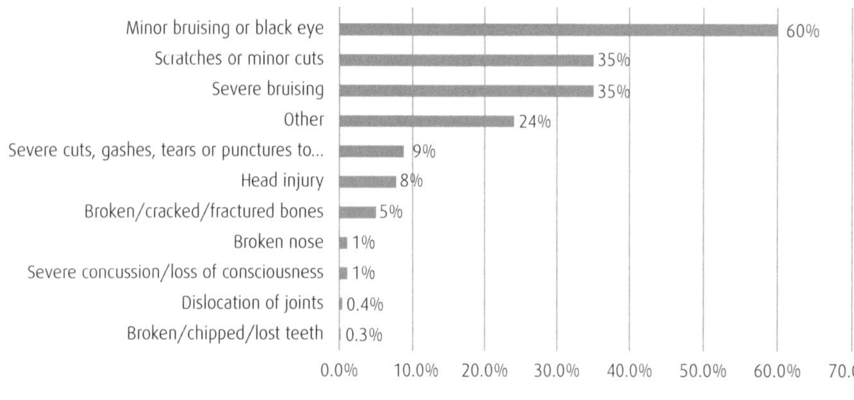

Physical impacts

Victims of crime may require medical attention and suffer long-term injury or scarring. People can develop anxiety disorders (PTSD), become depressed and have trouble sleeping.

Social and emotional impacts

Crime can cause people to feel unsafe and, in some cases, struggle to leave their homes. This can affect their employment and education. If someone is the victim of a burglary, for example, they may feel unsafe and anxious even in their own home.

	Violent crime	Property crime
Shock	30%	16%
Fear	26%	5%
Loss of confidence	16%	5%
Anxiety	16%	4%
Depression	6%	4%

Strong negative emotions felt by victims of crime

There is also an emotional impact when personal items are stolen or damaged. Across all SCJS crimes, the most common emotions experienced by the victims were annoyance (44%) and anger (45%). Other than annoyance and anger, victims of violent crime were more likely to experience other strong negative emotions than victims of property crime.

Offenders can also be emotionally affected by crime with feelings of guilt or fear of revenge.

Economic impacts

Some crimes have an immediate economic impact such as the theft of a handbag, where it costs to replace the stolen items. This type of crime can lead on to less obvious and long-term problems such as identity theft or fraud, which can take months to resolve.

Offenders may be economically affected by having to pay fines or compensation. Their employment, education and earning potential can be limited if they are given a criminal record.

COMMUNITY IMPACT

Unemployment and lack of opportunities

Communities can become run-down if crime is a regular occurrence, so people do not want to live or work there. The value of homes and businesses in those areas depreciates and there can be a lack of investment, so unemployment rises and prospects for individuals fall.

Areas with high crime rates can receive negative reputations, and people from these communities become stereotyped, especially young people.

Social exclusion

In crime blackspots, people may feel unsafe and avoid socialising, meaning there is no sense of community. Gangs and antisocial behaviour may instil fear of public spaces.

Drug and alcohol abuse

Lack of opportunities can lead to people looking for distractions to combat depression and social exclusion. This can mean increased alcohol or substance abuse.

Increased police and CCTV presence

Areas of high crime tend to have more police on the beat and high numbers of CCTV cameras in an attempt to prevent and tackle community problems.

ECONOMIC IMPACT

As businesses try to combat crime, they inevitably increase security, which means increased prices for the consumer. Some businesses cannot cope with these increased costs so shut down or downsize, impacting jobs in certain areas. Companies are also less likely to invest in areas of high crime. In 2015–16, the cost of crime to UK businesses was £8.7 billion.

Areas of high or regular crime may face high insurance premiums and low house values. People may have to spend more money on individual security measures such as house alarms.

POLITICAL IMPACT

The Scottish government may introduce or amend laws to tackle crime. Sometimes these laws can be viewed as controversial, such as the Offensive Behaviour at Football and Threatening Communications (Scotland) Act 2012. This Act was repealed (it is no longer a law) by Parliament in 2018 following a Members Bill by Labour MSP James Kelly. The government may also make changes to the powers of Police Scotland, which may reduce civil liberties.

Crime means the government has to spend valuable time and money (tax revenue) dealing with its consequences and prevention, which could perhaps be better spent elsewhere. For example, vandalism costs the City of Glasgow local authority around £8 million annually. This figure is actually conservative as many crimes of vandalism go unreported.

If a country has a high crime rate, it can affect its international reputation too.

THINGS TO DO AND THINK ABOUT

1 Essay practice: "Some crimes have a greater impact on society than others." Analyse the impact of different crimes on society. (12)
2 Explain how civil liberties are affected if police powers and tighter laws are introduced to combat crime.
3 Carry out a local crime survey in your area. You should aim to find out:
- what types of crime occur
- why people think these types of crime occur
- who is blamed for these crimes
- what people think can be done to tackle crime.

Think very carefully about who and what you'll ask and be prepared to present your findings.

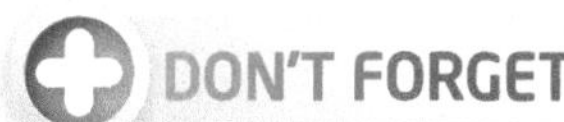

DON'T FORGET

Both businesses and individuals are also having to cope with new crimes such as **cyber-crime** where the internet is used to steal money, data or personal data of customers. Combating this type of crime requires investment in cyber-security. Cyber-crime and identity theft cost business in Scotland £394 million in 2016.

FACT

In 2015-16 crime cost the Scottish economy nearly £4.5 billion. This figure includes the cost of policing, courts, and disposals such as prisons and non-custodial sentences.

ONLINE TEST

Revise your knowledge of the impact of crime by taking the test at www.brightredbooks.net

DON'T FORGET

Some methods used by the police divide opinion. Consensual searches (where the officer requires the consent of the person) were used widely by Police Scotland in order to search for drugs and weapons such as knives. This policy was supported by the Violence Reduction Unit (VRU) but opposed by civil liberties groups and many politicians. The policy was ended in 2015 amid criticism that it unfairly targeted children as young as 12.

TACKLING CRIME IN SCOTLAND

Various organisations and groups, including the government, are focused on tackling and ultimately reducing crime in Scotland.

POLICE SCOTLAND: PROTECT, PRESERVE AND PREVENT

In April 2013, eight regional police forces merged with the specialist services of the Scottish Police Services Authority, including the Scottish Crime and Drug Enforcement Agency, to create one Scottish police service. This is now the second largest police force in the UK after the Metropolitan Police and it is headed by a Chief Constable. There are many civilian roles within Police Scotland and full-time officers are supported by many part-time voluntary Special Constables.

Police Scotland aims to protect people and property, preserve order at public events such as sporting events and protests, and prevent crime in general by visiting schools and working with communities.

Alongside the local policing divisions, there are a number of national specialist divisions. The **Specialist Crime Division** (SCD) provides specialist investigative and intelligence functions such as major crime investigation, public protection, organised crime, counter terrorism, intelligence and safer communities. It also incorporates the **National Human Trafficking Unit**, the **Border Policing Command** and the **Trunk Road Patrol Group (TRPG)**.

Community policing and initiatives

Within each police division there are community teams which set priorities based on specific community issues such as anti-social behaviour and protecting vulnerable people. Community-based officers work alongside community groups to gain trust and build relationships based on respect and local needs.

Some recent Police Scotland initiatives include:

- specific taskforces focusing on national child abuse, domestic abuse, national rape, hate crime
- firearms amnesties
- music festival safety
- student safety
- knife amnesties
- Smartwater – use of a marking solution only visible under UV light to safeguard residential belongings
- Weed Them Out - campaign to help landlords spot cannabis cultivation in properties in Forth Valley.

Violence Reduction Unit

The **Violence Reduction Unit** (VRU) works alongside Police Scotland and the Scottish Government to tackle violent crime in Scotland. The VRU uses a different approach to violent crime, particularly knife crime, treating it as a public health problem rather than a criminal problem. It has introduced initiatives such as Braveheart Industries which aims to reduce gang crime and allow members to instead access education and employment. However, the VRU also advocates tougher sentences for anyone involved in violence such as knife crime. The work of the VRU has been credited for a 69% drop in fatal stabbings in Scotland from 2006-07 to 2015-16. Following a spate of fatal stabbings in London in 2018, London Mayor Sadiq Kahn announced a similar scheme will be introduced in London.

FACT 

Phil Gormley became the second Chief Constable of Police Scotland in 2015 following the resignation of Sir Stephen House. However, Gormley resigned as Chief Constable in 2018 following a series of misconduct allegations. In August 2017, Iain Livingstone was appointed the new Chief Constable.

DON'T FORGET 

Law and order is a devolved matter, meaning that there are differences between Scottish and English police forces and Police Scotland only has authority in Scotland.

ONLINE 

Follow the Police Scotland link at www.brightredbooks.net

FACT 

Police Scotland introduced 101 calls, which provides a single number for the public to contact police if they don't need an emergency response. 999 remains the emergency number to call.

CLOSED-CIRCUIT TELEVISION

Closed-circuit television (CCTV) is used extensively in Scottish towns and cities. There are considerable arguments for and against the widespread use of CCTV.

Supporters of CCTV highlight that it is invaluable in fighting crime. The number of camera-assisted arrests remains high and CCTV can be in areas where police cannot be, making people feel safer and reducing the fear of crime, since CCTV can act as a deterrent. CCTV can also provide jobs for those operating the systems. Recently, Edinburgh City Council replaced their CCTV system with a new £1 million set of upgraded high-definition digital cameras which provide face and car number-plate recognition.

However, opponents of CCTV argue that CCTV costs a great deal of public money each year. Two local authorities in Scotland, Midlothian and Inverclyde, have proposed ending their use of CCTV to save money due to budgetary constraints. Civil liberties groups argue that there are too many CCTV cameras in Scotland and that CCTV is an invasion of privacy. There are also concerns that existing CCTV systems are out-dated and produce poor quality, blurry images which cannot be used as evidence in court. A leaked report by Police Scotland criticised the current 'piecemeal' system of CCTV cameras arguing for it to be replaced by a single, police-run national network using high-definition digital cameras costing at least £10m to install.

SCOTTISH GOVERNMENT INITIATIVES: A SAFE, JUST AND RESILIENT SCOTLAND

In 2017 the Scottish Government published its new justice strategy for 2017 to 2020:

- A new, smaller, women's prison to replace HMP Cornton Vale
- Two new **Community Custody Units** for female offenders with a greater emphasis on rehabilitation and reducing reoffending
- Earlier interventions in the lives of people with poor physical and mental health who may have or be at risk of experiencing traumatic events and therefore at a much greater risk of being drawn into offending (20 times more likely)
- These approaches are already reducing youth offending where there has been a 78% fall in the number of under 18's convicted since 2006-07
- Following the recommendations of the **Christie Commission** which found that up to 40% of all public spending could have been avoided by using a preventative approach instead of interventions.

These new initiatives aim to support existing Scottish Government policies which have been operating for several years such as:

- **Cashback for Communities** which allows the proceeds of crime to be used to fund community projects to tackle crime
- Reducing reoffending programme in Scottish prisons
- Increasing mandatory sentencing from four to five years for carrying a knife
- The **Criminal Justice and Licensing (Scotland) Act 2010** which strengthened the law in terms of hate crimes
- Tackling misuse of firearms and air weapons.

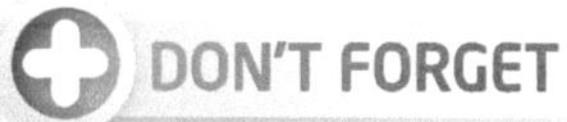

DON'T FORGET

Other funding, such as that provided by the National Lottery, can also help support anti-crime projects.

ONLINE

Read more about armed policing in Scotland at www.brightredbooks.net

ONLINE

Read more on Scottish community projects and charities dealing with crime at www.brightredbooks.net

DON'T FORGET

Note your sources and try to make them as recent as possible!

ONLINE TEST

Test your knowledge of tackling crime at www.brightredbooks.net

THINGS TO DO AND THINK ABOUT

1. Use a variety of sources (newspaper articles, interviews, documentaries, websites, blogs etc.) to investigate the following topics of discussion and debate:
   - Should all Police Scotland officers be armed?
   - Has the creation of Police Scotland been a success?
   - Why was Police Scotland created?
   - CCTV vs. Community Policing.
   - Does CCTV work?
   - Knife crime in Scotland.
2. Essay Practice: Evaluate Scottish government policies to tackle crime. (12)
3. Explain the different government agencies and organisations responsible for tackling crime.
4. Essay Practice: Evidence the effectiveness of CCTV in tackling crime. (12)

THE LEGAL SYSTEM IN SCOTLAND

OVERVIEW

The legal system of Scotland involves various agencies and organisations:

- UK Parliament
- Scottish Parliament including the Cabinet Secretary for Justice
- Crown Office Prosecution Service (COPFS)
- Scottish Courts Service
- Children's Reporter Administration
- Police Scotland
- The Scottish Prison Service including Young Offenders Institutions

All courts in Scotland are organised by the **Scottish Court Service** (SCS) led by the Scottish Government. They can deal with criminal and civil cases. If someone is tried under criminal law, the Scottish Government accuses them of breaking a law of Scotland, whereas if a case is civil, it involves a dispute between individuals or organisations.

THE PROSECUTION OF A CRIME IN SCOTLAND

When someone is accused of a crime, the police submit the evidence to the Crown Office and Procurator Fiscal Service (COPFS), who decide whether or not to prosecute.

There are two types of criminal court procedure, **solemn** and **summary**. In solemn procedure, a jury of 15 members of the public listen to the evidence and decide on the **verdict**. A judge is also present, who decides on any sentence that may be issued. Summary procedure is used for less serious cases and does not use a jury.

There are three main criminal courts in Scotland, the **High Court of Justiciary**, the **Sheriff Court** and **Justice of the Peace Courts**.

FACT

Between 2013 and 2015, the number of Sheriff Courts in Scotland was reduced by 10 whilst the number of Justice of the Peace Courts was reduced by 7. Cost savings of £1m a year in running costs and £3m in maintenance costs were the main drivers of the closures. However, the remaining courts will have better ICT provision installed including Wi-Fi and video link equipment.

SCOTLAND'S COURTS

The High Court of Justiciary

The High Court of Justiciary is the supreme criminal court in Scotland and deals with the most serious crimes such as murder (homicide), **culpable homicide** (killing without intention), rape, armed robbery, treason and serious sexual offences, particularly those involving children.

The High Court has unlimited sentencing powers such as life imprisonment (between 15 and 35 years) or an unlimited fine. Prior to 1965, the High Court had the power to issue the death penalty (capital punishment) where those found guilty of murder would be hanged. The death penalty was officially abolished for murder in 1965 but it wasn't until 1998 that it was officially abolished for the crime of treason.

The Sheriff Court

The Sheriff Court deals with crimes such as theft, assault, prostitution, possession of drugs or appeals from a Children's Hearing.

Under solemn procedure, sheriffs can issue sentences of up to five years in prison or an unlimited fine. Under summary procedure, which can also be heard in a Sheriff Court, a sheriff can issue fines up to £10 000 or prison sentences up to 12 months in prison.

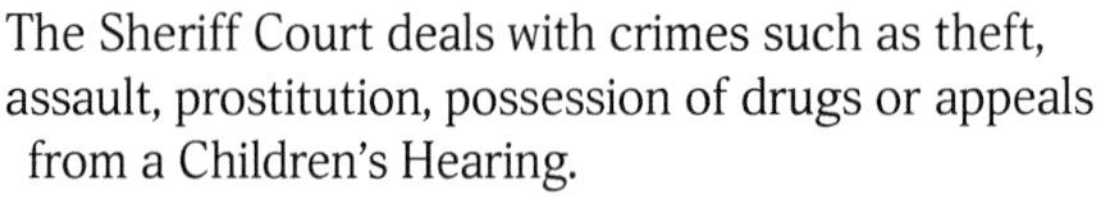

The Sheriff Court also deals with civil cases such as separation, divorce or dissolution of a civil partnership, adoption or custody of children.

Justice of the Peace Courts

Justice of the Peace Courts replaced the District Court in 2007 and are lay courts (business can be carried out

contd

anywhere) where a Justice of the Peace (JP) presides with the support of a legally qualified clerk. These courts deal with offences such as breach of the peace, drunk and disorderly, assault of a police officer and traffic offences.

A JP can issue a maximum **custodial sentence** of up to 60 days and a fine of up to £2500.

The Court of Session

The Court of Session is Scotland's supreme civil court and sits in Edinburgh. The Court of Session can be used as a court of appeal and is headed by a Lord President. In 2018, this court rejected an appeal by UK Government lawyers and ruled that there would need to be a House of Commons vote to ratify any Brexit deal before 29 March 2019. It then forwarded the case to the European Court of Justice to provide a definitive ruling on whether the UK could halt the article 50 process without needing the approval of all other 27 EU member states.

YOUTH CRIME IN SCOTLAND

In 2019, a Bill was passed by the Scottish Parliament which raised the age of criminal responsibility to 12, in line with the age of criminal prosecution. Children aged between 8 and 16 committed 14,615 offences which were subject to referrals to the Children's Reporter including 365 children who had committed ten or more offences. Police also made 215 referrals for non-sexual crimes of violence. It is important to remember that not all crimes recorded by the Police will be referred to the Children's Reporter and so the actual level of offending by under 16's will be higher than these figures. However, evidence does suggest that youth crime is decreasing.

THE SCOTTISH JUVENILE JUSTICE SYSTEM

Under the **Children (Scotland) Act 1995** Scotland has a separate juvenile justice system and the Procurator Fiscal decides whether or not to prosecute and refer a case to the **Children's Reporter**.

The Children's Reporter

The Children's Reporter receives referrals regarding children and decides if action is necessary, such as a hearing. Referrals can be made by the police, social workers, health and education professionals, members of the public and even children themselves.

Referrals have declined in recent years, from 46 899 children and young people being referred in 2008–09 to 13,240 referrals in 2017-18. However, it is important to remember that only a minority of referrals are made to the Children's Reporter on offending grounds. In 2017-18, only 3,063 referrals were made due to offending. The majority of referrals are made due to concern for the wellbeing of the child or young person.

The Children's Hearing system

The **Children's Hearings (Scotland) Act 2011** outlines the powers and proceedings of the Children's Hearing system. The aim of hearings is to target both offending behaviour and welfare concerns and to provide a safe environment for the child or children involved.

Hearings take place in the child's local area with the child present. There will also be a panel of three adult Children's Hearing members as well as the child's parents or guardians. The child can also bring another person of their choosing. The panel is made up of impartial male and female volunteers who have special training.

THINGS TO DO AND THINK ABOUT

1 Describe all the courts in Scotland, including types of crimes and sentencing powers.
2 Explain why there is a separate justice system for children.
3 Discuss the strengths and weaknesses of the Children's Hearing system.

DON'T FORGET

Compulsory Supervision Orders (CSOs) put children under the care of a social worker, a relative or foster carers. CSOs can also limit who the child can associate with and place them into rehabilitation programmes. They can also issue electronic tags (known as a **Movement Restriction Condition**).

ONLINE

Read about the decrease in youth crime at www.brightredbooks.net

ONLINE

Follow the link at www.brightredbooks.net for more on the Children's Reporter.

DON'T FORGET

The Children and Young People (Scotland) Act 2014 came into force in April 2015 and affects the rights of children and young people in Scotland.

FACT

The UK Supreme Court is the final court of appeal for Scottish civil cases. However, permission is required for an appeal case (which has already been heard by the Court of Session) to be considered by the UK Supreme Court. This is usually due to human rights issues (for example, in the Nat Fraser case) but can also be due to 'devolution issues' where it is believed that the Scottish Parliament or Scottish Government have exceeded their devolved powers

ONLINE TEST

Head to www.brightredbooks.net and test yourself on the legal system in Scotland.

CRIMINAL VERDICTS

There are currently three **criminal verdicts** available in Scottish courts. Eight out of fifteen jurors must agree to a verdict.

Verdict	Definition
Not guilty	Based on evidence, the accused did not commit any crime and is free to go.
Guilty	Based on the evidence, the accused committed a crime **beyond any reasonable doubt**.
Not proven	There is suspicion of guilt but not enough evidence to convict. The accused is free to go.

DON'T FORGET 

The 'not proven' verdict only exists in Scotland.

NOT-PROVEN VERDICTS

Case Study: Murder of Amanda Duffy

In May 1992, 19-year-old drama student Amanda Duffy from Hamilton was found mutilated and murdered after a night out with friends. Francis Auld, whom she had known since school, was accused of her murder when his dental records matched a bite mark on her body and he admitted he had been with her that night. He went on trial that same year defended by Donald Findlay QC, but the jury returned a not-proven verdict. The shocking details of her murder and clear connections to Auld put the not-proven verdict under intense scrutiny and shattered many people's faith in it.

In 1994, Auld was convicted of making threatening phone calls to former friends, telling them: 'You thought Amanda was the last – you're next' and, in 1995, Amanda's parents launched a civil suit against Auld. A judge found him responsible for her death and ordered him to pay £50 000 in damages.

The family claim to have received no payment and Auld went on to commit a series of minor offences in England before his death in 2017.

Arguments for and against the not-proven verdict

Arguments for not proven	Arguments against not proven
Allows judges and juries to express reasonable doubt.	Evidence suggests guilt.
It may be more satisfactory for victims and witnesses by reflecting the absence of necessary proof without casting doubt on their evidence.	May leave a permanent mark on the character of innocent people.
	Traumatic for victims and families of victims; some victims of particular crimes may become more reluctant to come forward and there may not be a definitive result. In 2017 to 2018, Scottish figures showed there was a 'guilty' verdict in 87% of cases, with 5% found 'not-guilty' and 1% received 'not-proven' verdicts. However, for rape or attempted rape, 36% were found 'not guilty and 19% received 'not-proven' verdicts with only 43% found 'guilty'.
Juries can be unfairly influenced, particularly by the media.	Confusing to the public.

contd

In 2012, Labour MSP Michael McMahon launched a public consultation into the not-proven verdict after it was announced that Lord Carloway was reviewing Scots law. He said that reform would make the justice system simpler. '[Not proven] exists purely by accident of history and it seems to me illogical, inconsistent and confusing,' he said. However, the Law Society of Scotland were sceptical, and said that removal of the third verdict would mean the remaining two would be 'proven' and 'not proven'.

Mr McMahon and Lord Carloway recognised that removal of not-proven verdicts would lead to further changes within the justice system, perhaps requiring an increased majority within juries, increased from eight out of fifteen to ten. Ultimately, no changes were made on the basis of this consultation.

VIDEO LINK

Head to www.brightredbooks.net to watch a clip on this.

THE DOUBLE JEOPARDY (SCOTLAND) ACT 2011

In March 2011, the **Double Jeopardy (Scotland) Act** was introduced allowing a person to be re-tried for the same crime if there is 'compelling new evidence'. Angus Sinclair became the first person to be retried and convicted under the new rules in November 2014. He was found guilty of murdering Christine Eadie and Helen Scott, both 17, following a night out at the World's End pub in Edinburgh in 1977. A previous prosecution against Sinclair had collapsed in 2007.

The re-trial of Ronnie Coulter for the murder of waiter Surjit Singh Chhokar in Lanarkshire in 1998 resulted in Coulter being found guilty and sentenced to a mandatory life term in prison. However, the Crown Office failed to secure a retrial for Francis Auld in 2016 using the Double Jeopardy (Scotland) Act 2011. Francis Auld died of pancreatic cancer in 2017 aged just 45.

VIDEO LINK

Head to www.brightredbooks.net to watch clips on the issue of abolishing corroboration in Scotland.

CORROBORATION IN SCOTS LAW

In Scots law there is a need for two independent sources of evidence in criminal cases in order to secure a conviction. However, opponents of corroboration believe more rape, sexual offence and domestic abuse cases would be heard in court if the need for two sources of evidence was removed. Plans to end corroboration were brought forward by former Justice Secretary, Kenny MacAskill in 2013, who had said the "outdated rule" meant many victims were denied justice. The reform was supported by police and prosecutors but was strongly opposed by the legal profession, who raised concerns of an increased risk of miscarriages of justice. In 2015, the proposal was withdrawn from the Criminal Justice (Scotland) Bill by the then Justice Secretary Michael Matheson along with a related measure to increase jury majorities. However, Matheson also stated that there was a case for abolishing corroboration but more time was required to consider the issue.

ONLINE TEST

Want to revise your knowledge of this topic? Take the test at www.brightredbooks.net

THINGS TO DO AND THINK ABOUT

1. Should the not-proven verdict be abolished in Scotland? Provide detailed reasons for your answer.
2. Why might some people disagree with the Double Jeopardy (Scotland) Act 2011?
3. Give reasons for and against abolishing corroboration in criminal cases in Scotland.

SENTENCING IN SCOTLAND

HMP Polmont Young Offenders' Institution (YOI) near Falkirk is Scotland's national holding facility for young male offenders aged between 16 and 21. However, 110 female offenders, including young offenders have also been transferred here from HMP Cornton Vale in 2016 whilst a new 80-capacity national women's prison is built along with two, 20-capacity Community Custody Units (CCU's) for women in Glasgow and Dundee.

CUSTODIAL SENTENCES: PUNITIVE SOLUTIONS

Prisons and **Young Offenders Institutions** in Scotland are mostly managed by the **Scottish Prison Service** (SPS) under the jurisdiction of the Scottish Government and the Cabinet Secretary for Justice. There are 15 penal establishments in Scotland and the SPS aim to reduce reoffending and protect the public whilst hopefully transforming the lives of the offenders. Scotland still locks up more people than most other European countries and in 2019, following a decade of falling prison population, it steadily rose to over 8000 inmates, peaking at 8237 in December 2019. This figure was described as 'dangerously high' by the Scottish Chief Inspector of Prisons.

Young offenders

Young offenders can be sent to a young offenders' institution if they have been found guilty of crimes or while they are on remand awaiting trial.

Young offenders are kept separate from adult prisoners and can take part in educational programmes and gain skills and qualifications to help them gain employment on release.

ONLINE

Learn more about Scotland's prison population at www.brightredbooks.net

Case Study: HMP and YOI Grampian

At a cost of around £150 million to build, HMP and YOI Grampian in Peterhead began admitting its first prisoners in March 2014. The establishment, with a capacity of about 500 prisoners, including men, women and young offenders, replaced the previous HMPs Aberdeen and Peterhead and is the first community prison in the UK, so most of the prisoners will be from the Grampian area. In a move away from the traditional style of a Scottish prison, it will focus on rehabilitation and providing skills. However, former Peterhead inmate Johnny Steele says: 'at the end of the day a jail is still a jail regardless of what is available to the prisoners inside, whether that be TVs, swimming pools or whatever. It is still a prison.' The young offenders' hall has been empty since a riot in 2014 and it seems unlikely they will return in the near future.

FACT

In 2017-18, 27% of the Scottish prison population was made up of low-level offenders serving sentences of three months or less. This figure has fallen from 35% in 2010-11 partly due to a presumption against sentences of under three months. In June 2019, this presumption was extended to sentences of under 12 months.

DON'T FORGET

Crime and justice are devolved matters in Scotland.

MANDATORY SENTENCING

Mandatory sentencing (sometimes referred to as **Automatic Sentence** or **Required Custodial Sentence**) means that people convicted of certain crimes must be punished with at least a minimum number of years in prison. For example, the crime of murder carries a mandatory life sentence in Scotland. The aim is to act as a deterrent and provide uniformity in sentencing but courts may impose a less severe sanction where it would be unjust to impose the mandatory sentence. In the case of the crime of murder, the terms of the life sentence are set by a judge and the average time spent in prison is around 13 years. There are limits set on some crimes, for example, the maximum custodial sentence for a crime involving a knife is five years.

Automatic Early Release

Prisoners serving four years or more have to be released at the two-thirds point of sentence if they are still in custody in Scotland. Under the **Prisoners (Control of Release) (Scotland) Act** 2015, prisoners sentenced to four years or more for sex offences and ten years or more for other crimes will no longer be entitled to **automatic early release** from prison at any point in their sentence. Some MSPs would like automatic early release repealed altogether.

FACT

Each prisoner cost the taxpayer over £35 000 for the year 2018.

VIDEO LINK

Watch the clip at www.brightredbooks.net for more information about life for young offenders in HMP Polmont YOI.

NON-CUSTODIAL SENTENCING

Prison (custodial) sentences are only one of the sentencing options available to the courts. The table below shows the other options.

Fine/compensation	Offenders must pay money, either to the victim or to the court.
Fixed Penalty Notice (FPN)	On-the-spot fines issued by the police for low-level crimes such as littering.
Restriction of Liberty Order (RLO - electronic tagging)	The offender is given a curfew and their movements are restricted for up to 12 hours a day. They must wear a transmitter that alerts the police if they violate their agreed conditions.
Drug Treatment and Testing Order (DTTO)	This is a rehabilitation-based sentence. People are subjected to random drug testing and court reviews to monitor their withdrawal from drugs.
Home Detention Curfew	Offenders must be in an agreed address by a certain time each day. If the curfew is broken, they may be sent to prison.
Community Payback Order (CPO)	Introduced in 2011 to combine Supervised Attendance Orders, Probation and Community Service Orders, CPOs can be tailored specifically to offenders based on the nature of their crime and the underlying issues which may have led to it. This may include intensive supervision or unpaid work.
Antisocial Behaviour Order (ASBO)	Bans someone (over the age of 12) from causing disruption with their behaviour. ASBOs can be issued for crimes such as graffiti, noise pollution and littering. They also try to keep people away from certain areas. Broken ASBOs can lead to fines or up to five years in prison.

FACT

Non-custodial sentences are much cheaper than prison. For example, a Home Detention Curfew costs £126 per week compared to £610 per week to keep someone in prison.

THINGS TO DO AND THINK ABOUT

1 'HMP Grampian is money well spent.' Do you agree or disagree with this statement? Explain your answer.

2 Debate and research these topics:

- Automatic early release should be abolished.
- Life should mean life.
- The death penalty should be re-introduced.
- More non-custodial sentencing should replace prisons.
- More crimes should have mandatory sentencing.

3 Explain what is meant by mandatory sentencing.

4 Essay practice: Analyse policies which aim to reduce reoffending. (12)

ONLINE TEST

Test your knowledge of this topic online at www.brightredbooks.net

RESTORATIVE JUSTICE AND REDUCING REOFFENDING

REDUCING REOFFENDING

Reoffending is a continuing problem in Scotland. However, reconviction rates have improved over recent years. There has been a 16% decrease in the reconviction rate in the ten years from 2007-08. In 2017-18, 13% of people convicted (4992) had ten or more convictions, however this has also fallen from around 20% in 2010-11. Despite these improvements, the Scottish Government estimates that the total economic and social cost of reoffending remains around £3 billion a year.

Of the 37 191 people convicted of a crime in 2016-17, 27.2% were convicted of another offence in the next year. Aberdeen City has the highest imprisonment rate in the country with a reconviction rate of 33.3%. Inverclyde and Falkirk have the second and third-highest reoffending rates, 29.2% and 28.9% respectively. Fewer than six out of every ten (or 58%) offenders who serve short sentences (up to 3 months) end up committing another crime within one year, but just over three out of ten (31%) offenders who are instead given a **Community Payback Order (CPO)** reoffend within one year. Figures show that non-custodial sentences are more effective than short prison sentences in deterring convicts from reoffending.

Organisations like The **Scottish Consortium on Crime and Criminal Justice**, the **Howard League for Penal Reform** and the **Prison Reform Trust** agree that alternatives to custody such as Community Payback Orders, Drug Testing and Treatment Orders (DTTO's) and Supervision Orders are more effective in reducing crime. They believe that prison should only be used as an absolute last resort for the most dangerous offenders.

ONLINE

Read the Scottish Government's plans to reduce reoffending and its costs at www.brightredbooks.net

FACT

Men under 21 are the most likely group to reoffend. However, it is worth noting that the population of HMP Polmont YOI has fallen significantly in recent years. Following a critical inspection report in 2007, (when the population was over 1000 and the prison was described as dangerously overcrowded) Polmont's population has dropped substantially (300 16-21-year olds in March 2020).

RESTORATIVE JUSTICE: SOCIAL SOLUTIONS TO CRIME

There is a belief that a strong social service negates the need for a justice system intended to punish. Focusing on the crime is reactionary, in many cases unjust and, ultimately, impractical due to costs involved.

The **Safeguarding Communities Reducing Reoffending** (SACRO) programme aims to promote community safety across Scotland by providing high quality services to reduce conflict and offending. It provides services in conflict resolution, criminal justice and restorative justice and reparation.

A **restorative justice process** is a process where all those involved participate actively in addressing or repairing the harm that was caused, with the help of one or two trained facilitators. They discuss the facts, consequences and what needs to be done to repair a situation.

Restorative justice can be used by prison staff as an alternative, non-punitive way of dealing with the harm caused by misconduct, bullying, a breach of prison rules or violence.

DON'T FORGET

Community Payback Orders can involve a mixture of unpaid work along with a range of other possible requirements including supervision, compensation, treatment, residence, conduct or programmes. The requirements issued by the Sheriff will depend on the needs and circumstances of the offender.

WOMEN IN PRISON: A RADICAL NEW APPROACH

Women are far less likely to offend than men (15% of offenders were female in 2017 compared to 85% men), therefore there are far fewer women in Scottish prisons. However, Scotland has a higher female imprisonment rate than most other countries in Europe (second highest in Europe with 4.9% of the prison population female). HMP/YOI Cornton

contd

Vale, Scotland's national women's prison has been described as, "not fit for purpose," and, "disgracefully poor," in previous inspection reports. In response, radical changes are proposed by the Scottish Government.

The plan is to demolish Cornton Vale and replace it with a smaller, 80 capacity national prison near the current site, starting in 2018. The existing hall at HMP Grampian with capacity for 50 will also be retained. Two small regional units with 20 places each will also be built by 2021. The inspiration for these small units was an existing voluntary project: The 218 Centre in Glasgow. The changes to female imprisonment are supported by many organisations as well as most political parties in Scotland. The main arguments given in favour of these changes are firstly, the higher costs of imprisoning women compared to men and secondly, that prison is often unnecessary for many female offenders. Most female offenders are non-violent and suffering from a range of addictions, poor mental or physical health and trauma issues.

FACT

The 218 Centre is a 12-bed residential centre in Glasgow. Women are referred here by the courts and work on a mixture of compulsory and optional group work sessions and one-to-one support. It also has a clinic dealing with mental and physical health issues. A similar project known as the Willow Project operates in Edinburgh.

SCOTTISH COMPARED WITH SCANDINAVIAN JUSTICE

The rate of reoffending among prisoners in Norway is just under 20% which is the lowest rate in Europe where rates can be as high as 70%. What's the secret of success for Norway's prison service? The answer is simply offering a normal lifestyle, which allows reintegration through work, social life and free association.

Case Study: Bastøy Prison, Norway

Bastøy is an institution where people live in a community. It is often referred to as a **human ecological prison**. Six inmates share a six-bedroom wooden cottage. Each person has a room of their own. Inmates wake up early to work every morning and earn the equivalent of £6 a day doing a variety of jobs, from farming to repairing bicycles to working in the laundrette. There is a monthly fee of about £70 for buying goods in a local supermarket. For those who want to study, go to Mass or play an instrument, there is a library, a school, a church and a guitar teacher.

Visitors are struck by the air of optimism among inmates and comment on the lack of cynicism among guards, who appear to have a genuine sense of pride in their work. Bastøy is also one of the cheapest prisons in Norway to run.

Psychologists say that offenders need a realistic second chance, which is only possible by giving them respect and dignity. Perhaps this doesn't exist in Scottish prisons? One British prison officer is alleged to have said: 'We have to spend time away from our families to look after these vermin.'

ONLINE

Read more about Bastøy Prison at www.brightredbooks.net

VIDEO LINK

Watch the clip at www.brightredbooks.net for a look inside Bastøy Prison.

THINGS TO DO AND THINK ABOUT

1 Essay practice: Analyse the consequences for reoffending of a restorative justice process approach to crime in Scotland.

2 Role play – in a small group act out a restorative justice meeting. You will need at least one offender and one victim, or relative of a victim, as well as at least one facilitator.

There will need to be some background to the meeting, for example, what crime has been committed?

Is this appropriate for all crimes?

Why might both victim and offender be happy to participate?

Should anyone else be involved? Explain your answer.

Do you think this would reduce reoffending?

3 Essay practice: To what extent are non-custodial sentences move effective in dealing with those who break the law? (20).

ONLINE

Head to www.brightredbooks.net for advice on how to answer an essay question for this topic.

ONLINE TEST

Head to www.brightredbooks.net and test yourself on restorative justice and reducing reoffending.

CHINA

CHINA'S POLITICAL SYSTEM AND PROCESSES

Chinese constitution

CHINA'S POLITICAL SYSTEM AND CONSTITUTIONAL ARRANGEMENTS

China is a socialist republic and the political structure is outlined in the Constitution of the People's Republic of China, adopted in 1982. China's people are expected to strictly adhere to the Constitution which states that all citizens 'have the duty to uphold the dignity of the Constitution and ensure its implementation'. China is a single-party state which has been governed by the **Communist Party of China** (CPC) since 1949. The CPC permits eight other, non-communist, democratic, political parties to exist in China. However, these parties are small in terms of their membership and are fully controlled by the CPC. Political consultation also involves a number of socially influential mass organisations including the **All-China Federation of Trade Unions** (ACFTU) and the **All-China Women's Federation** (ACWF).

ONLINE

For additional information on China's system of **multi-party cooperation and political consultation** including an overview of the eight political parties which play a very limited role in the way in which China is managed, visit www.brightredbooks.net

DON'T FORGET

Although there are eight other political parties operating in China, they do not act as opposition to the CPC. The CPC dominates all important aspects of Chinese life, including exercising full control of the country's media.

FACT

On 1 July 2021, the CPC, the world's second-largest political party, will celebrate its 100th birthday.

POLITICAL PARTIES

The Communist Party of China

The Communist Party of China is by far the largest political party in the world, growing from just 50 members in 1921 to almost 92 million members in 2020. The CPC is represented in every corner of Chinese society including both state-owned and private enterprises. The route to CPC membership normally begins by enrolling in the Young Pioneers of China (age 6–14), before advancing to the Communist Youth League (age 14–18) and finally, if selected, becoming a full member (age 18+). Many young Chinese citizens are attracted to CPC membership as they believe it will help them to secure benefits in education or employment, such as gaining a good job with a government agency or state-owned enterprise.

However, the party is often criticised for being largely inaccessible to, and unrepresentative of, much of Chinese society. For example, in 2019, only 27.9% of party members were female, despite the fact that women account for over 48.9% of the total Chinese population.

In recent times, the CPC, under the leadership of Xi Jinping, has made some progress in addressing the under-representation of both females and ethnic minorities within the party. Efforts have also been made to change the party's membership composition with younger, highly educated, White Collar workers being recruited to improve the party's human capital, a somewhat 'elitist' approach which is not representative of Chinese society as a whole.

Access to the CPC can be difficult for individuals who lack connections. The application process is complex. Prospective members must be proposed by existing CPC members in addition to having to meet strict entry criteria, including the successful completion of a 2–3-year probationary period.

contd

Corruption

Concern has been raised about the existence of nepotism within the CPC. A recent internal survey has indicated that many cadres (public officials) believe that they have lost out on deserving promotions due to corrupt senior CPC officials who have abused their position and favoured individuals who they are in some way associated with.

President Xi Jinping addressing CCDI in January 2021

Case Study: Xi Jinping's campaign against corruption

Xi Jinping, General Secretary of the CPC and President of China, addressed the Central Commission for Discipline Inspection (CCDI) in January 2014 stating 'the anti-corruption situation remains grim and complicated, the unhealthy influence of the corruption problem is malignant and needs to be solved quickly'. Seven years later, at the same conference, in January 2021, Xi Jinping reiterated that corruption remained China's biggest obstacle in achieving both its economic and political goals.

Since the beginning of Xi Jinping's anti-corruption campaign in 2013, it is estimated that somewhere in the region of two million officials have been punished for a number of crimes including bribery and stealing public money. Xi Jinping's consistent message has been that nobody, not even 'tigers' (high-ranking officials) would be safe from graft. However, some critics claim that Jinping's anti-corruption campaign is nothing more than an attempt to clear the landscape of political rivals, while some economists claim that the anti-corruption campaign is having a damaging economic effect by reducing public spending. In 2020, China ranked 78th out of 180 countries in Transparency International's Corruption Perceptions Index. The table below highlights some high-profile government officials who have fallen foul to China's hard-hitting anti-corruption measures.

Selected individuals found guilty of graft (2018–21)

Name	Position	Crime	Punishment
Li Wei	Vice-chairman of the Beijing Municipal Committee of the Chinese People's Political Consultative Conference	Abuse of power. Accepting money and gifts from property developers.	Expelled from CPC. Dismissed from public office. Sentence pending (2021)
Qin Guangrong	Yunnan Party Chief	Bribery	7-year prison sentence and 1.5 million yuan fine (2021)
Lai Xiaomin	Chairman of China Huarong Asset Management Company	Accused of taking bribes to the value of more than $276 million	Executed (2021)
Zhang Zhongsheng	Deputy Mayor, Luliang	Accused of taking bribes to the value of $120 million	Sentenced to death (2018)
Sun Zhengcai	Politburo member and Party Chief of Chongqing	Accused of taking bribes to the value of more than $26 million	Sentenced to life imprisonment (2018)

FACT

The CPC has recently called on local governments to be 'prudent' when enlisting party members in a bid to attract 'quality rather than quantity'. According to a report by the Xinhua News Agency, the party is now placing a greater emphasis on recruiting members who are 'enterprising' and can play 'exemplary roles'. Although traditionally family background was a key part of the membership selection process, college ranking is now more influential. The party has also called on its grass-roots organisations to welcome those who 'believe in Marxism, communism and socialism with Chinese characteristics'.

The United Front

The table below provides approximate membership figures for China's other permitted political parties, which make-up the United Front, in 2018.

Party name	Established	Number of members (approx)
China Democratic League	1939	282 000
China Democratic National Construction Association	1945	170 000
Jiusan Society	1946	167 000
China Association for the Promotion of Democracy	1945	157 000
Chinese Peasants' and Workers' Democratic Party	1930	145 000
China Revolutionary Committee of the Kuomintang	1948	128 000
China Zhi Gong Dang	1925	48 000
Taiwan Democratic Self-government League	1947	3 000

ONLINE TEST

Test yourself on China's political system and processes at www.brightredbooks.net

THINGS TO DO AND THINK ABOUT

1 China is described as a 'single-party state'. What does this mean? In what way does this differ from the United Kingdom?
2 Choose either the All-China Federation of Trade Unions or the All-China Women's Federation. Conduct some independent research and create a fact file summarising the role that the organisation plays in China's political process.
3 To what extent has Xi Jinping been successful in tackling corruption in China since taking up office?

CHINA'S POLITICAL INSTITUTIONS AND PROCESSES

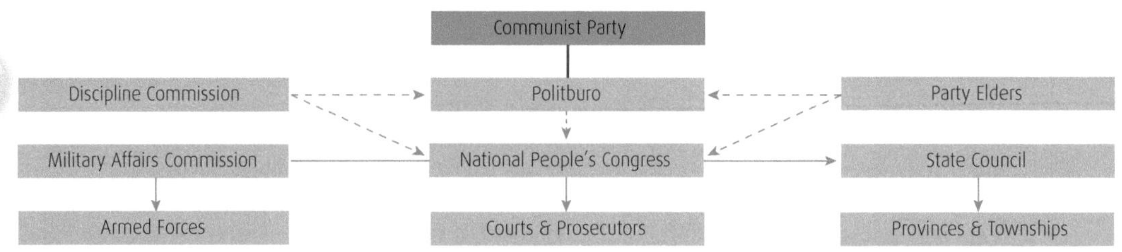

This flow chart gives an overview of the power structure in China

ONLINE

See the 'How China is Ruled: BBC Interactive Flowchart' via www.brightredbooks.net which provides an informative overview of China's main political institutions.

Meeting of National People's Congress.

THE NATIONAL PEOPLE'S CONGRESS

The **National People's Congress** (NPC) is China's legislature, and, according to Article 57 of China's Constitution, is 'the highest organ of state power'.

2980 delegates are elected for a five-year term. The NPC meets once each year for approximately two weeks as one half of the **Two Meetings** (the second meeting being the **Chinese People's Political Consultative Conference**). The vast majority of NPC delegates (approximately 70%) are CPC members.

Article 62 of China's Constitution outlines the NPC's functions and powers which include:

- electing the President of the Supreme People's Court
- enacting and amending basic laws governing criminal offences, civil affairs, the state organs and other matters.

However, according to some commentators, the NPC is nothing more than 'a rubber stamp for party decisions'.

The **National People's Congress Standing Committee** is made up of about 150 members who meet approximately six times per annum. Technically, this committee can change laws, but most of its members are members of the CPC, so the output from the committee is determined by the CPC.

The 2020 NPC was postponed from March until May due to the outbreak of Covid-19. Normally, during this week-long event, thousands of motions proposed by the NPC and Chinese People's Political Consultative Conference representatives are endorsed.

ONLINE

For full details of China's Politburo and Politburo Standing Committee, please visit www.brightredbooks.net

THE POLITBURO

The **Politburo** is China's 25-member decision-making body elected by the **Central Committee** of the CPC and made up of both military and civic leaders from across China. The current Politburo has only one female member, Sun Chunlan.

In reality, the most important decisions are made by the seven members of the **Politburo Standing Committee** (PSC). This group comprises China's main political heavyweights, including the Party General Secretary (Xi Jinping, the Premier (Li Keiang) and the Chairman of the NPC (Li Zhanshu).

The PSC meets regularly to discuss and take decisions on China's most important issues. The meetings are held behind closed doors and once a decision is made, all members of th PSC must stand united.

contd

Politburo Standing Committee: China's most powerful men

Xi Jinping (b. 1953); Party General Secretary; Chairman, Party and State Central Military Commissions; State President (Portfolio: Party, military, foreign affairs)

Li Keqiang (b. 1955); No. 2-ranked PSC member; Premier and Party Secretary of the State Council (Portfolio: government administration and economy)

Li Zhanshu (b. 1950); No. 3-ranked PSC member; Chairman, Standing Committee of the 13th National People's Congress (Portfolio: legislative affairs).

THE PEOPLE'S LIBERATION ARMY

The **People's Liberation Army** (PLA) is the largest defence force in the world with a well-equipped army, navy and air force.

The PLA is duty bound to defend the CPC. PLA officers are also CPC members. This further consolidates the CPC's unyielding power within China. Mao Zedong once said 'political power grows out the barrel of a gun'. Having control of a powerful army is important both nationally and internationally.

The CPC keeps a close eye on the internal workings of the PLA to ensure that army thinking consistently mirrors party thinking.

The PLA is answerable to the **Central Military Affairs Commission** (CMAC) which is headed up by the General Secretary of the CPC, currently Xi Jinping.

THINGS TO DO AND THINK ABOUT

1 To what extent to you agree with the viewpoint that the NPC is 'nothing more than a rubber stamp for party decisions'?

2 In your own words, explain why the Politburo is such an important and influential body.

3 'Women are grossly underrepresented at the higher echelons of Chinese politics.' Provide two pieces of evidence to substantiate this viewpoint. You may wish to refer to the Politburo, its Standing Committee and leadership of the CCP.

FACT

Previously China's President and Premier were only permitted to serve two consecutive five-year terms in office. This was changed in March 2018 when China's Congress voted to abolish presidential term limits.

Chinese citizens do not get the opportunity to vote directly for senior politicians who make up important groups such as the Politburo. The average citizen only has the opportunity to elect representatives at grassroots levels such as village, town or county elections.

ONLINE TEST

Test yourself on China's political institutions and processes at www.brightredbooks.net

GOVERNANCE, DEMOCRACY AND MEDIA CENSORSHIP

FACT 

China's 22 provinces are: Anhui; Hainan; Hunan; Qinghai; Yunnan; Fujian; Hebei; Jiangsu; Shaanxi; Zhejiang; Gansu; Heilongjiang; Jiangxi; Shandong; Guangdong; Henan; Jilin; Shanxi; Guizhou; Hubei; Liaoning; Sichuan

DON'T FORGET 

China's five regions with increased autonomy and sizeable ethnic minority populations: Guangxi; Inner Mongolia; Ningxia; Tibet; Xinjiang

FACT 

Xinjiang is China's largest administrative division which has a high Muslim Uygur population who have repeatedly clashed with China's authorities in the past few years over repression.

DON'T FORGET 

China's four municipalities: Beijing; Shanghai; Tianjin; Chongqing

DON'T FORGET 

China's two Special Administrative Regions (SAR): Hong Kong; Macau

REGIONAL GOVERNMENT

Administrative divisions of China

China is broken down into the following regions:

- 22 **provinces** (23 if you were to include Taiwan)
- five **regions** with increased autonomy and sizeable ethnic minority populations
- four **municipalities**, which are important cities controlled by central government
- two **Special Administrative Regions** (SAR). These regions operate under a capitalist system as opposed to a socialist one. **Hong Kong** returned to China from the UK in 1997 and **Macao** returned to China from Portugal in 1999. China promised not to interfere in each country's established social and economic systems – both countries were handed back to China under the 'one country, two systems' policy.

HOW DEMOCRATIC IS CHINA?

According to China's Constitution:

- citizens who are 18 years old or above are allowed to vote and stand for election
- citizens can enjoy freedom of speech, freedom of press, freedom of assembly, freedom of association and freedom of procession and demonstration, provided they abide by the Constitution and they:
  - pay taxes
  - defend China and perform military services
  - safeguard the unity of China
  - safeguard the security and honour of China.

However, in reality, opportunities for political participation in China are limited. Chinese citizens do not get the opportunity to vote for senior CPC leadership. Therefore, they have little say about which individuals get to make the most important decisions for China at a national level. For the vast majority of China's citizens, voting is restricted to electing village committees and local people's congresses. Even at a local level, only candidates endorsed by the CPC are permitted to stand for election, and, access to the party is unachievable for most. In some instances, Chinese citizens are allowed to protest about local matters of public concern such as pollution and poor quality housing, but any criticism of the Chinese government is strictly prohibited.

LOCAL DEMOCRACY

Local democracy

As villages and townships are the only level in Chinese politics where direct and regular elections take place, many believe that they play a vital role in the democratisation of China. However, it is also argued that local elections do nothing more than pay lip service to democracy, due to the behind-the-scenes involvement of the CPC in controlling election committees and selecting the candidates who are allowed to stand.

Village elections were first introduced in 1988 in order to help the Chinese government increase their influence in rural areas, which at that time, they were struggling to control.

Recent debate has looked to build on the successes of local democracy and further extend it to urban areas. For example, deliberative democracy would allow urban citizens to have a direct say in the way in which their communities are governed through attendance at meetings and participation in public consultation exercises.

Village elections take place every three years in approximately 950 000 of China's villages in order to elect the village chief and village committee, who manage all local affairs.

There have also been calls for greater transparency within the CPC and the need for power to be distributed more equally throughout party ranks. A movement towards a tenure system.

ELECTORAL REFORM AND PROTESTS IN HONG KONG

Back in September 2014, the National People's Congress Standing Committee caused anger and concern when they announced that they were making changes to the process by which the citizens of Hong Kong elect their leader, known as the **Chief Executive**. Although some Hong Kongers were involved in electing 'their leader' – Carrie Lam, in 2017, the vast majority of people were unable to vote and only the CPC approved candidates were able to stand for election, leading many to deem it 'a Beijing appointment'.

Chinese police firing tear gas at protesters outside a government building, June 2019

When Hong Kong transferred from British to Chinese rule in 1997, it was agreed that Hong Kong would be administered with a high degree of local autonomy over a fifty-year period until 2047. This arrangement had worked relatively effectively until 2014, but the decision to alter the voting process led to the emergence of protest movements such as Occupy Central with Love and Peace (now disbanded). Throughout 2019 and 2020, Hong Kongers took to the streets in protest of the new National Security Law, which they believed was an attempt by the Chinese government to exert further control over the SAR. Many Hong Kongers were fearful as the law will see those accused of serious offences tried in China where they could receive life sentences for acts of subversion and secession. Many Hong Kongers have now fled to the UK, where a new British National Overseas (BNO) status is granting them permission to live and work in Britain. This decision by the UK government has created tension between London and Beijing.

ONLINE

To access the 2020 World Press Freedom Index, please visit www.brightredbooks.net

FACT

According to a recent survey conducted by the Committee to Protect Journalists (CPJ), China is the 'world's leading jailer of journalists', detaining 47 people in 2020.

FACT

During the 2019 democracy protests, Chinese police used pepper spray, tear gas and rubber bullets to keep the protesters at bay. The protestors retaliated by throwing bricks and other foreign objects at the police.

MEDIA CENSORSHIP

The CPC does not tolerate open dissent from protestors, and **media censorship** is common. The Chinese government goes to great lengths to try to ensure that social stability is not threatened. However, some people argue that China is 'no longer the journalistic black hole it once was'. Instances of censorship include:

- state television failing to report large scale protests
- social media sites (such as Facebook, Twitter and Instagram) being blocked
- journalists being targeted by police for publishing negative reports about the CPC
- blogs being closed down for presenting information deemed to be politically sensitive
- limiting foreign news broadcasts by blocking websites and satellite signals
- widespread use of cyber police to monitor web activity.

'China is the world's biggest prison for journalists, bloggers and cyber dissidents.'

China is ranked 177th of 180 countries in Reporters without Borders 2020 World Press Freedom Index with a score of 78.48.

VIDEO LINK

Watch a 12 minute BBC video at www.brightredbooks.net that captures the plight of two young men fleeing Hong Kong to the UK due to the introduction of the National Security Law.

ONLINE

To find out more about Cheng Lei, an Australian journalist arrested on spying charges in February 2021, visit www.brightredbooks.net

THINGS TO DO AND THINK ABOUT

1. Which SAR was returned to China from Portugal?
2. Name China's four municipalities.
3. To what extent are the views of Chinese citizens represented within the Chinese political system?
4. What decision by the CPC, in June 2020, has led to many Hong Kongers fleeing their place of birth?
5. Why might it be problematic for journalists to report accurately when covering stories in China? Provide three reasons.

ONLINE TEST

Test yourself on China's political institutions and processes at www.brightredbooks.net

SOCIO-ECONOMIC ISSUES IN CHINA: ECONOMIC INEQUALITY

DON'T FORGET

The **Gini coefficient** for family income indicates the wealth gap that exists within a country. A Gini coefficient of 0 indicates perfect equality as opposed to a Gini coefficient of 1 which would indicate perfect inequality.

CHINA'S WEALTH GAP

China's **Gini coefficient** in 2019 was 0.465. This is down from 0.468 in 2018, but still above the UN's international warning level of 0.4 which indicates that a severe, possibly dangerous, level of income inequality exists within the country and that there is a possibility of social unrest. Research from Peking University's Institute of Social Science has suggested that 1% of Chinese families own 33% of the country's wealth, while the bottom 25% only own 1% of the country's wealth. Economic inequality in China is regarded as a serious social issue and, following the nation's rapid economic development of the past 45 years, China is now one of the most unequal countries in the world. The outbreak of Covid-19 in 2020 has exacerbated this inequality with China's poorest citizens being disproportionately affected, in terms of their earning capacity and their ability to withstand risk. Many Chinese citizens, such as Ning Shumei, a taxi driver from Beijing, have called for urgent government intervention to address the problem.

China's Gini coefficient from 2009 to 2019

Source: National Bureau of Statistics

'Income inequality is a serious issue. People are complaining about it, especially new graduates who are not paid well. They need to change this because I am sure it will affect the health and growth of China. I am not happy with the fact that people are not paid and respected according to what they can do. The rich remain rich, the poor remain poor.'

View of Ning Shumei, 51, taxi driver, Beijing.

A joint study between the University of Michigan and Peking University entitled 'Income Inequality in Today's China' highlighted a number of factors which are believed to contribute towards China's wage differentials. These factors include:

- head of household's level of education
- variations across Chinese provinces
- urban/rural gap
- family structure.

VIDEO LINK

To find out more about the gap between China's rich and poor, visit www.brightredbooks.net

ONLINE

Visit www.brightredbooks.net to find out which Chinese cities attract the country's wealthiest billionaires.

THE RICH, THE POOR AND THE MIDDLE CLASS

China is currently suffering from:

- sharp rises in the cost of living
- an ever-increasing income gap (the incomes of the poor are increasing, but the incomes of the rich are increasing at a much faster rate).

The table below gives an indication of the wealth gap that currently exists in China.

China's glaring wealth gap

Number of Chinese billionaires ($)	389 (2020)
Number of Chinese millionaires ($)	4.4 million (2019)
GNP per capita	10 410 (2019)
Number of Chinese people living in extreme rural poverty	6 million (2019)
Number of Chinese people living in relative poverty	130 million (2019)

contd

The urban elite

The super-rich tend to live in wealthy cities such as Shenzhen, Shanghai and Beijing.

Many of China's wealthiest citizens have amassed their wealth through successful property deals, private enterprise, investing in the stock market and holding senior positions within both domestic and multinational companies.

Many of the Chinese elite are impressed by a Western style of luxury and enjoy spending their money on expensive cars such as Lamborghinis and Ferraris. Many lead ostentatious lifestyles and have a passion for designer labels and vintage wine.

China's top 10 richest people (2020)

Position	Name	Source of wealth	Estimated fortune (US $)
1	Jack Ma	E-commerce	65.6 billion
2	Ma Huateng	Internet media	55.2 billion
3	Zhong Shanshan	Beverages/pharmaceuticals	53.9 billion
4	Sun Piaoyang	Pharmaceuticals	35.0 billion
5	He Xiangjian	Home appliances	32.2 billion
6	Wang Wei	Package delivery	32.2 billion
7	Colin Zheng Huang	E-commerce	30.6 billion
8	Yang Huiyan	Real estate	28.5 billion
9	Zhang Yiming	Software	27.7 billion
10	Hui Ka Yan	Real estate	27.1 billion

Source: Forbes (November 2020)

FACT

Only ten women feature in China's top 100 rich list. The highest, placing at number 8, is Yang Huiyan, who holds a 57% stake in property company Country Garden Holdings. Huiyan is estimated to be worth about $28.5 bn.

Yang Huiyan, China (and Asia's) richest woman

Country Garden Holdings Logo

The rural poor

Some of the poorest provinces in China are those heavily reliant on agriculture such as Guizhou, Sichuan, Tibet and Yunnan.

Many of China's poorest citizens work on farms. Their work is often carried out by hand as they do not have access to farm machinery. Chinese farmers work long days and, in many cases, work right up until they die.

China's less fortunate are forced to lead very basic lives. Many rural residents do not have access to household commodities such as refrigerators, washing machines and computers, which are taken for granted in the bigger cities. In fact, many villages are still deprived of electricity.

Chinese farmer in Xiaoyi County, Guangxi

The middle class

Almost 70% of Chinese urban households are deemed to be middle class.

China produces over approximately 9 million graduates each year, many of whom are confident that they will achieve the 'Chinese Dream'.

This new emerging middle class have experienced a 60% increase in their disposable incomes between 2013 and 2021 and, as such, have acquired a taste for higher quality goods, services and experiences. This group will exceed 550 million by 2022 and will play a key role in increasing domestic consumption within China and, in turn, fuelling economic growth.

VIDEO LINK

To find out about the lifestyles and spending habits of China's emerging middle class, visit www.brightredbooks.net

THINGS TO DO AND THINK ABOUT

1. According to University of Michigan Sociologist, Yu Xie, 'Income inequality in today's China is among the highest in the world'. What societal problems could this potentially cause?
2. State two reasons why it might be difficult for academics, both Chinese and otherwise, to produce accurate reports relating to socio-economic issues in China?
3. Why might the head of household's level of education be a main cause of wage differentials in China?
4. From the table 'China's Top 10 Richest People' select one company listed and investigate why it has been so successful. You may wish to visit the company homepage or, alternatively, carry out some press scanning.
5. Create a comparison table between Guangdong and Guizhou that includes information about population, economic base, life expectancy, minimum wage (this varies from region to region) and main problems experienced.

ONLINE TEST

Test yourself on the socio-economic issues in China at www.brightredbooks.net

REDUCING SOCIO-ECONOMIC ISSUES IN CHINA

CHINESE GOVERNMENT POLICIES TO REDUCE ECONOMIC INEQUALITY AND THEIR EFFECTIVENESS

The Chinese government has been highly successful in reducing the number of people living in extreme poverty by approximately 850 million since the late 1970s. Between 2012 and 2017, circa 13 million people were lifted out of poverty per annum, and in 2011, the national poverty line was increased to 2300 yuan per annum (approximately $1.03 per day). Today, the Chinese government intends to eradicate extreme poverty by July 2021, when the CCP will celebrate its 100th birthday. However, this will be no easy task, according to Wang Xiangyang, Assistant Professor at Southwest Jiaotong University, who states 'Some villages are in extreme poverty that is difficult to alleviate, because of natural conditions and the lack of infrastructure.'

According to China's calculations, there are currently approximately 6 million Chinese citizens still living in extreme poverty, this figure would be significantly more if you measured poverty levels in accordance with the World Bank's international poverty line of $1.90 per day. Furthermore, some academics estimate that there are still 130 million Chinese citizens living in relative poverty.

War on poverty

In the eight years between 2012–2020, over 250 million Chinese citizens were lifted above the national poverty line of 2300 yuan. Xi's 'war on poverty' included a range of measures such as relocating families, nurturing small towns, improving transportation infrastructure and providing more development opportunities for the poor. Increased government funding was made available and CCP officials led on poverty alleviation initiatives in rural settings.

Beijing Daxing International Airport opened in 2019 at a cost of $11 billion and is a huge employer.

Gini coefficient

According to the National Bureau of Statistics, China's Gini coefficient decreased year on year between 2008–2015, suggesting a reduction in income inequality. Income inequality may have narrowed as a result of measures such as limiting the annual income of company executives, providing tax breaks for small companies and making changes to the Chinese social security system including pension reform. Between 2015–2018, there had been a slight increase year on year to 0.468, but the figure fell significantly between 2018–2019 to 0.465.

Job creation

In the period between 2014 – 2020, the Chinese government managed to reduce the country's unemployment rate from 4.1% to 3.8%. In 2020 alone, China created almost 12 million new jobs, surpassing their 9 million target. Job creation was an important strand of China's 13th Five-Year Plan (2016–2020) which aimed to create an additional 50 million urban jobs and not to exceed a 5% unemployment rate. China achieved success in both areas.

Wage increases

Over the past few years, civil servants, public employees and employees of state-owned enterprises (SOEs) in a number of Chinese provinces have benefited from increases to the minimum wage. In China, the minimum wage varies from region to region. In 2020, Beijing workers received the highest minimum rate at 24 yuan per hour. According to researcher Wendy Liu, 'The pay hike indicates Beijing's goal of improving the quality of life for the average Chinese, after having extracted savings by curbing wasteful spending at government branches and SOEs.' Average salaries rose by 3.6% in China in 2020 placing it 8th in the league table of salary increases for the year.

contd

Regional investment

Some provinces have received huge government investment. Guizhou, in the south of the country, has received funding to improve its transport links in order to help the region become a more attractive tourist destination. The local economy has experienced rapid growth which has been supported by the creation of new roads and a new airport. The government has been criticised, however, in some instances, for providing poor quality infrastructure which serves no real purpose.

FACT

China's urban population has grown from roughly 18% of the total population in 1978 to about 61% of the population in 2021, making it one of the fastest growing urban population growth rates in the world. Although the Chinese government see urbanisation as paramount to China's economic growth, they are concerned about its impact on areas such as housing, social security and the environment.

SOCIAL INEQUALITY

Urbanisation

China now has over 200 million more urban residents in 2021 than it did in 2010. This number will continue to increase with World Bank figures indicating that urban areas are attracting a further 1.8 million migrants each month. Increasing urbanisation presents a number of problems for both rural and urban residents as well as the Chinese government which, in January 2015, was advised by the World Bank that it should attempt to reduce urban sprawl in a bid to make cost savings of almost $1.5 trillion over the next decade. The population in some cities is becoming less dense and this is leading to increased infrastructure development and spiralling maintenance costs.

'A country with more than 1.1 billion people has achieved a level of urbanisation and industrialisation in four decades that the Western countries took two centuries to realise'

Xie Fuzhan, President of the Chinese Academy of Social Sciences

Urban-rural divide

The table below highlights some notable differences between life in large towns and cities and life in the countryside.

FACT

According to Forbes Global 2000 list (2020), China and Hong Kong are home to 330 of the world's largest companies, a significant increase from 2003 when they were home to just 43. ICBC and China Construction Bank currently hold position 1 and 2.

Selected urban and rural disparities

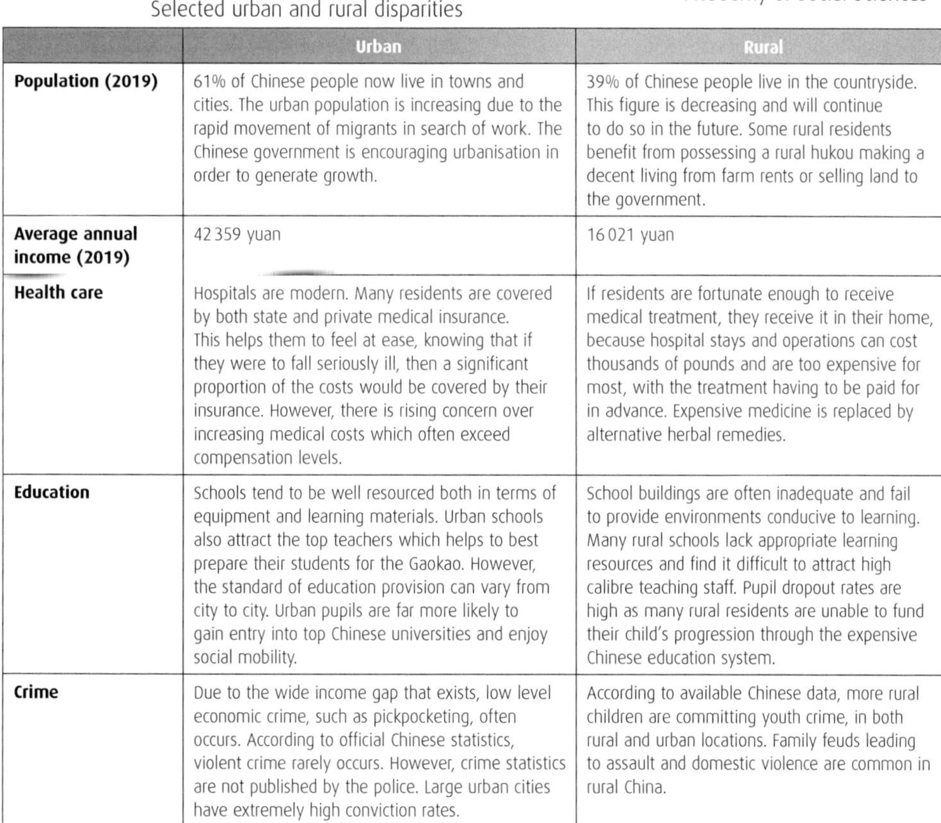

	Urban	Rural
Population (2019)	61% of Chinese people now live in towns and cities. The urban population is increasing due to the rapid movement of migrants in search of work. The Chinese government is encouraging urbanisation in order to generate growth.	39% of Chinese people live in the countryside. This figure is decreasing and will continue to do so in the future. Some rural residents benefit from possessing a rural hukou making a decent living from farm rents or selling land to the government.
Average annual income (2019)	42 359 yuan	16 021 yuan
Health care	Hospitals are modern. Many residents are covered by both state and private medical insurance. This helps them to feel at ease, knowing that if they were to fall seriously ill, then a significant proportion of the costs would be covered by their insurance. However, there is rising concern over increasing medical costs which often exceed compensation levels.	If residents are fortunate enough to receive medical treatment, they receive it in their home, because hospital stays and operations can cost thousands of pounds and are too expensive for most, with the treatment having to be paid for in advance. Expensive medicine is replaced by alternative herbal remedies.
Education	Schools tend to be well resourced both in terms of equipment and learning materials. Urban schools also attract the top teachers which helps to best prepare their students for the Gaokao. However, the standard of education provision can vary from city to city. Urban pupils are far more likely to gain entry into top Chinese universities and enjoy social mobility.	School buildings are often inadequate and fail to provide environments conducive to learning. Many rural schools lack appropriate learning resources and find it difficult to attract high calibre teaching staff. Pupil dropout rates are high as many rural residents are unable to fund their child's progression through the expensive Chinese education system.
Crime	Due to the wide income gap that exists, low level economic crime, such as pickpocketing, often occurs. According to official Chinese statistics, violent crime rarely occurs. However, crime statistics are not published by the police. Large urban cities have extremely high conviction rates.	According to available Chinese data, more rural children are committing youth crime, in both rural and urban locations. Family feuds leading to assault and domestic violence are common in rural China.

VIDEO LINK

To find out about the advantages and disadvantages of urbanisation in China, visit www.brightredbooks.net

DON'T FORGET

Improving living standards in rural areas and tackling poverty is a top priority for the Chinese government.

ONLINE TEST

Test yourself on the socio-economic issues in China at www.brightredbooks.net

THINGS TO DO AND THINK ABOUT

1. 'China's rural citizens experience vast inequalities in relation to their urban counterparts'. Provide three pieces of evidence to substantiate this viewpoint.
2. To what extent has Beijing been successful in its mission to 'eradicate poverty'?

SOCIAL INEQUALITY: HEALTH AND EDUCATION

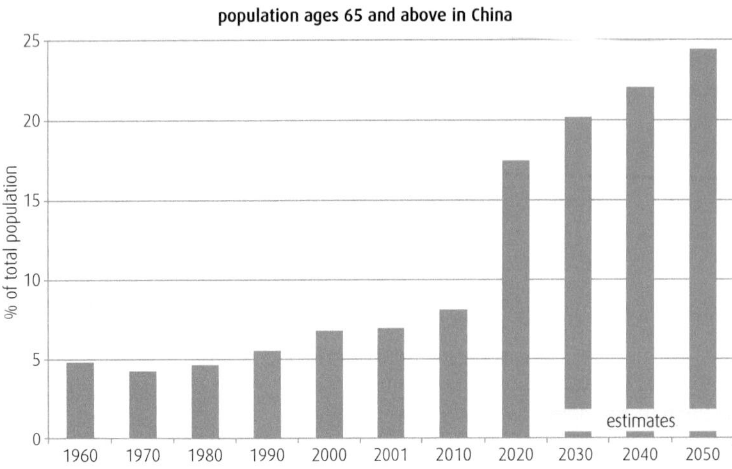

Bar chart of China's ageing population 1960–2050

PROBLEMS ASSOCIATED WITH AN AGEING POPULATION

China's population is ageing as a result of the **One-Child Policy** (OCP) which was implemented in the late 1970s. The factsheet provides key details of China's demographic change, and the problems it may cause for future Chinese leaders.

DON'T FORGET

Historically, Chinese women who violated the OCP were punished in a number of ways by the Chinese government. These punishments included forced sterilisation and forced abortion. The families of those breaking the law were also targeted and subjected to beatings, imprisonment and huge fines. Some people lost their livelihood. Despite the OCP being abolished in 2015, punishments remain severe for those families who have more than two children

FACTSHEET

- In the 1950s and 1960s China experienced a baby boom. As a result, by the early 1970s, over 50% of the Chinese population were of working age.
- The OCP was introduced in the late 1970s, and, China's birth rate decreased significantly as a result for the next three decades. In 2014, over 70% of China's population were of working age. This has been a key factor in China's unprecedented economic rise.
- The Chinese government recognised that an **ageing population** would have a negative impact on continued economic growth, and relaxed the OCP in late 2013, stating that couples could have a second child if either parent was an only child. They do not want the population 'getting older before it gets richer'.
- However, the change in policy did not have the effect that was intended. According to an article in the China Daily in January 2015, only 1 million of the 11 million eligible couples applied to have a second child.
- According to China's National Health and Family Planning Commission, 25% of China's population will be 60 or over by the early 2030s. China will then have one of the oldest populations in the world and a working-age population of just 56%.
- In 2016, the Chinese Government introduced a Two-Child Policy which allowed couples who lived in urban areas to have up to two children. It was hoped that this would be successful in changing China's current population trend. In 2018, an Independent Fertility policy was considered which would allow families to have as many children as they wanted. However, Beijing was, and still is, wary of the cost associated with a young population including healthcare and education.

FACT

One consequence of the OCP is a gender imbalance. In 2019, there are 114 males for every 100 females born.

FACT

Another issue is China's ageing population. There is concern over a '4-2-1' family structure which places strain on the limited young to look after the many old.

HEALTH CARE INEQUALITY

Although approximately 95% of the Chinese population have access to some form of medical insurance, the degree to which they are covered varies significantly. China has three state medical insurance schemes in place, but with a population of 1.44 billion, the Chinese government is unable to provide every Chinese citizen with fully comprehensive medical insurance. Consequently, access to certain specialised health care services is based on the individual's ability to pay. A health care divide therefore exists which has contributed to significant variations in life expectancy between urban and rural regions.

CURRENT HEALTH RISKS IN CHINA

In recent years, China's main health risks have changed from diseases associated with developing nations to those more commonly associated with developed countries. China is now suffering from an increase in deaths relating to a number of **non-communicable diseases** (NCDs) such as heart disease, diabetes, obesity and lung cancer. According to the World Health Organisation (WHO), NCDs are 'driven by forces that include ageing, rapid unplanned urbanisation, and the globalisation of unhealthy lifestyles'. China's ageing population, severe levels of pollution, high tobacco consumption, increasingly unbalanced diets and reduction in exercise have all played a major part in the rise of NCDs within Chinese society. Combatting the rise of NCDs is an important priority for the government of the most populous country in the world.

EDUCATION INEQUALITY

'Children in Liangshan of Sichuan Province are picking up scraps for a living, and homes where children in Shanghai live are worth tens of millions...in universities and colleges, students from families of migrant workers or farmers eat only one meal a day, while some wear luxury products from head to toe.'

Richard Li, 21, Law Student (2020)

China's education system is extremely unequal, with many urban children only gaining access to a high quality education due to the wealth of their parents. Corruption is rife and many families pay exorbitant sums of money to ensure that their child has access to the best schools in a bid to increase their life chances. Some parents also abuse their position within society by exploiting business networks to give their child an unfair advantage. Children who live in rural provinces are at a severe disadvantage due to the poor quality of many rural schools in terms of teachers, equipment and learning resources. Children who follow their parents to the cities are often worse off, as the Hukou system means they are unable to gain entry to urban schools. They are also frequently the victims of societal discrimination.

A disadvantaged group: the educated?

A recent China Household Finance Survey highlighted that the less-educated were more likely to secure employment than those with university degrees. One potential reason for this is China's economic boom driven by the manufacturing and construction industries, both of which do not create an abundance of opportunities for the more academic in society.

Furthermore, the number of Chinese graduates has increased tenfold since 1999 to an astonishing 9 million. It is estimated that anywhere between 1 million and 2.3 million Chinese graduates could form 'an army of educated unemployed' due to a lack of graduate job opportunities. According to Chinese sociologist Lian Si, the term **ant tribe** describes the high number of unemployed or underpaid graduates who may be unable to realise their potential as a result of failing to secure appropriately satisfying work. The Chinese government are concerned about the potential unrest that may occur from anxious graduates desperate for wealth and success.

THINGS TO DO AND THINK ABOUT

1 Name two consequences of the One Child Policy. What problems do these issues present for Chinese society?

2 According to the New York Times, 'an applicant from Beijing is 41 times more likely to be admitted to a Peking University than a comparable student from the poor and largely rural province of Anhui.' In what way may this restrict the life chances of the rural citizen?

3 What is the Household Registration System? How has it been reformed?

FACT

China has witnessed a 20% increase in the number of its people who are living with HIV and Aids. According to Chinese health officials, over 1.5 million people are affected. It is estimated that circa 150000 people per annum and contracting HIV and Aids transmitted through sex.

DON'T FORGET

The **Household Registration System** or **Hukou** is a registration record which connects an individual with an area. It acts as a barrier to mobility as individuals are required to remain in their place of birth in order to access various forms of social welfare such as pensions, education and health care.

ONLINE

To find out more about China's Hukou system, visit www.brightredbooks.net

VIDEO LINK

To find out about some of the difficulties in accessing rural education in China, visit www.brightredbooks.net

ONLINE TEST

Test yourself on the socio-economic issues in China at www.brightredbooks.net

SOCIAL INEQUALITY: URBAN HOUSING, WOMEN AND MIGRANT WORKERS

CHINA'S URBAN HOUSING PROBLEM

The past 15 years or so has witnessed a housing boom which has played an integral part in China's economic growth. According to Tospur Real Estate Consulting the average price of a new private home in 60 tier-three and tier-four cities rose by 30% between 2016–2018. However, in the early stages of the Covid-19 outbreak, house sales temporarily stalled as a result of China's economy closing. In July 2020, Hayden Briscoe of UBS Asset Management stated 'Urbanisation and upgrading are key demand drivers. Property prices are recovering and developer profitability is improving.' The property market has also presented the Chinese government with a number of serious challenges that they must tackle if future success is to continue. Two of these challenges are summarised below.

Chenggong, Chinese ghost town

Over-supply of private housing

Although rapid urbanisation has occurred, it has not occurred fast enough to fill the vast number of properties that have been built. Supply is currently outstripping demand partly due to the fact apartment prices are extremely high in comparison to Chinese incomes. This has resulted in the emergence of ghost towns which pose a threat to developers, financial institutions and regional economies.

Lack of affordable urban housing for migrant workers and the urban poor

Accommodation in urban settings is highly sought after but it is also far too expensive for migrants and vulnerable groups such as the elderly or disabled to rent, never mind purchase. Cities, such as Beijing, have experienced huge population and average-income growth between 2000–2021 and, as a result, have witnessed residential property prices increase seven-fold further exacerbating the problem. People have suffered as a result of the government's decision to abolish public housing provisions. Many are forced to live in slums and basements and experience health problems as a direct result.

ONLINE 

For access to more detailed information on China's socio-economic challenges, access the China National Human Development Report 2019 via www.brightredbooks.net

A DISADVANTAGED GROUP: WOMEN

Despite the fact Mao Zedong once exclaimed that 'women hold up half the sky', serious concerns continue to exist about gender inequality in China. Males are viewed as being superior to females and this is clearly reflected in China's 2019 birth rate with 144 males being born for every 100 females. Women also experience widespread employment discrimination. According to a recent article in the South China Morning Post, women professionals now feel they experience more sexual discrimination in the workplace than they did in 1993. This, along with the #Metoo movement, has led the Chinese government to introduce a Civil Code in January 2021 to help tackle the issue.

In her book, *Leftover Women: The Resurgence of Gender Inequality in China,* Dr Leta Hong Fincher highlights:

- For some time now, the Chinese government have been aggressively pushing marriage in order to promote social stability. Many women are made to feel inferior and leftover if they do not marry by the time they are 27. This agenda is amplified by the Xinhua News Agency who paint a rather negative image of women who do not marry.
- 70% of women help to buy their home, but only 30% of them have their name on the deeds for the property. It is claimed that many of the women are so desperate to marry that they are prepared to compromise their independence and financial security in order to ensure that they find a husband.

VIDEO LINK 

To find out more about gender discrimination in the workplace in 2020 China, visit www.brightredbooks.net

contd

- Chinese women are less likely to own their own homes compared to Chinese men. One reason for this is that Chinese parents are far more likely to help their son buy a home than their daughter. They feel that the responsibility should lie with their daughter's future husband to purchase the marital home.

FACT

As in many countries, lockdown has resulted in increased instances of domestic violence in China. Hubei province witnessed cases surge from 47 in 2019 to 162 by April of 2020.

A DISADVANTAGED GROUP: MIGRANT WORKERS

Back in 2013, President Xi Jinping and Premier Li Keqiang announced that the Hukou system was going to be reformed between 2014 and 2020. This led to increased urbanisation, but it has still remained difficult for rural migrants to gain access to the highly populated cities where the most lucrative opportunities often exist. The Hukou has been one of the main barriers preventing the integration and social mobility of migrants since its introduction in the 1950s.

Some new generation migrants also leave the countryside in order to pursue the Chinese Dream in cities such as Shanghai.

About 300 million young Chinese migrant workers have travelled from rural to urban provinces to escape extreme poverty.

Many of the migrants are in low-paid jobs in factories (44.4%) and building sites (9.8%). Some are forced into prostitution. The work can be hazardous and many suffer from illnesses related to their occupation.

Migrant workers have no fixed abode and are often forced to live in severely overcrowded accommodation. They may be forced to sleep in their place of work, living in conditions which can damage their health.

Migrant workers are more likely to be the victims of crime, but they are also more likely to commit crime. A 2010 study estimated that about 33% of urban crime was connected to new generation migrants.

The **'mingong'** travel from one town to the next to find work and to secure a regular monthly income. The vast majority of migrants retain their rural status. This prevents them from accessing social security if they encounter difficult times (**institutional exclusion**).

Migrant workers are subjected to much hostility. Many city dwellers believe that the migrants provide stiff competition for jobs and keep wage rates low.

Migrant youths are more likely to be sent to prison by Chinese courts than urban youths. This is partly due to the ability of the richer urban youths to pay compensation to their victims.

Case Study: A migrant worker

Name	Lui Young
Home province	Anhui (left home in pursuit of work when she was 17).
Age	20
Employer	Langsha Knitting (World's largest underwear manufacturer). Approximately 4000 employees (mostly migrants). Lui produces 1400 pairs of stockings per day.
Likes	The fact she gets weekends off.
Hates	Standing for 12 hours per day (7am–7pm) Monday–Friday.
Earns	$7 per day – enough to live and send money home to parents.
Accommodation	Lives in a dormitory with 9 of her fellow workmates.
Interesting facts	Lui hasn't seen her parents in 3 years. Langsha Knitting is 'the centre of her life'.

VIDEO LINK

To find out more about the lives of China's left behind children, have a look at the following BBC animation at www.brightredbooks.net

THINGS TO DO AND THINK ABOUT

1 Describe two of the housing problems that the Chinese government currently face.

2 Covid-19, at least in the short-term, has had a detrimental impact on China's social and economic progress. Can you identify two areas which have been affected?

3 Provide a detailed explanation as to why migrant workers are classed as a disadvantaged group.

4 Describe, in detail, two problems many Chinese women face. Do you think the Chinese government is doing enough to tackle these issues?

ONLINE TEST

Test yourself on the socio-economic issues in China at www.brightredbooks.net

GOVERNMENT POLICIES TO REDUCE SOCIAL INEQUALITY AND THEIR EFFECTIVENESS

VIDEO LINK

To find out about how the World Bank-supported Ningbo Countryside Development Project has provided wastewater services and improved water supply to tens of thousands of people, visit www.brightredbooks.net

FACT

China has the world's second largest economy. China's growth dipped from 6% in 2019 to 2.3% in 2020 due to Covid-19. The economies of other wealthy countries such as Germany and USA did not fare so well. China is predicted to have circa 8% growth in 2021.

WELFARE: ACHIEVEMENTS

The implementation of the 2011 National Social Insurance Law has improved the living standards of many Chinese citizens. Between 2012 – 2016 there were a number of improvements to the Chinese social security system including an additional 99 million covered by the basic pension scheme, 211 million more by basic medical care in urban areas, 28 million more by unemployment insurance and 30 million more by maternity insurance.

HOUSING: ACHIEVEMENTS

The Chinese government is committed to providing housing for those on low incomes. Between 2016–2020, as part of the 13th Five-Year Plan, the Chinese government built over 100 million affordable homes. They also re-developed tens of millions of dilapidated properties and provided government subsidies to make homes affordable.

In 2019 alone 6 million urban properties and 2 million rural properties were renovated, over 18 million subsidised homes were built and a further 12 million houses in poverty-stricken areas were refurbished.

The Chinese government also launched a joint home ownership scheme which has been rolled out across six cities to help disadvantaged young people get a foot on the property ladder.

However, the government has been criticised for cutting corners in order to meet its targets, by using poor quality materials, selecting highly inappropriate building locations and renovating existing properties to a less than acceptable standard.

HEALTH CARE: ACHIEVEMENTS

China's 13th Five-Year Plan Healthcare Achievements (according to State Council Information Office)

- 95% of Chinese citizens now covered by basic medical insurance.
- Average life expectancy increased to 77.3.
- Almost $22 billion invested in public health.
- 84% of county-level hospitals reached second-level hospital standards.

The Healthy China 2030 programme reflects the UN's SDG of universal health coverage, and aims to build on the work of the 2020 programme and help China overcome its many health challenges. The Chinese Ministry of Health set a number of targets to ensure that sufficient progress is made. These targets include:

- A life expectancy of 79 (currently 77.3 in 2021).
- An increase in people's health literacy.
- Development of healthy lifestyles.
- A reduction in Non-communicable Diseases (NCDs) such as cancer and heart disease.
- Promotion of health science and technology innovation.

A joint report produced by the World Bank and Chinese government highlighted that without the type of changes documented in the Healthy China 2030 programme, health spending would reach an eye-watering $2.5 trillion in 2035, up from $543.5 billion 2015.

EDUCATION: ACHIEVEMENTS

Chinese Senior Pupils, Wuhan, May 2020

China has succeeded in ensuring that over 95% of its total population is literate, which has been a main factor in driving its economic success. Many Chinese students perform well in subjects such as science and mathematics and the country is outperforming many Western nations in the OECD's Programme for International Student Assessment (PISA).

Hukou reform has resulted in increased rural access to early, primary and secondary education.

The Chinese government spent almost $750 billion on education in 2019. In 2021, government has attempted to address inequality in education in a number of ways including:

- Recruiting and assigning more teachers to rural areas (including the provision of incentives).
- Providing subsidies/financial support to poorer students to help them complete their compulsory education (free textbooks/nutrition improvement programme).
- All primary schools receiving 650 yuan per year per student.
- All Junior High Schools receiving 850 yuan per year per student.
- Additional support to schools affected by Covid-19.
- Allowing some migrant children to attend urban schools.
- Introducing admission quotas to allow students from poor provinces access to college and university.

Recently, the Chinese government has invested heavily in improving the educational experience of ethnic minority children in rural locations. In 2014, the Ministry of Education, supported by UNICEF, carried out a pilot in 250 schools across five poor regions to promote social and emotional teaching and learning to better engage the young people. The Chinese government felt the pilot was a success and therefore adopted the **National Child Friendly School Standards** which was rolled out further throughout 2015. This initiative is similar in many ways to the Scottish Curriculum for Excellence in relation to developing the confidence and skills of young people.

GENDER: ACHIEVEMENTS

Gender equality is now an important priority for the Chinese government. Recent developments have included:

- implementation of a law on domestic violence (2016)
- increased access to education and the workplace (particularly for poor rural females)
- increasing attention paid to All-China Women's Federation (ACWF) by Chinese government
- Chinese government priority of equal involvement in economy for women
- introduction of the Civil Code to ensure employers deal with sexual harassment in the workplace (2021).

ONLINE

To read about China's education targets in the 14th Five-Year Plan (2021–2026), visit www.brightredbooks.net

DON'T FORGET

Despite its phenomenal economic growth, China is still officially classified as a developing nation, even though many areas of the country are actually very advanced.

ONLINE TEST

Test yourself on this topic at www.brightredbooks.net

THINGS TO DO AND THINK ABOUT

1 To what extent is the Chinese government effectively tackling housing inequality?

2 To what extent is the Chinese government effectively tackling education inequality?

3 To what extent is the Chinese government effectively tacking gender inequality?

INTERNATIONAL RELATIONS 1

CHINA'S MEMBERSHIP OF INTERNATIONAL ORGANISATIONS

China is the world's largest regional power and holds membership of hundreds of international organisations. Although not always the case in the past, China is currently an active member of a diverse range of organisations of great importance to Asia, and, the world at large. These organisations are concerned with matters such as delivering global security, protecting the environment, promoting human rights and stimulating economic growth. The table below details ten of the key organisations that China is a part of and highlights the year in which it gained entry.

China's membership of selected key international organisations

Name of organisation	Year of entry
African Development Bank (AfDB)	1985 (non-regional member)
Asian Development Bank (ADB)	1986
International Labour Organisation (ILO)	1919
International Monetary Fund (IMF)*	1945 (regained entry 1980)
Shanghai Cooperation Organisation (SCO)*	1996
United Nations (UN) General Assembly and Security Council*	1945 (PRC, 1971)
United Nations Educational, Scientific and Cultural Organisation (UNESCO)	1946
World Bank (WB)*	1945 (regained entry 1980)
World Health Organisation (WHO)	1948
World Trade Organisation (WTO)	2001

**denotes China as being a Founding Member*

FACT

In 2020, with loans of over $4.5 billion, India was the Asian Infrastructure Investment Bank's (AIIB) largest borrower. This is a trend that is expected to continue in the post-Covid era.

FACT

Judge Xue Hanqin, having been re-elected in 2020, is China's current representative in the International Court of Justice (ICJ). Judge Hanqin has been a Member of the Court since 2010 and in 2018 was promoted to the role Vice President. A first for a female, Chinese national

ONLINE

For a detailed and up-to-date overview of China's ongoing contribution to the UN's main bodies, visit www.brightredbooks.net

DON'T FORGET

When exploring an international issue, it is important to refer explicitly to the country in question. Therefore, when writing about China, it is vital to use Chinese examples in your answers.

CHINA AND THE UN

Judge Xue Hanqin

China is a member of the General Assembly of the **United Nations** and a permanent member of a number of other UN main bodies including the Security Council (UNSC) and the Trusteeship Council.

In 2021, Chinese nationals lead four out of the fifteen UN specialised agencies:

1. The Food and Agricultural Association (FAO) – Director General – Qu Dongyu
2. The UN Industrial Development Organisation (UNIDO) – Director General – Li Yong
3. The International Telecommunication Union (ITU) – Secretary General – Houlin Zhao
4. The International Civil Aviation Organisation (ICAO) – Secretary General – Fang Liu.

China is often criticised by the USA for its lack of financial contributions to some UN agencies with some commentators alleging 'minimal money for maximum influence.'

In recent years, China has become increasingly active in many of the international organisations that it belongs to, including the UNSC. Since 2011, China has regularly used its veto in relation to the crisis in Syria. One such occasion was in February 2012, when China, along with the Russian Federation, failed to back an Arab Peace Plan which called for the removal of Syrian President Bashar al-Assad. In October 2020, almost 40 UN member countries, including Canada, Germany and the UK, condemned Beijing for its continued human rights violations, particularly in relation to the treatment of the Muslim minority in Xinjiang. Addressing the UN General Assembly's Third Committee, the German Ambassador to the UN, Christoph Heusgen, stated 'we call on China to respect human rights.' Politically, China regularly receives support from countries such as Cuba, India, Pakistan, Russia and Syria.

contd

UN peacekeeping

Chinese UN Blue Berets

To date, China has provided over 50 000 peacekeeping personnel to the UN. According to 2020 official UN statistics, China is currently the ninth largest contributor to UN peacekeeping, making available over 2520 peacekeeping personnel to support worldwide operations. These personnel are made up of 7 police, 29 military experts, 48 staff officers and 2436 troops. China is the second largest financial contributor to the peacekeeping budget providing circa $9 billion per annum, which accounts for 15% of the total spend.

FACT

China contributes approximately 12% to the total UN budget, making it the second largest financial contributor behind the USA.

VIDEO LINK

Watch a short video looking at the huge contribution made by Chinese peacekeepers to UN worldwide peacekeeping operations at www.brightredbooks.net

SHANGHAI CO-OPERATION ORGANISATION

Formerly known as the **Shanghai Five**, the **Shanghai Cooperation Organisation** (SCO) was established in April 1996 by the presidents of China, Kazakhstan, Kyrgyzstan, Russia and Tajikistan. Its purpose is to improve security for its member countries of central Asia. This aim continues, and there is now a strong emphasis on fighting international terrorism. A sixth member, Uzbekistan, joined the SCO in 2001, followed by India and Pakistan in 2017, taking the total membership now to eight. Traditionally, China and Russia have played leading roles in the SCO. The SCO is notable as an international organisation with no representation from either the European Union or the USA.

ONLINE TEST

Test yourself on China's role in international relations at www.brightredbooks.net.

THINGS TO DO AND THINK ABOUT

1 From the table **China's membership of selected key international organisations**, identify the organisations which have predominately economic aims.

2 Create a spider diagram or an infographic which illustrates China's involvement in the UN. (You may wish to refer to China's inclusion in the UNSC and its contribution to UN peacekeeping operations.)

3 Given the success of the Chinese economy in recent decades, do you think China should increase its financial contributions to support the work of international organisations?

4 China regularly receives political support from countries such as India, Russia and Syria. Provide three reasons why this might be the case.

INTERNATIONAL RELATIONS 2

DON'T FORGET

Remember, one aim of the G20 is to create global economic stability. Have a quick look at p82 of Bright Red's N5 Modern Studies Study Guide for a brief overview of the G20.

ONLINE

The **BRICS Post** is a news website containing information about China and the other emerging economies of Brazil, Russia, India and South Africa. Why not check it out on Facebook (www.facebook.com/thebricspost) or follow it on Twitter (@TheBricsPost)?

CHINA AND THE G20

China values its status within the G20. Although traditionally dominated by Western powers, the G20 is now an economic institution where China can play a leading role in determining the global political economy. Speaking 'virtually' at Session 1 of the 15th G20 Leaders' Summit on 21st November 2020, President Xi Jinping delivered a keynote speech which focused, in part, on the collective fight against Covid-19. He stated 'China is ready to strengthen co-operation with other countries, and work to make vaccines a global public good accessible and affordable to people around the world.' Since hosting the 2016 Hangzhou Summit, China has become more involved in the G20's leadership, and, as a result, global economic governance.

Contributing to a recent article in the BRICS Post, He Fan, Deputy Director of the Institute of World Economics and Politics at the Chinese Academy of Social Sciences (CASS) wrote 'China needs G20 and G20 needs China. China should seek to strike a fine balance between the developed and the developing countries granting a credibility to G20 that is badly needed.'

SINO-US RELATIONS

Recent Sino-US tensions

In 2020, China had the world's second largest economy. According to official figures from the IMF, and calculated by purchasing power parity (PPP), China's economy was estimated to be worth $14.9 trillion against the USA's $20.1 trillion. Economists expect the gap to narrow moving forward, due to the poor economic performance of the USA in the aftermath of Covid-19 and, as a result, of China's significant progress in tackling in-country poverty. Washington is concerned by the vast economic growth experienced by China and does not want to see the top spot, which it has occupied for over 145 years, threatened.

US Warships carried out drills in South China Sea, July 2020

The power struggle that exists between China and the USA has continued to escalate over the past few years and US-Sino relations are currently at their lowest point in decades. This could be attributed to a number of factors including former President Trump's accusations about the origins of Covid-19. China has recently been the subject of a WHO investigation but received intense criticism from the international community for failing to allow investigators access to all areas. Speaking in February 2021, US National Security Adviser Jake Sullivan stated 'China should take part in a transparent and robust process for preventing and responding to health emergencies.' Beijing have also been critical of Washington's weak leadership in response to the pandemic.

FACT

Although initially adversely affected by the Covid-19 pandemic in the early part of the year, China was the only major economy to experience economic growth in 2020, with its economy expanding by approximately 2.3%.

China has also had disputes with Vietnam and the Philippines, both of whom are American allies. The USA believes that China is becoming overly aggressive in re-claiming territory in the South China Sea (a strategic shipping route that is rich in oil and gas reserves) with the threat of military action where its perceived sovereignty is concerned. A tribunal at The Hague in 2016 concluded that China had no legal basis to claim historic rights to the South China Sea, but that has not prevented Beijing from reclaiming over 3000 acres since 2014. Tensions also arose between China and the USA when China played an instrumental role in establishing the Asian Infrastructure Investment Bank (AIIB) in late 2014. The USA believed it was an attempt by China to increase its influence and power in Asia at the expense of the USA and other nations such as Japan. Between 2017–20, China and the USA were embroiled in a trade war over 'steel dumping' on international markets and industrial subsidies which restricted competition through the provision of an unfair advantage. This trade war is far from over and will be of huge political concern to both Xi Jinping and newly elected President Biden. This ongoing situation is covered in more detail in the USA section of this Study Guide.

CHINA'S POWER AND INTERNATIONAL INFLUENCE

Economic power

The rise of China's powerhouse economy looks set to continue for decades to come as the nation wrestles to increase its economic and political power within the global marketplace. It is only a matter of time, experts predict, before China overtakes the USA to become the largest economy in the world. Although China has made very good progress in raising GDP per capita and lifting millions of people out of poverty, controversially, it is still regarded as a developing nation. This means that the country receives preferential treatment from international organisations in relation to trade and aid. Moving forward, China must work hard to improve infant mortality, life expectancy and adult literacy rates. Some commentators argue that China is an 'emerging' or a 'hybrid' nation due to the extreme variations between the prosperous and poverty-stricken regions.

Cultural influence

Beijing spent $40 billion to deliver the 2008 Olympic Games sending a message to the world's global powers that China was on the rise and it had matured diplomatically. In 2022, it will once again take centre stage as it hosts the 2022 Winter Olympics. China is now actively promoting its brand to a worldwide audience through innovative partnerships with Western media outlets including the commissioning of cultural programming.

'I want to build a strong relationship between the U.K. and China. To do that, I want to show that this is a relationship that delivers, both for people in China and for people in the United Kingdom'

Caroline Wilson, British Ambassador to China, December 2020

Military strength

Although conflicting sources of information exist, it is estimated that China's annual defence spending is over $270 billion, second only to that of the USA. The People's Liberation Army is by far the largest military force in the world and over the past decade it has developed highly advanced weaponry, including the Dong Feng-21D Anti-Ship Ballistic Missile and the Chengdu J-20 Fighter, the 'Sky Hawk' stealth drones and grenade launching assault rifles. Without question, China is a global military power on the rise and enjoys showcasing its military strength to the wider world. China is estimated to have over 350 nuclear warheads. China contributes more peacekeepers to the UN than any other permanent member of the UNSC and plays an active role in maintaining global security.

'When you get rid of Huawei, it sends out a very wrong message. You punish your image as a country that can conduct independent policy. It means you succumb to foreign pressure and you cannot make your own independent foreign policy. I always say Britain can only be great when it can have its independent foreign policy'.

Liu Xiaoming, Chinese Ambassador to the UK (2010-21), July 2020

UK-Sino relations

In October 2020, Caroline Wilson was appointed as the British Ambassador to China. This was a challenging time for Caroline to assume this role due to ongoing disagreements between Britain and China. Relationships became strained as a result of Boris Johnson's decision to extend British citizenship rights to Hong Kongers and the UK's decision to ban Huawei equipment across Britain's 5G network.

China is still viewed with suspicion by some G7 nations who are monitoring its relationship with North Korea and the former G8 member, Russia.

THINGS TO DO AND THINK ABOUT

1. Discuss the importance of China occupying a leading position within the G20.
2. Why do you think the prospect of losing the status of the world's largest economy would concern Washington?
3. To what extent is China influential in international relations?
4. Why do you think some Western countries would challenge China's label as a 'developing nation'?
5. When Liu Xiaoming states 'It means you succumb to foreign pressure and you cannot make your own independent foreign policy' What do you think he is implying?

Test yourself on China's role in international relations at www.brightredbooks.net

UNDERDEVELOPMENT IN AFRICA

THE SCALE OF UNDERDEVELOPMENT

DON'T FORGET

Africa is not a country, it is a continent made up of 54 independent nations.

FACT

Current statistics indicate that, during their lifetime, African women give birth to, on average, 4.5 children, compared to 1.6 in Europe. West African nations have the highest fertility rate in the world at 5.6 children per woman.

Africa's 54 nations

Map showing the division between Africa and Sub-Saharan Africa

OVERVIEW

Africa is the second largest continent in the world, both in terms of land mass and population. The continent covers an area of over 30 million square kilometres and boasts a population in excess of 1.2 billion people. The demographics are changing dramatically, however, as sub-Saharan Africa is experiencing unprecedented population growth. It is estimated by the Population Reference Bureau that by 2050, the African population will have more than doubled to reach almost 2.6 billion.

The October 2020 edition of *Africa's Pulse*, the World Bank's bi-annual African economic analysis, projected a reduction in economic activity by circa 3.3% in 2020 leading to the region's first recession in a quarter of a century. The Covid-19 pandemic has obliterated much of economic progress made since 2010 and it is estimated that anywhere up to 40 million people could be plunged into extreme poverty. Pre-Covid, sub-Saharan Africa had experienced moderate GDP growth fuelled by significant progress in some the region's largest economies such as Angola, Nigeria and South Africa.

However, despite the fact many African economies are now growing faster than the economies of many developed nations, and despite the fact Africa has received over $600 billion in international aid since the 1950s, it continues to remain the world's poorest continent. According to *Africa's Pulse* 'poverty and inequality remain unacceptably high and the pace of reduction unacceptably slow'.

THE POOREST COUNTRIES IN THE WORLD

The following table is based on data obtained from the International Monetary Fund (IMF)and identifies the poorest countries in the world based on GDP per capita. All ten are found in Africa.

Rank	Country	GDP per capita($)
1	Burundi	727
2	Central African Republic	823
3	Democratic Republic of the Congo	849
4	Eritrea	1,060
5	Niger	1,106
6	Malawi	1,240
7	Mozambique	1,303
8	Liberia	1,414
9	South Sudan	1,602
10	Sierra Leone	1,690

(IMF, October 2019 data, based on PPP)

THE SUSTAINABLE DEVELOPMENT GOALS

Superseding the eight **Millennium Development Goals** (MDGs), the seventeen Sustainable Development, or Global Goals, came into effect in January 2016. These goals are:

1 No poverty
2 Zero hunger
3 Good health and well-being
4 Quality education
5 Gender equality
6 Clean water and sanitation
7 Affordable and clean energy.
8 Decent work and economic growth

contd

9 Industry, innovation and infrastructure
10 Reduced inequalities
11 Sustainable cities and communities
12 Responsible consumption and production
13 Climate action
14 Life below water
15 Life on land
16 Peace, justice and strong institutions
17 Partnerships for the goals.

According to the latest Sustainable Development Goals Report published in 2020, although some progress is being made in many areas of the 2030 Agenda, there is still much work to be done, especially in Sub-Saharan Africa. The following list shows the **scale of underdevelopment** that still exists in the region:

- Post Covid-19, sub-Saharan Africa is projected to see one of the largest increases in extreme poverty with over 25 million people living below the international poverty line.
- The incidence of HIV for women of reproductive age in sub-Saharan Africa is currently 2.58 per 1000 uninfected people, again, this is much higher than the global incidence of 0.26 per 1000 uninfected people.
- Some of the lowest participation rates in early childhood and primary education are found in sub-Saharan (41%) and Northern (52%) Africa.
- Many countries in Northern Africa have a water stress level above 70%. This means there is a high probability of future water scarcity.
- In 2019, 36% of children affected by chronic undernutrition (stunting) live in sub-Saharan Africa.

Factfile: Burundi

President is Évariste Ndayishimiye. He has held office since 18 June 2020 when he replaced Pierre Nkurunziza following his death. Nkurunziza was Burundi's longest serving President, holding office for almost 15 years.

Capital city is Gitega (changed from Bujumbura in 2019 by Nkurunziza).

Population is approximately 11.9 million (2020).

Languages spoken are Kirundi, French and Swahili.

The main ethnic groups are Hutu (85%) and Tutsi (14%).

Ranked 185th of 189 countries in the 2020 United Nation's Human Development Index (HDI)

Burundi's development has been heavily restricted by the Hutu-Tutsi civil war. It is estimated that approximately 300 000 civilians were killed in the period between 1993–2005 and over one million people have been displaced.

Burundi suffers from a number of infectious diseases including malaria, hepatitis A and typhoid fever.

In 2020, the average life expectancy was 60.9 for males and 64.6 for females.

VIDEO LINK

To find out more about the impact of Africa's population boom on the wider world, please visit www.brightredbooks.net

ONLINE

To read the full UN Sustainable Development Goals Report 2020, visit www.brightredbooks.net

VIDEO LINK

Visit www.brightredbooks.net to watch a short video about some of the ongoing challenges facing many African nations.

VIDEO LINK

To view a short video clip showing how torrential rains devastated Sudan in September 2020 visit www.brightredbooks.net

ONLINE

To access the UNDP's 2020 Human Development Report which highlights the scale of global inequality, visit www.brightredbooks.net

THINGS TO DO AND THINK ABOUT

1. Explain why the average African birth rate is much greater than that of the UK. Provide two reasons.
2. a. Explain why, despite receiving over $600 billion of aid in recent decades, Africa is still the world's poorest continent.
   b. Provide two reasons why this might be the case and explain your logic.
3. Have a look at the 2020 Sustainable Development Goals Report. Identify some of the key challenges African countries face in relation to the 2030 Agenda.
4. The 2020 SDG Report highlights that 36% of children living in sub-Saharan Africa suffer from chronic undernutrition. Which SDG aims to tackle this problem? What impact do you think the Covid-19 Pandemic will have on progress?
5. Watch the video clip that highlights some of the ongoing challenges facing many African nations. What percentage of Africans live on less than $1.90 per day? Why is this figure significant?

ONLINE TEST

Head to www.brightredbooks.net and test yourself on the scale of underdevelopment.

CAUSES AND EFFECTS OF UNDERDEVELOPMENT: SOCIAL BARRIERS

There are many social, political and economic factors causing African underdevelopment.

FACT 

According to Avert, based on 2020 UNAIDS data, HIV prevalence in East and Southern Africa is on the rise. 75% of adults and 58% of children living in these regions are on antiretroviral treatment.

VIDEO LINK 

To watch the Director-General of the WHO talk about the need for an increased response to tackling malaria, visit www.brightredbooks.net

ONLINE 

To find out more information about the rise of ebola between March 2014 – present, visit www.brightredbooks.net and access an interactive map which highlights worldwide outbreaks.

DON'T FORGET 

Although there have been numerous outbreaks of EVD between 2014-2021 across Africa, the disease is nowhere near as widespread as other African killer diseases such as malaria and tuberculosis.

SOCIAL BARRIERS TO AFRICAN DEVELOPMENT

Inadequate access to health care

In order to enjoy internationally acceptable living standards and achieve sustainable economic growth, a country's workforce needs to be healthy and must be able to access an appropriate health care system in times of need. Unfortunately, **inadequate access to health care** severely limits the development of almost all sub-Saharan African nations. These nations are particularly susceptible to a number of serious diseases which have widespread social and economic consequences. The most serious are detailed below.

Africa's killer diseases 2019

Disease	Number of deaths	Description
Lower respiratory tract infections	1 million + deaths	Examples include pneumonia and influenza.
HIV/AIDS	760,000 deaths	HIV targets the immune system which makes it difficult for an individual to fight infection. People who are HIV + are particularly susceptible to tuberculosis.
Diarrhoeal diseases	643,000 deaths	Results in death by dehydration. Can be caused by contaminated water supplies.
Stroke	451,000 deaths	Death by stroke is common throughout the world, not just in Africa. Risk of stroke can be increased by smoking and other lifestyle choices such as having a poor diet.
Ischaemic heart disease	441,000 deaths	Essentially death is caused by a heart attack due to arteries becoming narrower and getting blocked.

(WHO Data)

HIV/AIDS FACTSHEET

- HIV is one of the world's leading infectious killers, responsible for around 700 000 deaths in 2019 alone.
- HIV is prevalent throughout East and Southern Africa. In 2019, 20.7 million people in these regions were living with the disease. In 2020, 27% of Eswatini's (previously known as Swaziland) population had HIV
- HIV can be transmitted in a number of ways including having unprotected sex and sharing contaminated needles.
- Across East and Southern Africa, in 2018, there were approximately 1.1 million children with HIV, having contracted the infection from their mother during pregnancy, childbirth or breastfeeding.
- If more African people had access to antiretroviral therapy (ART), the transmission of the disease from the HIV positive partner to the HIV negative partner would be reduced by well over 90%.

contd

Case Study: Ebola in Africa

What is Ebola Virus Disease (EVD)?

The Ebola virus **causes** an illness which, if left untreated, is potentially fatal. It can be passed to humans from wild animals such as fruit bats or monkeys and apes. It is passed on from human to human via bodily fluids.

What are the symptoms of Ebola?

Initial symptoms include fever, fatigue, muscle pain, headache and sore throat, followed by vomiting, diarrhoea, rash, symptoms of impaired kidney and liver function and internal and external bleeding.

Treatments, vaccines, prevention and control

A number of potential vaccines have been developed and tested, including rVSV-ZEBOV, which was widely used throughout the 2018-19 Ebola outbreak in the Democratic Republic of the Congo. Outbreaks can be controlled by quickly identifying individuals who have been in contact with people infected with Ebola and providing appropriate medical care, ensuring medical teams have access to well-equipped laboratories and are able to conduct safe burials.

DRC outbreak 2018–2020

In August 2018, the Ministry of Health of the Democratic Republic of the Congo announced an outbreak of EVD in North Kivu Province. Matshidiso Moeti, WHO Regional Director for Africa, stated *'We will work closely with health authorities and partners to support the national response'*. Tarik Jasarevic, a WHO colleague, commented *'experience has shown us that it only takes one case to set off a fast-moving outbreak'*.

As of 26 June 2020 almost 3500 cases of Ebola were identified which was estimated to result in about 2287 deaths. This outbreak was declared a public health emergency of international concern and was the world's second largest Ebola outbreak ever.

Affected African countries (2014–2020)

The 2014–2016 West African Ebola epidemic affected six of Africa's poorest countries with the most basic health care systems and infrastructure – Guinea, Liberia, Mali, Nigeria, Senegal and Sierra Leone. According to the Centres for Disease Control and Prevention, there were 28,646 cases and 11,323 deaths. The Democratic Republic of the Congo has been plagued by Ebola since the mid-1970s. Some of the most recent outbreaks are detailed below:

DRC Ebola Outbreaks (2014–2020)

Year	Cases	Deaths
2020	130	55
2018–2020	3470	2287
2018	54	33
2017	8	4
2014	66	49

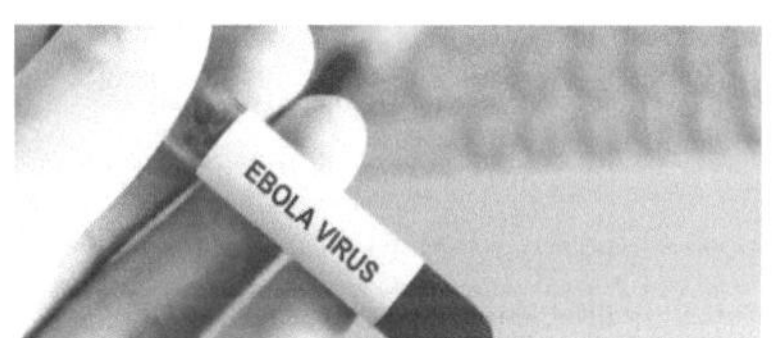

Eleventh outbreak in DRC, November 2020

Source: Centres for Disease Control and Prevention WHO

Inadequate access to education

A high-quality education system and skilled workforce are two essential components of a developed and prosperous economy. Unfortunately, despite a number of measures introduced to improve the learning experience of African children, including a strong focus on achieving Global Goal #4 (Quality Education), the situation in sub-Saharan Africa remains grim. Many countries have low literacy rates. Problems include lack of finance, lack of resources and large class sizes. According to the **Africa Learning Barometer**, the continent suffers from four major educational problems. These are:

- a high, and increasing number, of non-attenders at school
- a high school drop-out rate
- varying standards of education – many children receive an insufficient quality of education
- educational inequality.

According to UNICEF in October 2020, over 40 million children and young people across West and Central Africa were missing out on their education, a figure which accounts for approximately one third of the world's out of school children. This crisis has been exacerbated by the Covid-19 pandemic which has also disproportionately affected marginalised groups such as girls and disabled children. In South Sudan, education is a priority because: 2.8 million children are out of school; 63% of teachers have had no formal training; and 33% of the country's schools have been damaged or destroyed.

THINGS TO DO AND THINK ABOUT

1 Choose two of Africa's poorest countries and try to establish some of the main reasons why they are so poor.

2 In developing regions, such as Africa, diseases like pneumonia and influenza can often result in death. Why do you think this is particularly alarming?

3 In what ways has the Covid-19 Pandemic further exacerbated educational inequality?

ONLINE

To find out more about the response to the DRC's tenth outbreak of EVD (2018–2020), visit www.brightred.net

FACT

According to the WHO, historical outbreaks of Ebola have resulted in fatality rates ranging from 25%–90% and averaging at 50%.

FACT

Two-thirds of Nigerian children are likely to never attend school.

FACT

According to UNESCO's Institute for Statistics, schools in Cameroon suffer greatly from a lack of resources with a ratio of 1 mathematics textbook to every 14 pupils.

ONLINE

Have a look at the 'Building Schools for Africa' website by visiting www.brightredbooks.net

DON'T FORGET

Absolute poverty is when individuals struggle to access the basic necessities of life such as clean water, food, shelter and access to health care

ONLINE TEST

Test yourself on the causes and effects of underdevelopment at www.brightredbooks.net

CAUSES AND EFFECTS OF UNDERDEVELOPMENT: SOCIAL AND POLITICAL BARRIERS

SOCIAL BARRIERS TO AFRICAN DEVELOPMENT

High youth unemployment

Many African countries, such as Ghana, have high levels of both **youth unemployment** and **underemployment**. This is a significant barrier to development. High levels of unemployment may often result in increased instances of crime and conflict due to the inequality it creates. A highly unequal society has the potential to threaten a country's social stability, especially when there is a significant percentage of the population living in absolute poverty. According to African Union, the Covid-19 Pandemic could see almost 20 million jobs destroyed, resulting in increased unemployment, vulnerable employment and in-work poverty. Currently:

- 70% of Africans are below 30 years old
- 50% of these young Africans are unemployed
- every year 10–12 million new workers need to find work
- the African labour market is unequal and prone to **corruption**
- working in the informal sector is common. This means that employment may be infrequent, working conditions may be dangerous and poverty is inherent.

In future, many African countries must take urgent action to create sustainable employment opportunities for their young. This is especially true given the fact that by 2050, the African youth population will have soared to 830 million which will account for 50% of the world's total youth population.

POLITICAL BARRIERS TO AFRICAN DEVELOPMENT

Civil war, conflict and insurgency

For decades, Africa has been plagued by ongoing **civil war**, conflict and insurgency, all of which have had a devastating effect on the continent's development. Current crisis spots include Libya, Nigeria, Somalia and South Sudan. As of June 2019, the humanitarian group Mercy Corps reported that almost 4 million people had been displaced and circa 7 million people were experiencing famine and food insecurity in South Sudan. The following spider diagrams highlight both the human and economic cost of the South Sudanese conflict.

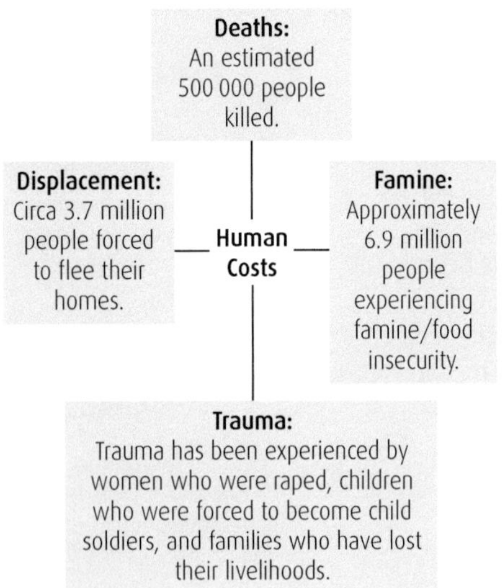

Reduced Economic Activity:
This occurred as a result of the country diverting from 'productive' to 'non-productive' activities. Money was used to buy weapons and ammunition as opposed to being spent on infrastructure projects which promote development. Destruction of key buildings and towns and loss of life have also resulted in a reduction in economic activity.

International Impact:
The international community would unquestionably benefit from improved relations within South Sudan and would save billions of dollars as a result of not having to provide humanitarian aid and peacekeeping troops.

Economic Costs

Environmental Degradation:
Large swathes of South Sudan have been destroyed as a result of warfare. Natural resources have been exploited and ecosystems and wildlife have suffered as a result of the continued violence. Costs have also been incurred as a result of polluted water supplies, the destruction of agricultural land and the loss of livestock.

Regional Impact:
The economies of neighbouring countries including Ethiopia, Kenya, Republic of the Sudan, Tanzania and Uganda have suffered as a result of limited trade with South Sudan.

(Source: South Sudan: The Cost of War, Frontier Economics in collaboration with CECORE)

Case Study: Boko Haram insurgency

Who are Boko Haram?	Boko Haram is Nigeria's largest Islamist extremist group (estimated to have between 6000–20 000 members) originally founded by Mohammed Yusuf in 2002. Since 2009, the group has been led by Abubakar Shekau. The US government is offering a reward of $7 million for information about Shekau's location. In 2016, IS announced Abu Musab al-Barnawi as leader, however this is disputed by Shekau.
What does Boko Haram mean?	Boko Haram means 'Western education is forbidden' or 'People committed to the propagation of the Prophet's teachings and jihad'.
Where does Boko Haram operate?	Initially Boko Haram caused havoc in Nigeria, having a strong presence in the north-eastern states of Adamawa, Borno and Yobe. It also operates in Cameroon, Chad and Niger.
Has Boko Haram carried out high profile attacks?	Boko Haram has carried out a number of large scale attacks and abductions of late including: • Kidnapping of 273 girls from a Nigerian boarding School (April 2014). • 2000 people massacred in Nigeria (January 2015) • Beheadings posted online (March 2015). • Multiple suicide bombings (March 2015). • Over 300 Nigerian schoolboys were kidnapped from a boarding school in Katsina (December 2020). • According to UNICEF, the group has been responsible for kidnapping more than 1000 children in northeastern Nigeria since 2013 (April 2018).
In what way has Boko Haram limited development in Africa since 2009?	• An estimated 36,000 people have been killed. • 4.5 million people affected by Boko Haram's campaign of terror including the displacement of circa 3 million. Vast sums of money have been stolen and extorted by the militants. Government buildings have been destroyed, military bases have been ransacked and homes have burned to the ground. Money has had to be redirected from worthwhile projects to help the Nigerian army combat Boko Haram.
What does Nigeria's President think about Boko Haram?	In April 2015, following his election as Nigerian President, Muhammadu Buhari claimed *'Boko Haram will soon know the strength of our collective will. We should spare no effort'*. However, in November 2020 after receiving intense criticism for failing to defeat Boko Haram since taking office, Buhari Tweeted 'Nothing is more important than ensuring the security of lives and property of Nigerians. Everything is secondary when security is at stake. I will ensure that more resources are made available to the military and other security agencies to prosecute the war against terrorism.'

Former First Lady, Michelle Obama, supporting the Twitter campaign raising awareness of the kidnapping of 273 Nigerian schoolgirls in May 2014 from their government secondary school in Chibok, Borno State, Nigeria. Despite some of the girls being returned in the past few years, in January 2021 there were over 100 of the girls still missing.

THINGS TO DO AND THINK ABOUT

1. 'The South Sudanese conflict has had a devastating effect on both the people and the economy of South Sudan'. Discuss.
2. Describe two ways in which the actions of Boko Haram have restricted development in Nigeria.
3. In a similar format to the Boko Haram Case Study, create your own case study for al-Shabab. You may wish to include – who they are, where they operate and how their actions have impeded development activity.

DON'T FORGET

An insurgency is a rebellion. In the case of Boko Haram, the insurgents are rebelling against the Nigerian government, led by Muhammadu Buhari. Boko Haram have pledged allegiance to Islamic State (IS).

Boko Haram logo

VIDEO LINK

To find out why President Buhari and the Nigerian government have struggled to defeat Boko Haram, visit www.brightredbooks.net

FACT

Boko Haram are also linked to the al-Shabab Islamist movement who were responsible for killing 100 people in Mogadishu in January 2020. Since 2006, the Somali militants have kidnapped and brainwashed many children to help them fight their opponents, who include the Federal Government of Somalia and the African Union Mission to Somalia (AMISOM).

ONLINE TEST

Take the test on the causes and effects of underdevelopment at www.brightredbooks.net

CAUSES AND EFFECTS OF UNDERDEVELOPMENT: POLITICAL BARRIERS

POLITICAL BARRIERS TO AFRICAN DEVELOPMENT

Corruption and ineffective governance

Africa's poorest countries receive billions of pounds of aid from developed nations, international organisations and non-governmental organisations (NGOs). However, according to a recent report published by the United Nations Conference on Trade and Development (UNCTAD), almost $90 billion per annum is lost through tax evasion and theft. In reality, corruption costs Africa much more annually than it receives in aid packages. **Corruption and ineffective governance** are widespread, and have severely hindered Africa's social, political and economic progress.

The table below shows selected data from the 2020 **Corruption Perceptions Index**. The level of corruption is determined by the country's score, where a high score denotes low levels of corruption and a low score denotes high levels of corruption. As you can see, nations such as Ethiopia, Mali and Somalia do not fare well and are perceived as being highly corrupt.

Corruption Perceptions Index 2020 (selected countries)

Rank	Country	Score
1	New Zealand	88
1	Denmark	88
11	United Kingdom	77
21	United Arab Emirates	71
25	United States of America	67
75	Ghana	43
94	Ethiopia	38
129	Mali	30
179	South Sudan	12
179	Somalia	12

ONLINE

To access Transparency International's Corruption Perceptions Index 2020, which includes an interactive map highlighting the perception of corruption that exists throughout the world, including all African countries, visit www.brightredbooks.net

FACT

According to the Corruption Perceptions Index 2020, Africa's most corrupt countries are Somalia, South Sudan, Sudan, Equatorial Guinea and Libya.

Corruption and ineffective governance as a barrier to development

Africa has the potential to generate vast revenues from its abundance of natural resources. However, corruption results in the loss of billions of pounds each year which could otherwise be spent on improving living standards across the continent. Examples of corruption and ineffective governance include:

- The disappearance of billions of pounds of oil revenues over a prolonged period in countries such as Angola and Nigeria. This lost revenue could have been spent on programmes aimed at improving education and agriculture.
- Multiple instances of money laundering and fraud, including the creation of 'phantom firms'. According to the grassroots organisation ONE, 'the DRC lost £880m in just five mining deals from 2010–2012 through mispricing of assets using phantom firms'.
- Alex Badeh, Nigeria's ex-defence chief was accused of stealing $20 million in 2016; in 2018 the The Economic and Financial Crimes Commission (EFCC) re-arraigned him for money laundering.
- In 2017, Uganda's President, Yoweri Museveni, promoted his own son to the position of 'Special Presidential Advisor'.
- In 2016, Zimbabwe's ruling party was reported to have spent approximately £575,000 on throwing a 92nd birthday party for former President Robert Mugabe at a time when many people in the country were suffering from extreme food shortages.

contd

- When people are denied basic human rights, made to feel worthless and are forced to live in absolute poverty, there is an increased chance that they may consider joining militant groups such as Boko Haram. This will lead to conflict and an increase in military expenditure.
- A number of Africa's leaders have been criticised for corruption and systematic abuse of power, including former Angolan President José Eduardo dos Santos and Equatorial Guinea's Teodoro Obiang Nguema Mbasogo.

DON'T FORGET

Phantom firms are companies which are extremely difficult to trace and are used by corrupt politicians and businesses to embezzle money.

President José Eduardo dos Santos

Former Angolan President Jose Eduardo Dos Santos was repeatedly criticised for selective distribution of Angola's oil reserves. His daughter, Isabel Dos Santos, is the richest woman in Africa. However, it is claimed that she was merely a custodian of the wealth for her father. After holding office for 38 years, Dos Santos was replaced by João Lourenço, who has annulled contracts worth over $20 billion which were allocated to Isabel by her father, an action which is currently being contested.

José Eduardo Dos Santos, former President of Angola

During his reign as President, Dos Santos was accused by Human Rights Watch of victimising and intimidating journalists who campaigned for a change in leadership.

Despite the fact Angola is a top oil and diamond producer, the country had an average life expectancy of 61.2 and an average literacy rate of just over 70% in 2020.

President Teodoro Obiang Nguema Mbasogo

President Obiang has exploited Equatorial Guinea's oil reserves for personal gain. In late 2014, Obiang's son lost a $30 million Malibu mansion on the grounds it was purchased with stolen cash. In 2017, he was given a three-year suspended prison sentence and fined 30 million euros by a French court for a number of offences including money laundering and embezzlement.

Africa's longest serving leader, Teodoro Obiang Nguema Mbasogo, President of Equatorial Guinea

Obiang has been heavily criticised for human rights violations including the use of torture and conducting unfair trials. Serious questions have been raised over the legitimacy of the country's elections.

Many people living in Equatorial Guinea lack access to safe water, electricity and education.

ONLINE TEST

Test yourself on the causes and effects of underdevelopment at www.brightredbooks.net

THINGS TO DO AND THINK ABOUT

1 Describe, in your own words, what is measured by the Corruption Perceptions Index.

2 Carry out your own research. Attempt to explain why Somalia is accused of being a corrupt country.

3 President Obiang has now held the Presidency for over four decades. Why might this be problematic for the people of Equatorial Guinea? Do you think holding office for such a long period of time should be allowed?

CAUSES AND EFFECTS OF UNDERDEVELOPMENT: ECONOMIC BARRIERS

ECONOMIC BARRIERS TO AFRICAN DEVELOPMENT

Africa's debt boom: key issues

High levels of **borrowing** are a significant issue in African economies. African countries are borrowing more money from private lenders than they are from traditional sources of finance such as the African Development Bank (AfDB), the World Bank (WB) and the International Monetary Fund (IMF). This could create difficulties if the borrower experiences unforeseen financial difficulty and requires an increase to the original loan agreement or requires the repayment period to be extended. In most cases, traditional lenders will be more flexible than private lenders. Many countries are also borrowing much more than they should be based on the size of their country's economy.

An increasing number of African countries including Ghana, Mozambique and Rwanda are now issuing **bonds** as a means of generating income to drive forward development. Many leading economists believe this approach is risky, as the countries are effectively gambling on their ongoing ability to perform well economically when their performance is often determined by external forces. For example, Nigeria has recently suffered due to the variations in the price of crude oil. According to the IMF, several African countries (such as Ghana, Egypt, Angola) are also now experiencing debt distress as a result of issuing Eurobonds collectively surpassing $100 billion across the continent.

The strong performance of the US dollar previously had a negative impact on the **value of African currencies**, such as the Ghanaian Cedi and the Gambian Dalasi. In 2014, the Dalasi fell by 12% against the dollar. This is problematic as it means that the Gambia is able to purchase fewer goods for its money, including, for example, much needed food supplies. This may lead to more long- and short-term borrowing for the country.

Many African nations are currently struggling to make their **debt** repayments due to a **drop in the prices of their key commodities or exports**. Examples include copper in Zambia and wood in the Gambia. If prices remain low, then these countries may need to request additional support from key international organisations.

A number of African countries including Djibouti, Eritrea, Mozambique and Zimbabwe spend significant proportions of their government revenue on repaying debt and have been near or at distressed levels. Between 2015–2019, Ghana borrowed $918 million from the IMF to stabilise its economy, and although significant progress has been made, the country still heavily relies on foreign loans from countries such as China, who in 2021, is the continent's single largest lender accounting for one fifth of all money borrowed.

Gross debt position for 10 of Africa's largest economies

% of GDP: 0, 35, 70, 105, 140

Algeria, Angola, Egypt, Ethiopia, Ghana, Kenya, Morocco, Nigeria, South Africa, Tanzania

2016, 2017, 2018, 2019, 2020, 2021

'Today's economic environment in sub-Saharan Africa is similar to the boom that preceded the bust in the debt crises in Africa and Asia in the 1990s, when western governments and banks wrote off billions of pounds of debt. Today billions of dollars are again at stake, not to mention the financial stability of the region.'

Judith Tyson, researcher

FACT

According to Development Reimagined, 84% of Africa's total debt belongs to only 16 countries.

VIDEO LINK

To watch a short clip which provides an overview of Africa's current debt crisis, visit www.brightredbooks.net:

contd

Barriers to trade

African countries have a strong desire to work their way out of poverty by making the most of their natural resources. However, although the African people appreciate the importance of local, regional and global trade in order to achieve economic growth, there are a number of barriers which prevent sub-Saharan countries from fully capitalising on lucrative trade opportunities. Some of these barriers are described here.

High import tariffs act as a financial barrier to trade by forcing the producer to increase the market price at which their product is sold in order to cover production costs and make an acceptable profit. This can make it extremely difficult for African exports to compete with domestic producers in a foreign market.

African farmers can often struggle to sell their produce in their own country and region due to the availability of **cheap foreign imports.** It is often possible for foreign competitors to produce their goods in a more cost-effective manner as they have access to more advanced production processes and machinery. Many countries also provide subsidies to their own producers in order to give their products a competitive advantage on the international stage.

Some African producers struggle to gain access to **strictly regulated foreign markets** due to very specific **quality requirements**, such as EU licensing regulations.

Some countries in Africa suffer from having to pay **high costs to transport** their goods to the market. In most cases, the countries do not have the **capital** to establish competitive industries.

In the past, many African countries have had huge amounts of debt written off through schemes such as the **Multilateral Debt Relief Initiative** (MDRI).

Africa's highly sought-after exports include oil, diamonds, copper, bauxite, iron ore, coal and timber as well as **cash crops** such as sugar, coffee, tea, maize, cotton, tobacco, bananas and cocoa.

THE EFFECTS OF UNDERDEVELOPMENT

The effects of underdevelopment

Underdevelopment	Effects
Lack of health care/ disease	Lower life expectancy, high number of deaths from avoidable illness, high infant mortality, poor maternal and child health, rapid population growth, high death rate from HIV/AIDS and other serious illnesses, high medical costs. Lack of production due to illness (resulting in reduced economic growth), high proportion of child carers, high number of orphans.
Hunger and malnutrition	Lower life expectancy, chronic malnutrition (especially in children under 5), lack of productivity from workforce, low economic development as a result, high infant mortality, high number of deaths.
Lack of education	High illiteracy rate, large class sizes, inability to secure and sustain employment as a result of being poorly educated, low paid jobs, low living standards, poverty, limited life chances, slow economic growth for the country due to a high proportion of the workforce being uneducated.
Lack of jobs and unemployment	Highly unequal society, a high rate of crime and conflict, a low standard of living for many (extreme poverty), an underperforming economy, increased reliance on international aid.
War and conflict	Government money being redirected from productive to non-productive activities, reduced economic activity, reduced trade, increased reliance on international aid, high number of deaths, denial of human rights, displacement, famine, use of child soldiers, child exploitation, sexual violence, high number of orphans.
Corruption and ineffective governance	Lost government revenue, increased debt, reduced political and economic progress, social instability, increased reliance on international aid.
Debt and barriers to trade	Increased borrowing from a number of sources, higher debt repayments, reduced infrastructure developments and reduced economic growth as a result, lack of international competitiveness, poverty.

DON'T FORGET

The people of many underdeveloped African nations suffer from a range of human rights violations including political oppression, torture, female genital mutilation and lack of religious freedom.

Climate change can result in severe flooding or drought which can lead to crop failure. This can have devastating effects on African countries who rely on the harvest, not only to eat, but also to sell as cash crops.

THINGS TO DO AND THINK ABOUT

1. Explain two reasons why a number of African countries may see their external debts rise if commodity prices fall or their currency weakens.
2. Some commentators argue that African countries borrow 'too much money for too much interest.' Using China as an example, collect evidence to support this statement and present your findings to the class.
3. Provide two reasons why many African producers may struggle to export their goods to the European Union.
4. Complete a spider diagram to show the range of ways underdevelopment impacts on African countries.

Head to www.brightredbooks.net and test yourself on the causes and effects of underdevelopment.

EFFECTIVENESS OF ATTEMPTS TO RESOLVE UNDERDEVELOPMENT

HOW DOES SCOTLAND SUPPORT AFRICAN COUNTRIES?

Despite the fact that Scotland is a small nation, the Scottish Government is determined to play a part in supporting developing countries, particularly those within sub-Saharan Africa. The Scottish Government's International Development Policy 'articulates the vision of Scotland's place in the world as a good global citizen, committed to playing its role in addressing the challenges faced by our world'. The majority of Scottish support is directed towards Malawi.

In August 2018, the then Minister for Europe, Migration and International Development, Ben Macpherson, announced 11 projects that will be funded in Malawi between 2018 and 2023 at a cost of £11 million. Collectively, these projects focus on a number of areas including healthcare, education and sustainability. The details of the funded projects are listed in the table below.

Projects funded from the Malawi Development Programme (2018–2023)

Organisation	Project	Total Funding
Chance for Change	Access to Justice	£949,333
Challenges Worldwide	CROPS	£998,074
Global Concerns Trust	Tools and training for livelihood in Malawi	£706,407
Mary's Meals	Mary's Meals pre-school and primary feeding programme in Malawi	£1,080,000
NHS Tayside	Scottish Emergency Medicine – Malawi Project	£1,007,504
St John Scotland	Community action and service access for maternal, new born and child health	£457,591
Sense Scotland	Promoting equal access to education in Malawi North	£1,239,488
University of Edinburgh	Moving towards sustainability	£1,288,378
University of Glasgow	Towards a Dental School for Malawi – The Maldent Project	£1,312,424
University of Strathclyde	Rural energy access through social enterprise and decentralisation (EASE)	£1,332,533
Water Aid	Deliver life to mothers, girls and children in the southern region of Malawi	£1,012,500

Source: Scottish Government website

ONLINE

For full details of the organisations and programmes funded through the Malawi Development Programme, visit www.brightredbooks.net

DON'T FORGET

In November 2020, Jenny Gilruth announced £2 million funding for UNICEF from the Scottish Government's International Development Fund to tackle country-specific needs in Malawi, Rwanda and Zambia. This funding will also be used to support health systems prepare for the roll-out of the Covid-19 vaccine.

VIDEO LINK

To find out how Malawian engineers are attempting to widen access to electricity, visit www.brightredbooks.net

The Scottish Government also allocates smaller sums of money towards a **Small Grants Programme.** The seven African projects which received funding awards in the 2020–21 allocation operate in Malawi, Zambia, Kenya and Tanzania. A number of these programmes have received feasibility grants or capacity building grants to tackle the issue of underdevelopment. Some of these are highlighted in the table below.

Selected beneficiaries of the Scottish Government's Small Grants Programme (2020–21)

Organisation / Type of funding	Beneficiary	Amount	Award Focus
Smileawi *(feasibility study grant)*	Malawi	£13,470	To introduce limited dental provision in rural areas
Wasteaid *(feasibility study grant)*	Malawi	£15,000	To improve waste management in north and south Malawi.
Lake Victoria Disability Centre Scotland *(feasibility study grant)*	Tanzania	£15,000	To trial the implementation of a mobile clinic to treat club foot
On Call Africa *(capacity building grant)*	Zambia	£15,000	To improve monitoring and evaluation systems used by community health workers
International Voluntary Service *(capacity building grant)*	Kenya	£14,985	To produce more effective digital tools for training, communications, partner relationship management and monitoring and evaluation
Africa on the Ball *(capacity building grant)*	Zambia	£15,000	To evaluate and strengthen skills and resources in fundraising, governance and monitoring and evaluation

Source: Scottish Government Website

Using funds received from the Scottish Government, NGOs, both large and small, have been able to make a considerable difference in Africa by providing voluntary aid. Farming is a good example which illustrates the progress that has been made. Many rural farmers have been educated in effective farming techniques by Oxfam Scotland and, as a result, have managed to increase the productivity of their farms. They have been taught how to

contd

Scotland remains fully committed to our support of international development – playing part in tackling shared global challenges cluding poverty, injustice and inequality, as well as responding to pressing emergencies. So am I.

Jenny Gilruth MSP, December 2020

maximise their harvest and use the most appropriate irrigation methods to adapt to the damaging effects of climate change. Many farmers have moved away from subsistence farming and now generate a surplus which allows them to grow and sell cash crops. The producers can feed their families, increase their living standards and help to address Africa's food shortages.

The Scottish Government funds projects which helps African countries to work towards achieving the SDGs and recognise the **Paris Declaration on Aid Effectiveness.**

FACT

The Paris Declaration (2005) aims to ensure that aid provided by a donor country is used in an effective manner by the recipient country. It outlines five principles in order to make aid as effective as possible – ownership, alignment, harmonisation, results and mutual accountability.

UK SUPPORT FOR AFRICAN COUNTRIES: BILATERAL AID

The UK Government is keen to ensure that it carefully selects recipient countries so that aid is provided to the people who need it most. The government is also keen to ensure that the money is used for the purpose for which it was intended, and has introduced a **payment by results** system where additional monies are only issued if promised development comes to fruition. It is now widely recognised that money alone will not solve Africa's underdevelopment issues. Despite major cash injections, many African nations are now worse off in 2021 than they were in the 1980s.

In September 2020, under the instruction of Prime Minister Boris Johnson, the Department for International Development (DFID) and the Foreign and Commonwealth Office (FCO) merged to become the Foreign, Commonwealth and Development Office (FCDO).

In 2019, the UK Government, through the then DFID, made £330 million available to Ethiopia in bilateral country specific aid, which made it the second largest recipient after Pakistan. Nigeria also received £258 million in Official Development Assistance (ODA) from the UK in 2019. This money was spent mainly on improving health and education, helping to protect the environment and deal with the effects of climate change and providing disaster relief in times of crisis. This spider diagram gives an indication of some of the DFID's main priorities in Ethiopia.

FCDO current priorities in Ethiopia

- Supporting economic development
- Advance gender equality
- Develop democratic institutions
- Build resilience to avoid, and better respond to, future humanitarian crises
- Empower women and girls
- Promoting the private sector

Source FCDO

ONLINE

To find out which countries benefited from UK aid in 2019, visit www.brightredbooks.net

UK SUPPORT FOR AFRICAN FEMALE ENTREPRENEURS

In January 2020, the DFID announced that it was going to provide additional funding to African women entrepreneurs in Ghana, Kenya and Nigeria to help them access global markets. It was anticipated that the £3.5 million funding would support job creation for women, reduce poverty and drive economic growth. It has been estimated that this investment could add $12 trillion to the global economy by 2025.

In November 2020, UK Foreign Secretary Dominic Raab announced that future aid will only be provided to countries who align with the UK in relation to development, security and economic interests.

THINGS TO DO AND THINK ABOUT

1. Apart from the Small Grants Funds, describe the range of ways in which Scottish Government aid has helped the people of Malawi.
2. Choose one of the beneficiaries of the Scottish Government's Small Grants Fund. Find out more detail about the project and present your findings in a spider diagram or an infographic.
3. Use the FCDO's Development Tracker (https://devtracker.fcdo.gov.uk/) to find out how much ODA the UK will provide to the Africa Region in 2021-22.
4. Create a group presentation on either Ethiopia, Nigeria, South Sudan, Somalia, DRC or Tanzania. You may wish to highlight some of the key problems faced by the country as well as the support provided by the FCDO to help combat the issues. You may also wish to showcase some recent success stories and future opportunities the country may be able to exploit.

ONLINE TEST

Test yourself on the response to underdevelopment at www.brightredbooks.net

RESPONDING TO UNDERDEVELOPMENT: TIED AID AND AID EFFECTIVENESS

DON'T FORGET

Tied aid is aid that restricts the recipient country to spending financial aid in the donor country. Alternatively, there may be other strict conditions to the aid being granted.

FACT

In September 2020, the USA stopped $130 million of aid to Ethiopia due to a breakdown in negotiations relating to the construction of the Grand Ethiopian Renaissance Dam. Some commentators argue this was a political decision driven by America's allegiance with Egypt.

VIDEO LINK

To find out how UNICEF helped Latifatou and her fellow villagers in Burkina Faso, visit www.brightredbooks.net

FACT

In March 2021, Ngozi Okonjo-Iweala became the first women, and the first African, to become Director-General of the World Trade Organisation.

TIED AID

Recent decades have witnessed a significant reduction in the provision of **tied aid**, with increasing international support for a total ban. Countries who often have very little option but to accept tied aid have greatly reduced purchasing power because they are required to buy goods directly from the donor country. This means that they cannot benefit from the fairest international price for required materials. This can severely limit economic growth as the recipient country has less money available to purchase the materials required for desired infrastructure development. However, 2019 figures from the OECD's Development Assistance Committee (DAC) indicate the situation is significantly improving with untied aid from the world's richest countries increasing from 41% in 1999 to 87% two decades later.

By 2021, UNICEF and its partners aim to increase immunisation, tackle stunting and malnutrition, provide access to quality education, reduce child marriage, violence and exploitation, increase birth registration and improve sanitation across West and Central Africa.

Many experts argue that the acceptance of tied aid by countries can often result in them becoming worse off. Following the acceptance of a loan from the IMF in 2009, many Ghanaians fell further into poverty as the government was prohibited from granting rice subsidies if they wished to receive future aid. This had a hugely negative impact on Ghana's growing rice industry and led to the Ghanaians having to import rice from countries such as the USA. It is widely argued that poor African nations would be better served by support rather than aid.

International organisations and multilateral aid

The UK provides funds to over 40 international organisations which provide invaluable support to African countries including:

- the Food and Agriculture Organisation (FAO)
- the Global Fund to Fight AIDS, TB and Malaria (GFATM)
- World Food Programme (WFP)
- World Health Organisation (WHO).

Example: UNICEF

The **United Nations Children's Fund** (UNICEF) is a UN **Specialised Agency**. Established in 1946, UNICEF carries out a number of functions including:

- protecting children from violence, exploitation and abuse
- helping children to survive by providing clean water, food and medicine
- helping children overcome barriers to gain access to education
- providing humanitarian support in times of disaster.

Throughout 2017, UNICEF and its partners were responsible for achieving a number of key successes including treating 2.5 million children for malnutrition, providing almost 30 million people with access to clean water and helping 5.5 million children access some form of education.

Example: United Nations Development Programme

The **United Nations Development Programme** (UNDP) helps African countries with:

- poverty reduction and achievement of the SDGs
- democratic governance
- crisis prevention and recovery
- environment and energy for sustainable development.

The UNDP helps to develop democracy in order that everyone can share the benefits of economic growth. The UNDP is helping countries like Benin, Sierra Leone and Niger become more democratic in a number of ways including increasing political awareness:

Case study: Drylands Investment

Between 2021–2026, the World Bank will invest circa $5 million to improve livelihoods and agricultural activity across 11 African nations. It is hoped that the investment will not only support the Covid-19 recovery, but it will also mitigate against the devastating effects of climate change. The programme will help to combat a number of the continent's long-standing problems such as food insecurity, inadequate rural infrastructure and lack of access to renewable energy.

The African Union

The **African Union** (AU) was set up in 2002, replacing the Organisation of African Unity (OAU).

The AU's vision is for 'an integrated, prosperous and peaceful Africa, driven by its own citizens and representing a dynamic force in the global arena'. The AU has a number of objectives including promoting unity between African nations, promoting social, economic and cultural sustainability, promoting peace and security across Africa and eradicating preventable diseases through effective international partnerships.

The AU is credited with a number of successes including:

- helping to create strong economies in a number of African countries
- encouraging African countries to allocate 10% of their annual budgets to farming
- helping to reduce political instability in countries such as Madagascar
- devising **Agenda 2063**, a 50-year plan which looks to build on progress which has already been made across the continent.

The AU has been criticised for hindering development by requesting funds from some of its members that they could not afford to part with and for failing to intervene in conflicts quickly enough, such as the civil war in Libya.

ONLINE

To find out more about the way in which the World Bank is helping African countries to tackle climate change, read the following blog at www.brightredbooks.net

FACT

In January 2021, President of the Democratic Republic of the Congo, Felix-Antoine Tshisekedi, took over as chairperson of the African Union. This is a ceremonial role which lasts for a year. Previous controversial appointments include Robert Mugabe, in 2015, who was perceived as a dictator responsible for carrying out multiple human rights offences.

African Union symbol

AID EFFECTIVENESS

Many African countries have benefited from reconstruction aid which has been provided in times of disaster and emergency. However, 'most independent research suggests that foreign aid has no positive consequences in the long run and that it may come with unintended and unwanted side effects' according to the Institute of Economic Affairs.

Although many would argue against this stance, most would agree that recipients and donors must do more to ensure aid is converted into sustainable development. No matter how good the intention, questions can be raised about whether financial aid is spent in the most appropriate ways. In October 2014, the Guardian newspaper reported that the **Independent Commission for Aid Impact** (ICAI) felt that the DFID was unsuccessful in tackling everyday corruption, claiming that UK aid often made little impact and, on occasion, actually made developing countries worse off. At the inaugural meeting of the **Global Partnership for Effective Development Cooperation** (GPEDC) in April 2014, it was also concluded that there was a greater need for increased partnership working between a number of groups, including donors, recipients, countries with growing economies and private industry. Furthermore, leading NGOs such as Oxfam believe that the way in which aid is delivered is equally as important as the amount of money that is spent.

ONLINE TEST

Head to www.brightredbooks.net and test yourself on the response to underdevelopment.

THINGS TO DO AND THINK ABOUT

1. 'Tied aid can restrict growth within African countries.' Discuss. (20)
2. Describe two ways in which UNICEF helps Africa's children.
3. Describe the role of the African Union in promoting development in Africa.
4. Name three of the main criticisms of foreign aid.
5. Explain, in detail, at least two political barriers to African development.
6. Evaluate the extent to which the international community has been effective in its attempts to promote African development. Provide at least two points for and against in your answer. (12)
7. In what way is climate change having a negative impact on countries like Ghana, Mozambique and Tanzania?

ONLINE

Head to www.brightredbooks.net for advice on how to approach these essay questions and sample answers.

USA

USA'S POLITICAL SYSTEM AND PROCESSES

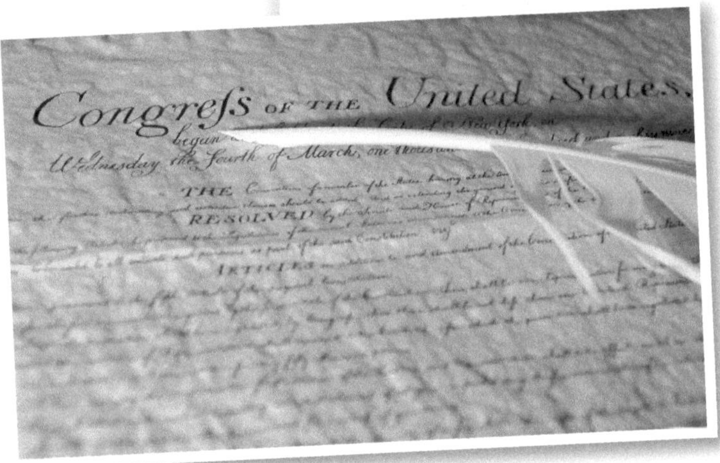

The US Constitution

USA'S POLITICAL SYSTEM AND CONSTITUTIONAL ARRANGEMENTS

The USA's political system is a federal constitutional republic and its structure is outlined in the US Constitution which was written in 1787. The Constitution determines how power should be shared between the federal government's **legislative**, **executive** and **judicial** branches, and also describes the rights and responsibilities of state governments.

The USA is essentially a **two-party system.** Historically, and currently, practically all seats in the legislature are held by Republicans or Democrats. This is largely because, at national level, smaller parties lack both the support and financial resources to challenge the two established parties, and they would find it impossible to win a majority of Electoral College votes.

ONLINE 

To find out more about the US Constitution, visit www.brightredbooks.net

POLITICAL PARTIES

Although the US political system is dominated by the Democrats and the Republicans, American citizens have, in theory, a choice of political parties for which they can vote. However, this choice may be more limited depending on the state in which they live.

American political parties can be grouped according to their level of prominence/popularity throughout the USA.

FACT 

In 2020, Mississippi had the most (13) ballot-qualified parties of all the US states including the Justice Party of Mississippi and the Reform Party of Mississippi.

The **Big Two** – major political parties recognised across **all** US states

The Democrat Party
The Republican Party

Largest third parties, recognised in **10+** US states*

The Libertarian Party (35 states)
The Green Party (22 states)
The Constitution Party (15 states)

Selected other political parties, recognised in **5 or less** US states*

Mountain Party (1 state – West Virginia)
Natural Law Party (2 states – Michigan and Mississippi)
Progressive Party (2 states – Oregon and Vermont)
Better for America Party (1 state – New Mexico)

*Source: Ballotpedia Research – accurate as of November 2020, but figures subject to change as a result of a party failing to meet various 'ballot status' requirements.

DON'T FORGET 

Some candidates opt to stand as **independents** at various levels throughout US politics. This means that they are not attached to any political party. The only President ever to be elected as an independent was George Washington in 1789.

contd

The Republican Party

Republicans believe in conservatism (low taxation, less government interference in the economy, etc.) and that traditional marriage is the bedrock of society. Many Republicans are opposed to highly emotive issues such as abortion and same-sex marriage.

The late George H.W. Bush (1989–1993) and his son, George W. Bush (2001–2009) were Republican Presidents.

Twitter: @GOP

Traditionally, the Republican Party has enjoyed popularity in 'sun-belt states' such as Arizona and Georgia. However, in the 2020 Presidential Election, there was a notable blue shift in these states. Biden narrowly took Arizona and Georgia by 10 457 and 12 670 respectively. This led to Trump's lawyers attempting to challenge and overturn the results.

The Republican Party enjoys support from much of corporate America and traditionally has a strong following from the wealthier white middle class.

Donald J. Trump was inaugurated as the 45th President of the United States of America on 20th January 2017, after defeating Hillary Clinton in the 2016 US Presidential election.

Republicans believe that the most effective way to stimulate economic growth is by adopting free market policies such as creating competitive working environments. They are against raising the minimum wage and providing company subsidies as they believe these methods are short-term fixes which will not support the achievement of long-term economic prosperity.

The Democratic Party

Democrats believe in liberalism (federal and state support to allow individuals to succeed, for example, in employment or education) and that 'America succeeds when everyone gets a fair shot, everyone does their fair share, and everyone plays by the same rules'.

Barack Obama (2009–2016) and Bill Clinton (1993–2001) were Democratic Presidents.

Twitter: @TheDemocrats

The Democratic Party is popular in north-east and western states such as New York, Illinois and California.

The Democratic Party attracts greater support from poorer groups in society, especially in urban areas, as well as people from minority ethnic groups.

Joe Biden was inaugurated as the 46th President of the United States of America on 20 January 2021, after defeating Donald J. Trump in the 2020 US Presidential Election

Democrats believe that the most effective way to stimulate economic growth is to reduce income inequality which will increase consumer demand, and in turn, will benefit businesses and the overall economy.

THINGS TO DO AND THINK ABOUT

1. Using the 2020 US election results, provide evidence that supports the statement that 'the USA has a two-party system'.
2. Explain the difference between the terms 'conservatism' and 'liberalism'.
3. Again, using the 2020 US election results, how did support differ for Joe Biden (Democrat) and Donald Trump (Republican) in terms of voter demographics?

FACT

The Republican Party is also known as the Grand Old Party (GOP).

ONLINE

For a comprehensive breakdown of how President Biden won the 2020 Presidential Election state by state, access an interactive map at www.brightredbooks.net

ONLINE

To find out more about the Republican Party, including the policies outlined in its platform (manifesto), visit www.brightredbooks.net

FACT

Following WW2, there have been 5 US Presidents who have served two full terms in office - Dwight Eisenhower, Ronald Reagan, Bill Clinton, George W. Bush and Barack Obama.

VIDEO LINK

To watch Joe Biden's Inauguration Speech on 20th January 2021 please visit www.brightredbooks.net

ONLINE

To find out about the Democratic Party stance on issues such as the environment, immigration and national security, visit www.brightredbooks.net

ONLINE TEST

Test yourself on the USA's political system and processes at www.brightredbooks.net

USA'S POLITICAL INSTITUTIONS AND PROCESSES

The powers of the US government are separated into three branches:

- legislative
- executive
- judicial.

Each branch has its own distinct powers. The US system of government aims to ensure that no one single branch of government has too much power. There are a number of **checks and balances** within the system to ensure that all branches of government must work together to make decisions.

LEGISLATIVE BRANCH

The legislative branch comprises elected senators and representatives who meet in **Congress**. Congress meets in the capital of the USA in Washington D.C.

Congress is known as a **bicameral legislature** and is America's highest law-making body. It is responsible for creating federal legislation that governs the country. Congress also has the responsibility of authorising government spending.

Congress is split into two houses or chambers, the **House of Representatives** and the **Senate**.

Rioters storming Capitol Hill in January 2021

The House of Representatives (the lower chamber) is made up of 435 elected members who are elected for a two-year term.

The Senate (the upper chamber) is made up of 100 elected members (two representatives from each state) who are elected for a six-year term. One-third of the Senate are elected every two years.

The legislative branch may limit the power of the executive branch (the President) by impeaching a president or over-riding the presidential veto if two-thirds of each house of Congress agree. In January 2021, the House of Representatives voted to impeach Donald Trump due to his alleged role in inciting the Capitol Hill riots on 6th January following his election defeat to Joe Biden. Trump was acquitted in February 2021 due to the Democrats failing to reach the required two-thirds majority (57 found Trump guilty in the vote and 43 found him not guilty).

The legislative branch may limit the power of the judicial branch by rejecting presidential nominations to the judiciary.

Congress is an important feature of the US democratic process as it allows the views of everyday Americans to be heard at national level through their elected representatives. These views can help to influence the passing of legislation.

ONLINE

Use the BBC Interactive Flowchart entitled **Guide to the US government** via www.brightredbooks.net to see an informative overview of the American government's three branches.

FACT

The number of representatives a state has in the House of Representatives is determined by its population. California is a large state with a population of 39.9 million people and has 53 representatives, whereas Rhode Island is a small state with a population of approximately 1.06 million people and only has 2 representatives.

DON'T FORGET

Unlike the President, who can only be elected for a maximum of two terms (eight years), members of the House of Representatives and the Senate can hold their position for as long as they continue to be elected.

VIDEO LINK

To watch a video of Nancy Pelosi, Speaker of the House of Representatives, address Congress in January 2021, and condemning the Capitol Hill riots and the behaviour of Donald Trump, visit www.brightredbooks.net

EXECUTIVE BRANCH

46th President of the USA, Joe Biden and Vice President Kamala Harris, Inauguration Ceremony. January 2021.

The executive branch comprises the **President** of the USA, the **Vice President**, the **Cabinet** and **federal organisations and agencies**. The president's official residence is the White House in Washington D.C.

The President has the responsibility to implement and enforce laws that have been passed by Congress (Article II of the Constitution). The President is also head of state and Commander-in-Chief of the military.

The President appoints a cabinet, which has to be approved by the Senate. The fifteen members of the cabinet each head up an executive department, such as the Department of Commerce or the Department of Justice.

The executive branch exercises influence over the legislative branch, because the President has the power to propose legislation to Congress and can veto acts of Congress that he/she does not agree with.

The executive branch exercises influence over the judicial branch as the President is responsible for nominating Supreme Court and Federal Court judges (which the Senate must approve) and also has the power to 'extend pardons for federal crimes, except in the case of impeachment'.

The President or the Vice President are elected by the Electoral College, and not directly by US citizens.

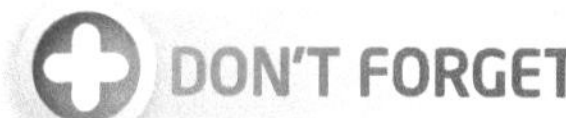

DON'T FORGET

The Electoral College is made up of 538 electors – the 435 State Representatives, the 100 State Senators and 3 electors from the District of Columbia.

JUDICIAL BRANCH

The judicial branch comprises the **Supreme Court** of the USA and **lower federal courts**. The Supreme Court meets in the US Supreme Court Building in Washington D.C. The Supreme Court is the highest court in the land.

As of 2021, the Supreme Court is made up of one chief justice and eight associate justices. This is determined by Congress and can change.

US Supreme Court Building

The judicial branch exercises influence over the executive branch through judicial reviews which can deem executive actions to be unconstitutional. Also, as justices remain in post until they choose to leave or they are removed by the Senate, they are unlikely to compromise justice due to political influence.

The judicial branch exercises influence over the legislative branch as it determines whether US laws are unconstitutional.

The President is responsible for appointing the justices, but the Senate must approve the President's nominations. In September 2020, former President Donald Trump replaced Ruth Bader Ginsburg, the second woman to ever serve on the Supreme Court, with Amy Coney Barrett. Other junior courts also exist. These include districts courts and courts of appeal.

DON'T FORGET

You can keep fully up to speed with all White House developments via a range of social media platforms including Facebook, Instagram and Twitter.

VIDEO LINK

To watch a short video clip which provides an overview of the executive branch, visit www.brightredbooks.net

THINGS TO DO AND THINK ABOUT

1 Why is there a system of checks and balances within the US system of government?
2 Describe the powers of the US President. Make at least three points.
3 Describe three powers of the legislative branch of the US system of government.
4 Describe the role of the US Supreme Court in the US system of government.

ONLINE TEST

Test yourself on the USA's political institutions and processes at www.brightredbooks.net

GOVERNANCE, DEMOCRACY AND MEDIA INFLUENCE

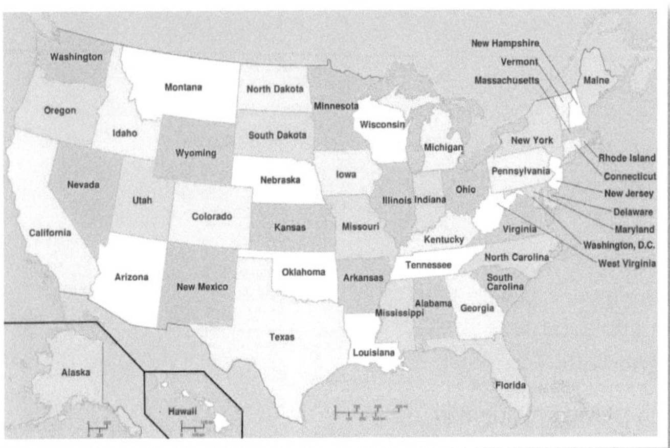

The fifty states of the USA

FEDERAL GOVERNMENT

The US federal government is responsible for dealing with issues that affect all US states. This includes currency, defence, foreign affairs, immigration and civil rights.

The federal government:

- consists of three branches, legislative, executive and judicial
- requires the election of candidates to the executive branch such as the President or Vice President. American citizens do not vote for these individuals directly
- requires the election of senators and representatives (congressional officers) to the legislative branch.

STATE GOVERNMENT

US states are responsible for dealing with domestic criminal matters as well as establishing a state constitution, issuing marriage licences and organising elections.

State governments also consist of the three legislative, executive and judicial branches. Within the executive branch, voters can elect **state governors**. Within the judicial branch, some states hold elections for **court judges**. Within the legislative branch, voters make up **legislative districts** and can vote for both a **senator** and a **representative**.

DON'T FORGET

Senior federal posts have strict qualification criteria that an individual must meet in order to run for the post. For example, the president of the USA must be a natural-born citizen of the USA, have lived there for the last 14 years and be at least 35 years old.

LOCAL GOVERNMENT

Local government is responsible for providing services such as parks and recreation, education and police services. American citizens have the opportunity to vote for public offices such as city council member or mayor.

DON'T FORGET

Similarly, senators must live in the state they represent, have been a US citizen for 9 years and be at least 30 years old. Entry to the House of Representatives requires an individual to live in the state they represent, have been a US citizen for 7 years, and be at least 25 years old.

HOW DEMOCRATIC IS THE USA?

The average US citizen is able to enjoy many freedoms as a result of a series of amendments to the US Constitution. These freedoms include: freedom of speech, freedom of religion, freedom of assembly, the right to bear arms, the right to own private property. There are also many ways for American citizens to participate in politics. They can:

- vote in federal, state and local elections for a range of elected representatives
- join a political party (remember, there are more than just the big two)
- stand as a candidate in federal, state and local elections
- join an interest group such as American Medical Association (AMA), the National Rifle Association (NRA) or the American Federation of Labour and Congress of Industrial Organisations (AFL–CIO).

FACT

In 2021, the basic salary of a Congress Member (Representatives and Senators) was $174,000 + benefits.

However, despite the fact that the USA prides itself on its democratic principles, and boasts that there are many opportunities for political participation, there are also a number of criticisms:

- According to the 2019 Electoral Integrity Project, US elections between 2012–2018 scored 61 out of 100 in relation to the integrity of electoral laws, voter registration and voting processes which was the lowest of all rich, democratically mature countries, and the same score as countries such as Mexico and Oman. Countries who performed well included Denmark (86), Finland (85) and Sweden (83).

contd

- The average American citizen does not get the opportunity to vote directly for the President.
- Many billionaire businessmen are accused of using their vast wealth to influence political decisions. The overall cost of the 2020 Presidential Election was estimated to be circa $14 billion. The largest donors were casino magnates Sheldon and Miriam Adelson who donated circa $173 million to Republicans and conservative groups.
- Following the US Supreme Court's **Citizens United** decision in 2010, there is no limit on what individuals like the Koch brothers can spend on media campaigns.
- Some people question the extent to which average American citizens can influence key decisions.

THE MEDIA

The freedom of the press is an important part of a democratic society. US citizens continue to benefit from access to a wide range of broadcast, print, online and social media which provides them with a vast array of information, some of which is based on facts, to help them form an opinion and make their decision.

Social media

According to the social media marketing platform Social Bakers, over 70% of US citizens of voting age use some form of social media platform. It is believed that social media played a heightened role in the 2020 Presidential Election due to the Covid-19 pandemic. Both the Biden and Trump campaigns used social media platforms extensively and, when, Donald Trump was permanently banned from Twitter in January 2021, he had almost 90 million followers.

Trump made multiple claims of election irregularities

US political parties appreciate the important role that social media platforms such as Facebook, Twitter and Tik Tok play in capturing the imagination and the votes of the electorate. However, rather disappointingly, the 2020 Presidential Election witnessed candidates and their supporters being particularly ruthless. There were also frequent instances of fake news, misinformation and the need for continuous fact checking.

THINGS TO DO AND THINK ABOUT

1. Describe the powers of both the federal and state governments.
2. Describe three ways American citizens can participate in US politics.
3. Give two possible reasons why the USA only scored 61 out of 100 in the 2019 Electoral Integrity Project. Do you find this to be surprising?
4. Use your mobile phone to follow or connect with five political organisations/ politicians in the USA. What important issues are they commenting about? Summarise your findings in a table and report back to the class.

DON'T FORGET

Interest groups are made up of a group of like-minded individuals who attempt to influence government policies in a number of ways, including lobbying, organising public protests or demonstrations and building relationships with individual politicians and political parties.

ONLINE

To find out more about social media coverage of the 2020 Presidential Election, visit www.brightredbooks.net

VIDEO LINK

To find out about the pitfalls of social media use in US politics, please visit www.brightredbooks.net

FACT

Between January 2019 – October 2020 Donald Trump and Joe Biden spent $107 million and $94 million respectively on Facebook advertisements.

ONLINE TEST

Test yourself on this topic at www.brightredbooks.net

SOCIO-ECONOMIC ISSUES IN THE USA: ECONOMIC INEQUALITY

US locations with the greatest income inequality

Rank	Location	Average Income of top 1% ($)	Average income of bottom 99% ($)
1	Los Angeles	1,803,340	53,904
2	San Francisco-Oakland-Hayward	2,812,641	82,321
3	San Jose-Sunnyvale-Santa Clara	3,445,220	99,486
4	Las Vegas	1,418,143	40,770
5	Fayetteville-Springdale-Rogers, Ark.-Mo	1,961,857	52,723
6	Cape Coral-Fort Myers, Fla	1,673,922	43,148
7	New York	2,425,384	61,550
8	North Port-Sarasota-Bradenton, Fla	1,810,660	42,021
9	Port St. Lucie, Fla	1,737,118	38,212
10	Miami	2,345,381	42,319

Source: 2018 Forbes

FACT

Across America, 568 000 people experience homelessness each night. Many of them in large cities such as Los Angeles and San Francisco. The Covid-19 pandemic is expected to further exacerbate this issue due to economic disruption and unemployment it will cause.

VIDEO LINK

To find out about some of the poorest cities in America and the problems they face in 2020, visit www.brightredbooks.net

ONLINE

To read about some of the wealthiest towns in America, visit www.brightredbooks.net

US INCOME AND WEALTH INEQUALITY

As you can see from the table, income inequality varies considerably across US states and is currently a significant issue facing the US government.

According to the OECD, the USA's 2017 Gini co-efficient was 0.39, which sits just below the UN's international warning level of 0.4. A Gini co-efficient of above 0.4 indicates that a severe level of income inequality exists within the country and that there is a possibility of social unrest because of the considerable income disparities that exist between the poorest and wealthiest in American society.

'After meeting fixed monthly expenses and paying income taxes to the federal and state authorities, there is no – I repeat, no – money left to be able to eat well or do anything in terms of discretionary spending.'

View of Donald, 72, Richmond, Virginia.

Many American senior citizens are too poor to retire and therefore have no other option but to work well into old age.

There are a number of factors which are believed to contribute towards the USA's income inequality. These factors include:

- **Wealth distribution** Many argue that the US federal government has failed to direct enough money to the poor Americans who need it most and have provided wealthy lobbyists and businessmen with overly-generous tax breaks.
- **Education** The slogan 'skills pay the bills' has never been more true. Changes in the US economy have meant that individuals without college or university educations struggle to find work, and when they do, the work tends to be low paid. Conversely, people with a high level of education are not only more occupationally mobile, but they also command higher salaries.
- **Technology** The number of relatively low-skilled manufacturing jobs has been greatly reduced as a result of technological advancements. In order for the USA to remain internationally competitive, it has outsourced many of its technology-based jobs to countries which command lower wage rates. This has had a serious impact on many middle-income families who can no longer secure permanent, full-time well-paid employment.

THE RICH, THE POOR AND THE MIDDLE CLASS

The USA is currently suffering from:

- significant rises in the cost of living which is made worse by the fact that wages have fallen or remained static
- a burgeoning wealth gap, where in 2019, America's richest 1% held $35 trillion of the country's wealth against $37 trillion held by the country's entire middle class, which accounts for about 40% of the population.

This table further emphasises the wealth gap that currently exists in the USA.

USA's wealth gap 2019–20

Number of American $ Billionaires	614
Number of American $ Millionaires	18.6 million
GNP per capita	$63 051
Number of American People living in relative Poverty	43 million (*annual income of less than $12 760*)
Number of American People living in extreme poverty	15 million

Multiple sources: Forbes, US Census, UN

contd

America's super-rich

The super-rich tend to live in wealthy states such as California, New York and Washington.

Many of the USA's wealthiest citizens have amassed their fortunes through innovative entrepreneurship, investing in the stock market, or by making a name for themselves in highly paid professions such as medicine and law.

The American super-rich have a passion for fast cars. For example, rapper Jay Z is the proud owner of an $8 million Maybach Exelero. The richest man on the planet, Jeff Bezos, on the other hand, prefers to travel by air, and owns two Gulfstream G-650ER private jets worth a combined $150 million.

USA's top 10 rich list

Position	Name	Source of wealth	Estimated Fortune ($)
1	Jeff Bezos	Amazon	179 billion
2	Bill Gates	Microsoft	111 billion
3	Mark Zuckerberg	Facebook	85 billion
4	Warren Buffett	Berkshire Hathaway	73.5 billion
5	Larry Ellison	Software	72 billion
6	Steve Ballmer	Microsoft	69 billion
7	Ellon Musk	Tesla/SpaceX	68 billion
8	Larry Page	Google	67.5 billion
9	Sergey Brin	Google	65.7 billion
10	Alice Walton	Walmart	62.3 billion

Source: Forbes 400 (2020)

Walmart is officially the USA's largest retailer

Oprah Winfrey – US billionaire defying the racial wealth divide (worth $2.6 billion in 2020)

America's poor

America's poorest states include Mississippi, Arkansas and Louisiana. Many of the USA's poorest citizens work as cooks, bank tellers, housekeepers, childcare workers or retail sales clerks. These jobs are low paid which makes it extremely difficult for many Americans to escape the poverty trap.

In-work poverty in the USA is high, with almost 75% of working families accessing public benefits such as rent subsidies or food stamps.

America's middle class

In modern day America, what constitutes America's middle class? The median household income in the USA has barely changed in the past 15 years, despite significant increases in the cost of housing, health care and education.

According to a study by the Pew Charitable Trusts, all 50 US states have witnessed a reduction in the number of middle-class families between 2000 and 2013. The Trust defines middle class as having an income between 67% and 200% of the states' median income.

The middle class are credited with being the driving force behind America's great economic success. Many politicians believe that the reduction in the numbers of the middle-class people will result in the disappearance of the American Dream. Winning the middle-class vote was a top priority for both Trump and Biden during the 2020 Presidential Election.

THINGS TO DO AND THINK ABOUT

1. Describe the societal problems that an average Gini coefficient of above 4.0 could bring to the USA in the future.
2. Describe two factors associated with the rise of income inequality in the USA.
3. What is the 'Fight for 15' movement? (Watch the recommended video clip to help you).
4. Explain why a falling number of middle-class Americans would be of concern to American politicians.
5. Essay practice: Analyse the causes of wealth inequality in the USA.

With the prospect of a new 'green agenda' expected to come to the forefront in 2021, Elon Musk, owner of the electric car company Tesla, is suspected to surge up the rich list. Watch out Jeff Bezos!

In 2020, fashion & cosmetics entrepreneur, Kylie Jenner, purchased a $36.5 million mansion in Holmby Hills, California, adding to her already extensive property portfolio

FACT

The Walton family, who own Walmart, are the USA's wealthiest family with an estimated fortune of over $200 billion.

FACT

The ratio of white-to-black US billionaires is 88:1. In 2020, the USA only had seven black billionaires – Tyler Perry *($1billion)*, Jay-Z *($1billion)*, Kanye West *($1.3 billion)*, Michael Jordan *($1.6 billion)*, Oprah Winfrey *($2.6 billion)*, David Steward *($3.7 billion)* and Robert Smith *($5.2 billion)*

VIDEO LINK

To find out about the US-wide #Fightfor15 protests demanding that the minimum wage is increased to $15 per hour, watch the following Twitter video at www.brightredbooks.net

ONLINE TEST

Test yourself on the socio-economic issues in the USA at www.brightredbooks.net

REDUCING SOCIO-ECONOMIC ISSUES IN THE USA

DON'T FORGET 

Depending on where in the US you live, unemployment benefit can also be referred to as unemployment insurance or unemployment compensation.

US GOVERNMENT POLICIES TO REDUCE ECONOMIC INEQUALITY AND THEIR EFFECTIVENESS

For some time now, income inequality has been a significant economic concern for the US government, and was a considerable factor in the 2020 Presidential Election. According to official poverty figures, one in seven American citizens currently live in poverty.

US government success

US government intervention has been critical in fighting poverty. The three most effective government poverty-reduction measures have been:

- social security (for example, unemployment benefit)
- refundable tax credits (for example, Earned Income Tax Credit (EITC))
- Supplemental Nutrition Assistance Programme (SNAP, previously known as food stamps).

Barack Obama attempted to reduce inequality by increasing the taxes imposed on the more affluent sections of society, and through legislation such as the **Affordable Care Act**, also known as 'Obamacare', while, at the same time, providing tax credits for those most in need. In January 2015, Obama outlined plans to provide free community college education and reduce mortgage insurance premiums for middle-class Americans. However, this announcement sparked controversy, as this could only be financed by further progressive taxation. When Donald Trump won the election in 2016, he continually tried, with limited success, to repeal Obamacare. Although it remained in place, Trump went to extreme lengths to weaken the ACA by reducing opportunities for people to enrol in it and by cutting subsidies to insurance companies offering coverage on the exchanges. In January 2021, President Biden announced he was going to reopen enrolment on the ACA exchanges.

DON'T FORGET 

Developed by the US Census Bureau, the SPM measures the extent to which social programmes such as EITC impact on the economic security of American families. Using the Consumer Price Index, the SPM takes inflation into consideration.

Temporary Aid to Needy Families

Under the **Temporary Aid to Needy Families** (TANF) programme, individual states receive funding from the federal government to devise initiatives which provide funding and/or support services to needy families, in order to help to create and maintain the traditional family unit, promote self-sufficiency and reduce the need for state assistance. Forms of support include both employability and childcare support. In 2019, the US government spent $16.5 billion on the TANF programme.

FACT 

In 2018, New York City, under the direction of Mayor Bill de Blasio, reduced the number of people living in poverty to an historic low of 17.3%. This 3.6% reduction since 2013 was achieved through a range of measures including securing a $15 minimum wage, freezing rents and increasing the number of free pre-kindergarten places.

SOCIAL INEQUALITY

Current health risks in the USA

According to the National Health Expenditure Accounts (NHEA), the USA spent $3.6 trillion on healthcare in 2018. However, many Americans die from non-communicable diseases (NCDs) such as heart disease, diabetes, obesity and lung cancer which are preventable and are linked with unhealthy lifestyles including excessive alcohol consumption, lack of exercise and unhealthy diets. These diseases have a significant economic cost, not only in terms of the cost of treatment, but also the cost of reduced workforce productivity.

The following diseases are of particular concern to the US government:

- **Cardiovascular disease (CVD)** – responsible for 33% of all American deaths.
- **Obesity** – According to the Centres for Disease Control and Prevention, 31.4% of American adults were defined as being clinically obese in 2019.
- **Non-alcoholic fatty liver disease (NAFLD)** – In 2019, approximately 100,000 Americans are believed to have NAFLD, caused by a build-up of excess fat in the liver. NAFLD is closely linked to obesity and will result in increased need for liver transplants.

Health care inequality

The graphic highlights the variation in life expectancy (in years) by ethnic group. Male Asian Americans (86.5) and Female Latino Americans (82.8) fare particularly well compared to Male African Americans (74.6) and Female Native Americans (76.9).

Many African Americans grow up in environments which do not make securing longevity easy. For example, lack of income, poor living conditions and increased exposure to violence can often result in premature death.

African American
74·6 years
US life expectancy

Native American
76·9 years
US life expectancy

White American
78·9 years
US life expectancy

Latino-American
82·8 years
US life expectancy

Asian-American
86·5 years
US life expectancy

American life expectancy
Source: Centers for Disease Control and Prevention (CDC)

According to the report, **Health Insurance Coverage in the United States: 2017**, over 28.5 million Americans had no access to medical insurance in 2017, including 46.5% of the Hispanic population. Of those that did, many relied on Medicaid. This illustrates the income inequality that exists between different ethnic groups. A key aim of Obama's Affordable Care Act was to reduce the numbers of Americans without access to government and private health care – the so-called 'Medigap'.

THINGS TO DO AND THINK ABOUT

1. Describe three of the US government's most effective poverty reduction measures.
2. Explain how the Obama administration tried to reduce wealth inequality.
3. Explain why obesity and Alzheimer's pose a significant risk to the USA.
4. What conclusions can be drawn about life expectancy between each of the different minority ethnic groups in the USA? Provide statistics to support your answer.
5. Essay practice: Evaluate the success of a recent US government policy to reduce poverty in the USA.

FACT

The Trump administration argued that it successfully supported black African Americans. 2019 highlights include real median income growth of 7.9%, poverty rates falling below 20% (for the first time) and an increase in the number of households earning more than $100000.

VIDEO LINK

To To find out more about Joe Biden's stance on the Affordable Care Act, before he became President, visit www.brightredbooks.net

DON'T FORGET

African Americans tend to have lower life expectancies than all other ethnic groups. They are more likely to suffer from the most common killer diseases such as heart disease, cancer and diabetes. They are also more likely to die young as a result of violence.

ONLINE TEST

Test yourself on reducing socio-economic issues in the USA at www.brightredbooks.net

SOCIO-ECONOMIC ISSUES IN THE USA: SOCIAL INEQUALITY

'To see that young African-American students – or babies, as I call them – are being suspended from pre-kindergarten programmes at such horrendous rates is deeply troubling... It's incredible to think about or fathom what pre-kindergarten students could be doing to get suspended from schools.'

Leticia Smith-Evans, Interim Director of Education Practice at NAACP Legal Defence and Educational Fund

EDUCATION INEQUALITY

Variations in public school spending and the widening gap in educational attainment

The USA spends about $649 billion per annum on education. However, according to Sheryll Cashin, professor of Law at Georgetown Law School, the quality of education a child receives is 'a lottery of birth'.

Schools in run-down areas are unable to spend enough money on essential resources, whereas schools in more affluent areas have resources in abundance. According to Annual Survey of School System Finances, in 2018, New York City's school district spent $24 040 on each of its 976 711 students, almost double the national average of $12 612, and considerably more than Utah, where the spend was circa $7 628 per student.

Research indicates that only 10% of students from the poorest American families (the bottom 12.5% of earners) gain entry to the country's top 146 colleges. This clearly indicates that wealth and academic performance are inextricably linked, and that many less affluent schools are not preparing their students adequately for the college entry **Scholastic Aptitude Test** (SAT).

Racial inequality in education

In 2021, the National Centre for Education Statistics reported 'growing or barely narrowing gaps' between white and black and white and Latino students in literacy and numeracy test scores. Further data obtained from a recent Civil Rights Survey carried out by the US Department of Education concluded that racial inequality was inherent throughout the US education system. Selected key findings were that some ethnic groups, particularly those of African American, Native American and Hispanic origin were disadvantaged in relation to:

- **Quality of teacher** – African American, Native American and Hispanic students (3–4%) were more likely to be taught by partially qualified (probationer) teachers who lacked experience, when compared to white students (1%).
- **Access to curriculum** – African American, Native American and Hispanic students were much less likely to be able to study science, technology, engineering and maths (STEM) beyond introductory level than white students. The findings indicated that: 'A third of the schools with the highest percentage of African American and Hispanic students did not offer chemistry'.
- **Discipline** – African American and Native American students were found to be excluded from school at disproportionate rates. This was evident from pre-school stage, where African Americans accounted for nearly 50% of repeat suspensions despite only making up 18% of school enrolment. African American females were excluded from school more than all other ethnic females, and most males.

US schools are under fierce pressure to improve the treatment and attainment of minority Americans, in order to mitigate against the risk of America losing its global competitiveness.

DON'T FORGET 

To recap on the general characteristics of suburban and ghetto schools in the USA, see page 101 of BrightRED's National 5 Modern Studies Study Guide.

ONLINE TEST 

Test yourself on the socio-economic issues in the USA at www.brightredbooks.net

FACT 

With almost 50% of Asian and Pacific Islanders (AAPIs) over 25 having an undergraduate (or bachelors) degree, they are the most educated of all US ethnic groups.

DON'T FORGET 

The Covid-19 pandemic has disproportionately affected ethnic minority groups. Many African American families lacked the savings to respond to the challenges of remote learning such as paying for internet access and electronic learning devices. This is known as Digital Poverty and it widens the racial attainment gap.

HOUSING INEQUALITY

According to the **National Low Income Housing Coalition** (NLIHC), demand for housing in the USA outstrips supply, with 31 affordable homes available for every 100 families who need them. Renting a home is fast becoming the only option for many American families due to reduced savings and bad debt, partly due to the global recession. African Americans are 45% more likely than white Americans to rent rather than own their homes.

contd

There has been a significant decline in homeownership rates among African Americans and Hispanics – Whites and Asians are more likely to be approved for mortgages.

Many Americans are forced to move area in order to reduce their housing spend. There has also been an increase in the number of families who co-habit.

Over 57% of African Americans rent their home, considerably less than America's white population. This problem has been amplified by the particularly damaging effect that the recession had on the wealth of African Americans, reducing their total wealth by almost 50%.

The Covid-19 pandemic also disproportionately affected low-income ethnic minority groups.

The charts on the right illustrate the significant differences in home ownership rates between whites, Black African Americans and Hispanics.

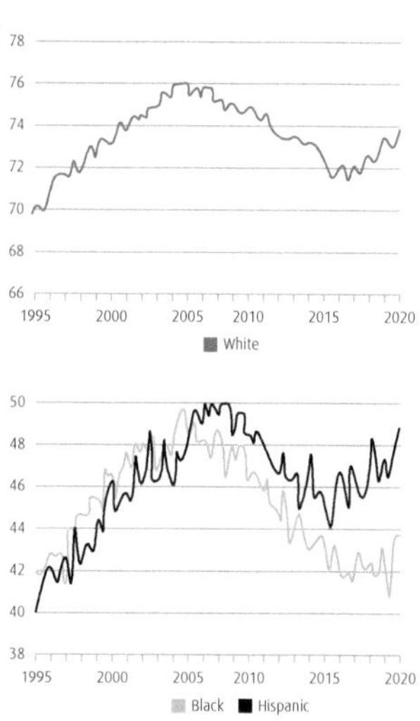

Homeownership rates recover for White and Hispanic householdsd

INEQUALITY IN THE US CRIMINAL JUSTICE SYSTEM

In August 2013, the **Sentencing Project**, a group that attempts to address racial disparities within the US criminal justice system, submitted a report to the UN Human Rights Committee which asserted that the USA was violating the International Covenant on Civil and Political Rights. The report argued that racial minorities in the USA were more likely than whites to be arrested, convicted and sentenced. In February 2021, the Sentencing Project evidenced that racial inequality in the criminal justice system persisted:

- One in every ten black men in his thirties is in prison or jail in any given day
- American Indian youth are three times as likely as white youth to be held in a juvenile detention facility
- In every state, black youth are more likely to be incarcerated than their white peers, about five times as likely nationwide
- Latino youth are 42% more likely than their white peers to be incarcerated
- After arrest, youth of colour are more likely to be detained pre-adjudication and committed post-adjudication

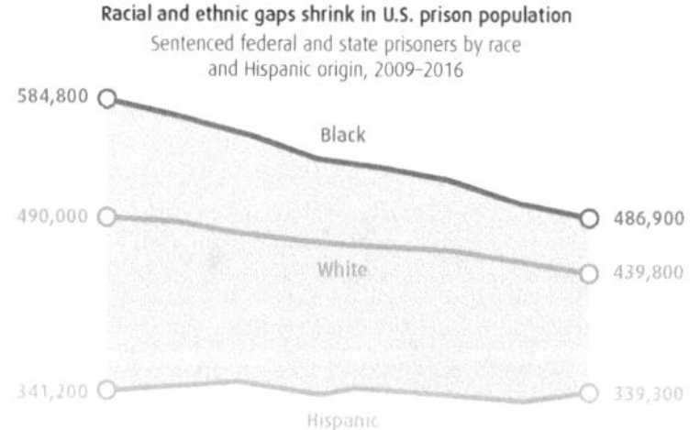

Criticism continues to be directed towards white police officers who use unnecessary force on African Americans. One of the most high profile examples of late took place in May 2020, when George Floyd, an African American man, died following arrest. A white police officer, Derek Chauvin, was arrested for murder after kneeling on Mr Floyd's neck. On twenty separate occasions, Mr Floyd said he was unable to breathe. When a video of the incident was made public, it led to a series of protests throughout Minneapolis where police property was vandalised. In April 2021, Derek Chauvin was found guilty of second-degree murder, third-degree murder and second-degree manslaughter. George Floyd's death resulted in America's largest civil rights protests in years, re-igniting the 2013 Black Lives Matter movement and propelling it into the media spotlight.

Black Lives Matter Protests at Capitol Hill, June 2020

According to the Sentencing Project, 'since the nature of law enforcement frequently requires police officers to make snap judgements about the danger posed by suspects and the criminal nature of their activity, subconscious racial associations influence the way officers perform their jobs'.

THINGS TO DO AND THINK ABOUT

1 Explain why many African Americans experience racial inequality in education. Think about long-standing factors as well as new problems which have surfaced as a result of Covid-19.
2 Black African American are more likely to own their own homes than white Americans. Do you agree with this statement? Provide detailed evidence to support your position.
3 Organisations, like the Sentencing Project, argue that ethnic minorities are treated unfairly by the US criminal justice system. Why do you think this might be the case?

'The United States now incarcerates more African Americans as a percentage than apartheid South Africa did.'

Nicholas Kristof, *New York Times*.

GOVERNMENT POLICIES TO REDUCE SOCIAL INEQUALITY AND THEIR EFFECTIVENESS

The **Affordable Care Act** (ACA) was introduced by President Barack Obama and was his flagship domestic policy, which aimed to roll out affordable health insurance across the USA. The policy attempted to achieve this in a number of ways including increased provision of Medicaid, increased provision of tax credits (to both individuals and employers), increased progressive taxation (to ensure the rich contribute more) and a reduction in wasteful health care spending.

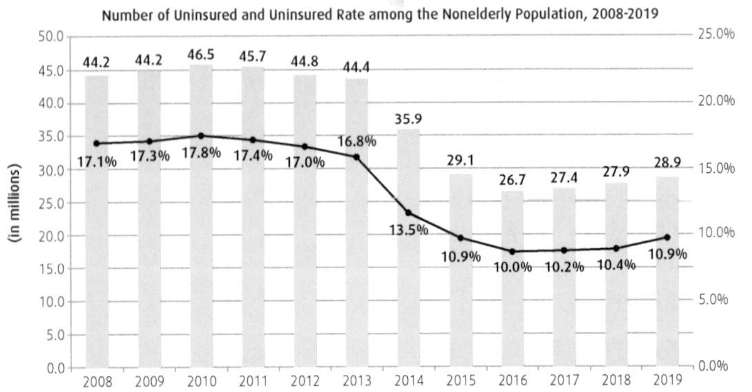

HEALTH ACHIEVEMENTS: HOW SUCCESSFUL IS THE ACA?

Successes

The graph illustrates the decline of uninsured Americans during the second term of Obama's presidency.

Trump's term as President witnessed a 0.9% increase in the number of uninsured Americans from 26.7 million in 2016 to 28.9 million in 2019.

The ACA has helped to tackle poverty within vulnerable groups including African Americans and Hispanics, with both groups experiencing significant reductions in uninsured rates.

The former Obama administration invested more money in preventing and treating medical ailments which result in a higher death rate among African Americans. Groups such as Asian American Pacific Islanders (AAPIs) are no longer prevented from joining health care plans due to pre-existing medical conditions such as hepatitis B which is particularly prominent among young AAPIs (19–24). Over 1000 community health centres, where one-third of all patients are Hispanic, have witnessed an increase in funding. According to Obama, 'this law is saving money for families and businesses. This law is also saving lives'.

Criticisms

- Approximately 63% of Americans wish the law to be abolished.
- The **Congressional Budget Office** (CBO), estimated that by 2023, over 30 million Americans will still be uninsured.
- The CBO estimated that Obamacare, over the next ten years, will drastically exceed the programme's forecast budget of $1 trillion by 0.8 trillion, costing the USA circa $1.8 trillion.

EDUCATION ACHIEVEMENTS

Successes

The former Obama administration invested heavily in the US education system and aims to make education accessible for all. Approximately $40 billion has been invested in **Pell Grants** to help America's less affluent pay for college. Pell Grants have benefited over 60% of African American students and almost 25% of Hispanic and AAPI students. Almost $3 billion has also been invested in **Historically Black Colleges and Universities** (HBCU) to encourage more African Americans to matriculate to higher education.

Within the **American Recovery and Reinvestment Act** (2009), programmes such as **Race to the Top** and **Head Start** have resulted in:

- $4 billion in funding to support 22 million students
- 1.5 million teachers employed to improve the education of 42 000 students in 19 states
- creation of projects to raise student attainment in states such as Tennessee.

contd

DON'T FORGET

Named after US Senator Claiborne Pell, a Pell Grant is financial support provided by the US Federal Government which helps students of low-income families attend college or university.

- $5 billion to fund early learning programmes, such as Head Start, which has had significant enrolments from minority groups including Hispanics (37%). Over 11,000 AAPI children have also enrolled in Head Start.

The **No Child Left Behind Act of 2001** (NCLB) has continued to ensure that federal government funds are available for poor school districts in a bid to raise the attainment and educational opportunity of students from low-income families.

NCLB has been commended for:

- attempting to narrow the attainment gap between whites and ethnic minorities
- creating a climate of increased accountability for teachers and schools. Schools, districts and states must report on overall performance and the academic scores of disadvantaged groups such as low-income, disabled and ethnic minority students.

Criticisms

The Race to the Top Programme has received criticism for being inaccessible to a number of states due to strict conditions attached to gaining the grants. This obstacle has affected states such as California, where the Governor considered making changes to the state's education system in order to help improve their chances of securing funding.

No Child Left Behind (NCLB) has received criticism for creating a culture where staff and schools are under pressure to raise attainment or lose funding. NCLB was replaced by Every Student Succeeds Act (ESSA) in 2015.

HOUSING ACHIEVEMENTS

Successes

In recent years, the US Department of Housing and Urban Development (HUD) announced funding for projects to assist vulnerable groups, including:

- $1.8 billion for public housing authorities to significantly improve their housing stock
- $150 million to help low-income disabled people pay their rent
- $24 million for the **Jobs-Plus Pilot Programme** to help the residents of nine public housing authorities increase their earning power to become more self-sufficient
- $65 million to help over 9000 homeless veterans find a home.

Criticisms

- **High taxpayer costs** – According to the Cato Institute, in 2014, the cost of HUD was $341 per US household. This is estimated to increase to over $46 billion in 2015.
- **Financial mismanagement** – It has been asserted that HUD has provided some programmes with funding that has been abused.
- **Vouchers** – The value of HUD vouchers does not accurately reflect market conditions, resulting in some landlords refusing to accept them.

CRIMINAL JUSTICE SERVICE ACHIEVEMENTS

Successes

Recent developments have included:

- the 2010 **Fair Sentencing** Act which reduced sentencing disparities between blacks and whites in relation to drug possession
- $263 million to increase police officers' use of body-worn cameras
- a team of researchers funded to look at racial bias in law enforcement and to suggest possible interventions to improve the situation.

Criticisms

Despite efforts from the US government to improve the treatment of minority groups, tensions still run deep, with some US police departments being accused of racism. Consequently, violence has continued to occur in areas like Ferguson, Missouri.

THINGS TO DO AND THINK ABOUT

1 To what extent has the US government effectively tackled inequality in education?
2 To what extent has the US government effectively tackled inequality in housing?
3 What evidence is there that ethnic minority groups are treated less favourably than whites in the American criminal justice system?

DON'T FORGET

HBCUs were established in the early 1960s with the purpose of accommodating African American students. Today, there are still over 100 HBCUs in the USA, although many of them now attract high percentages of non-African American students also.

ONLINE

To read a comprehensive list of the Trump Administration's accomplishments including a number of economic successes, visit www.brightredbooks.net

VIDEO LINK

To find out how President Biden intends to improve American education, visit www.brightredbooks.net

ONLINE

For up to the minute press releases on all HUD activity, visit www.brightredbooks.net

VIDEO LINK

To explore the role of the Sentencing Project in tackling racial inequality in the criminal justice system, visit www.brightredbooks.net

ONLINE TEST

Test yourself on the socio-economic issues in the USA at www.brightredbooks.net

INTERNATIONAL RELATIONS: USA'S INVOLVEMENT IN INTERNATIONAL ORGANISATIONS

US membership of selected key international organisations

Name of organisation	Year of entry
Food and Agriculture Organisation* (FAO)	1945
Asia-Pacific Economic Cooperation* (APEC)	1989
International Monetary Fund* (IMF)	1945
World Bank* (WB)	1945
Nuclear Energy Agency* (NEA)	1976
United Nations (UN) General Assembly and Security Council*	1945
Group of 7* (G7)	1975
International Fund for Agricultural Development* (IFAD)	1977
World Trade Organisation* (WTO)	1995
World Meteorological Organisation (WMO)	1949

*denotes USA as being a founding member

IMF Factfile

Membership	190 countries
Established	1945
Headquarters	Washington D.C.
Key aims include:	• Promoting international monetary cooperation. • Facilitating the expansion and balanced growth of international trade. • Making resources available to members experiencing balance of payments difficulties.
Key functions include:	• Surveillance – keeping a close eye on the international monetary system and 'financial policies of members' • Lending – providing loans to member countries in times of need. • Technical assistance – providing guidance, support and training to member countries to improve their economic policy and better manage their finances.

Source: IMF

USA'S MEMBERSHIP OF INTERNATIONAL ORGANISATIONS

The USA continues to be the most influential country in the world. It has been a founder member of many of the world's leading international organisations and continues to play an active and effective part in these organisations. The USA is at the centre of many of the key global decisions and exercises dominance over matters ranging from international economic policy to global security. The table shows US membership of ten key international organisations and highlights the year in which it gained entry.

USA and IMF

With 16.52% of voting shares, the USA is the IMF's most powerful and influential member and is the only country able to veto changes to the organisation's rules and governance. In recent years there have been attempts to restructure decision-making within the IMF by allowing other nations (such as the so-called BRICS countries) a greater say. However, reform has been blocked by the US Congress leading to allegations that the US is putting its own self-interest before that of the greater global economic good.

The USA's reluctance to approve IMF quota and governance reforms has led some countries to question America's commitment to the IMF and other multinational institutions. The BRICS nations have identified this as an opportunity and have created institutions such as the New Development Bank (NDB) and the Asian Infrastructure Investment Bank (AIIB) to provide existing IMF members with a choice about where they obtain future finance, a situation that has concerned some senior US officials.

In January 2021, following a video call with the newly appointed US Treasury Secretary, Janet Yellen, the IMF's Managing Director, Kristalina Georgieva, deemed 2021 to be a 'critical year of action' and tweeted 'we agreed that fighting the pandemic, boosting growth, combating income inequality and tackling climate change are top priorities, and that global engagement to support low-income countries is essential.' In February 2021, President Biden proposed a $1.9 trillion economic stimulus plan, which according to IMF Chief Economist, Gita Gopinath, could boost GDP by circa 5% over a three-year period.

FACT 

2021 sees the UK take on the Presidency of the G7. However, back in March 2014, the USA, supported by Canada, France, Germany, Italy, Japan and the UK decided to suspend Russia from the G8 in retaliation to Vladimir Putin's annexation of Crimea from the Ukraine. As a result, the G8 became the G7.

The **Asia-Pacific Economic Cooperation** (APEC) forum was established in 1989 with an initial membership of 12 (currently 21). Its main aim is to have free trade across the Asia-Pacific region by 2020, achieved by trade and investment liberalisation, business facilitation and economic and technical cooperation.

Membership of APEC greatly benefits the USA. It provides trade opportunities in an immense market which accounts for 48% of world trade and represents circa 60% of world GDP.

The USA imports more goods from APEC countries than it exports to them. In 2017, the trade deficit was $620 billion.

The 21 member economies of APEC are home to 2.9 billion people. This is approximately 40% of the world's total population.

contd

USA and the United Nations

The USA is a founding member of the UN, holds a permanent seat on the United Nations Security Council and plays a full role within the organisation. Today, New York City is home to the UN's official headquarters and five out of the six main UN organs; the General Assembly, the Security Council, the Economic and Social Council, the Trusteeship Council and the Secretariat.

Case Study: US Support for Syria

In June 2020, the former US Special Representative for Syria Engagement Ambassador, James F. Jeffrey, announced an additional $700 million in additional humanitarian assistance for the Syria crisis. This makes the USA the largest donor of humanitarian aid to Syria, having provided in excess of $12 billion in assistance between 2012–2020. USAID humanitarian assistance reaches 4.5 million Syrians each month.

US Government Humanitarian Funding for Syria (2012–2020)

Total USAID/Bureau for Humanitarian Assistance Funding for Syria	$6 153 700 050
Total State/Bureau of Population Refugees and Migration Funding for Syria	$6 050 511 437
Total USG Humanitarian Funding for Syria	**$12 204 21 487**

Source: USAID Factsheet 3 (2021)

Previously, the USA had attempted to address a number of human rights concerns through its participation in the United Nation's **Human Rights Council** (HRC). The USA was actively involved in renewing mandates and passing and opposing resolutions affecting countries such as Myanmar and Israel. However, in 2018 under President Trump, the USA withdrew from the HRC claiming it was a 'protector of human rights abusers'. In February 2021, the US Secretary of State, Antony Blinken, confirmed that the US would be rejoining as an observer highlighting the Biden administration's commitment 'to a foreign policy centred on democracy, human rights and equality.'

Linda Thomas-Greenfield replaced Kelly Craft, as the United States Permanent Representative to the UN on 25 February 2021

US Support to the UN

The USA is the largest financial contributor to the UN, a situation that has been consistent since the organisation was founded in 1945. In line with UN membership rules, the USA is required to pay the maximum assessed contribution to the UN regular budget (22%) which is based on the country's gross national product (GNP). In 2018, the USA contributed over $10 billion to the UN. In addition to being the largest contributor to the regular budget, the USA was also the largest financial contributor to UN peacekeeping operations and was required to pay 27.89% in 2020–21.

However, despite being a high financial contributor to the aforementioned budgets, the USA is often criticised for making an insufficient human contribution in terms of police, troops and military experts. As of December 2020, the USA provided 30 troops (military and police personnel) to UN peacekeeping operations. This contribution is miniscule compared to countries like Bangladesh and Rwanda, who contributed 6798 and 6383 peacekeepers respectively during the same time period. Some of this imbalance is due to US public and political opinion which is largely against US soldiers being placed under the command of anyone other than the US military.

THINGS TO DO AND THINK ABOUT

1 'The USA is an influential member of the IMF.' Provide detailed evidence to support this statement.
2 Explain why many nations, including the BRICS countries, are sceptical about the USA's level of influence in the IMF.
3 Explain why the USA might be concerned with the New Development Bank (NDB) and the Asian Infrastructure Investment Bank (AIIB).
4 What arguments are there for and against the view that the USA contributes too little to the UN in terms of peacekeeping?
5 Why is it important that UN member states pay their contributions on time and in full?

ONLINE

To find out more about the ongoing humanitarian emergency in Syria and the USA's efforts to support the Syrian people, have a look at a USAID factsheet from January 2021 at www.brightredbooks.net

VIDEO LINK

Watch US State Department, Ned Price, confirming that the USA would be rejoining the HRC in February 2021 www.brightredbooks.net

ONLINE

For a detailed and up-to-date overview of USA's ongoing contribution to the UN's main bodies, visit www.brightredbooks.net

FACT

In May 2020, the US Government announced $225 million in emergency aid to support the UN's World Food Programme's work in Yemen which provides aid to 24 million people, including 10 million people at risk of famine.

DON'T FORGET

In January 2021, it was reported that the USA was $2 billion in arrears with its payments to the UN, 50% of which was for peacekeeping dues.

ONLINE TEST

Test yourself on USA's role in international relations at www.brightredbooks.net

INTERNATIONAL RELATIONS: USA'S RELATIONSHIPS WITH OTHER COUNTRIES

Which one country anywhere in the world do you consider to be the United States' greatest enemy today?

2016	2018	2020
North Korea (16%)	North Korea (51%)	Russia (23%)
Russia (15%)	Russia (19%)	China (22%)
Iran (14%)	China (11%)	Iran (19%)
China (12%)	Iran (7%)	North Korea (12%)

(Source: Selected findings from Gallup's World Affairs Poll, 2016–2020)

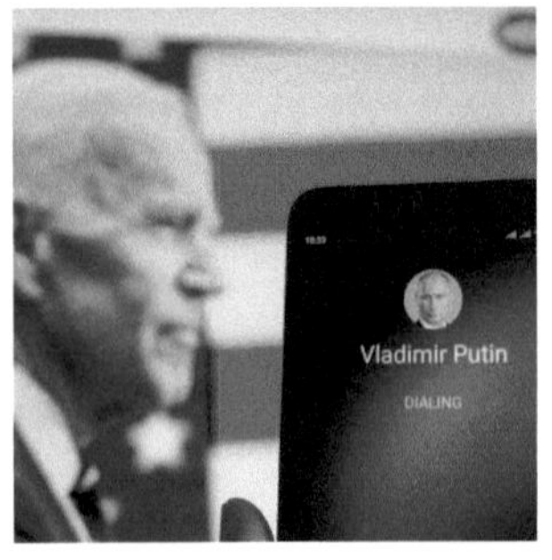

Tensions between Russia and the USA are currently high over a number of issues including Russia's continued interference in US politics and Putin's support of Syrian President, Bashar al-Assad.

In August 2018, Apple Inc. became the world's first public company to reach the $1 trillion market value due to the success of products such as the iPhone XR.

USA's STRAINED RELATIONSHIPS

Recent US-North Korea tensions

The results of Gallup's 2020 World Affairs Poll indicate that the USA's perceived relationship with North Korea has improved in recent years. Previously, between 2016–2018, relations were strained due to a number of North Korean missile tests and a number of bitter exchanges between Kim Jong Un and Donald Trump. The situation improved, however, in June 2018, when both leaders met and signed a pledge agreeing to repair their fractured relationship. A second summit went ahead in February 2019, which proved to be less positive, with Trump bringing it to an early close. Kim Jong Un recently showcased his largest intercontinental ballistic missile during a military parade in Pyongyang, which gained the attention of the Biden administration.

North Korean leader, Kim Jong Un, meeting former US President Donald Trump for a second historic summit in Hanoi, Vietnam (February 2019).

Recent US-Sino tensions

From 2018, China and the USA have been embroiled in a bitter trade war with the USA placing over $360 billion of tariffs on Chinese goods and China retaliating by placing over $110 billion of tariffs on US goods. The USA accused China of unfair trading practices and Intellectual Property (IP) theft and China accused the USA of breaching WTO rules and attempting to stifle China's economic ascent. In 2020, it was estimated by the Federal Reserve Bank of New York that the Trade War had wiped $1.7 trillion from US companies' market value. In 2021, the trade war rumbles on, with President Biden recently placing sanctions on some of China's leading technology firms. To find out more about Sino-US tensions, refer to the China section of this Study Guide.

USA'S POWER AND INTERNATIONAL INFLUENCE

Economic power

In 2020, the USA remained the largest economy in the world with a GDP of over $20 trillion. The USA has held the number one spot since 1872. However, from an economic perspective, 2020 was a challenging year for America, which witnessed its economy shrink by 3.5% as a result of the Covid-10 pandemic. The USA is an economic powerhouse as a result of:

- Output and innovation – the USA is responsible for producing about 20% of the world's total output. The USA is home to many entrepreneurs and has created many iconic products which are highly sought after around the world.
- GDP per capita – the USA has one of the highest GDP per capita in the world.
- Natural resources – the USA has access to a multitude of natural resources including farmland, oil and fresh water.
- Political system – the USA has one government and one currency which helps the country maintain a strong economic position.

contd

Cultural influence

The USA's cultural influence extends across the world, reaching a global audience of about two billion people. American entertainment such as TV sitcoms, films, music and computer games are extremely popular and have resulted in widespread **Americanisation**. American influence is further emphasised around the globe through uptake of American sports such as baseball, basketball and American football, and demand for American food outlets such as Burger King, KFC and Pizza Hut.

TV shows	Films	Business	Singers
The Masked Singer	Godzilla v Kong	Nike	Jay Z
Dancing with the Stars	Mortal Kombat	Apple Inc.	Miley Cyrus
Chicago P.D.	Cruella	Amazon	Ariana Grande
House of Cards	Venom: Let there be Carnage	Microsoft	Cardi B
Game of Thrones	Matrix 4	Walt Disney	Bruno Mars

Although the vast majority of the two billion people making up the audience for American entertainment will have never visited the USA, they will be aware of most of the personalities and brands shown in this table.

Military strength

Despite recent findings from the **2021 Index of US Military Strength**, which concluded that the USA's Navy was weak in terms of capacity, the USA is without question the most powerful military nation on earth. The USA's 2020 defence spend was estimated to be $700 billion, which is more than that of China, Russia, Saudi Arabia, France and the UK put together. The USA has 1.4m active frontline personnel and a reserve force of 1.1m who have access to state-of-the-art weaponry and are highly trained. The US military has a well-stocked arsenal which includes 20 aircraft carriers, almost 14 000 aircraft (including the B-2A Spirit stealth bomber), 72 submarines and approximately 8848 tanks. The US government is constantly developing new technology, for example, the US Navy's new Electromagnetic Railgun, which has the capability to intercept incoming missiles. The USA has allies throughout the world, and is unrivalled in terms of nuclear warheads with over 7 700.

World significance

The USA enjoys enormous political, economic and military strength, and, as a result, has many influential allies throughout the world including the UK, Canada, Japan and Germany. The USA has a dynamic and innovative workforce, excellent infrastructure and access to an abundance of natural resources which help to fuel its successful economy.

However, following the rise to prominence of countries such as China, India and Russia, the extent of the USA's significance is now being increasingly questioned. A recent poll by Forbes Magazine ranked Xi Jinping as the most powerful man in the world, followed by Vladimir Putin in second place and Donald Trump in third place.

Controversially, the USA is often regarded as the 'policeman of the world', due to its active involvement, some would say interference, in the domestic matters of other countries. In February 2021, the Biden administration announced the reversal of Donald Trump's decision to deem the Houthis movement in Yemen to be a terrorist group. The US Secretary of State, Antony Blinken, stated 'We have listened to warnings from the United Nations, humanitarian groups, and bipartisan members of Congress, among others, that the designations could have a devastating impact on Yemenis' access to basic commodities like food and fuel...By focusing on alleviating the humanitarian situation in Yemen, we hope the Yemeni parties can also focus on engaging in dialogue.'

THINGS TO DO AND THINK ABOUT

1 Explain why Russia, China and North Korea were each seen as the USA's greatest enemies in Gallup's 2020 World Affairs Poll.
2 Explain two factors which have helped the USA to maintain its position as an economic superpower.
3 What evidence is there that the USA remains the world's most powerful military nation?
4 The USA spends disproportionately more on its military than most other developed countries. What consequences might exceptionally high military spending have on domestic spending such as education, health care and housing?
5 Some people argue that the USA is no longer as influential as it once was. Can you think of any reasons why this might be the case?

ONLINE

If you are interested in this topic, and want to explore it in more detail, access the Heritage Foundation's 2021 Index of US Military Strength at www.brightredbooks.net

USS Gerald R. Ford, $13.2 billion Aircraft Carrier

VIDEO LINK

Watch the video clip which shows former US President Barack Obama speaking about the USA's influence in the world from its historical involvement in Kosovo and Bosnia to current diplomatic efforts in Palestine, Israel and the Ukraine at www.brightredbooks.net.

ONLINE TEST

Test yourself on the USA's role in international relations at www.brightredbooks.net

ONLINE

Head to www.brightredbooks.net for advice on how to approach these essay questions and sample answers

EXTERNAL ASSESSMENT COMPONENT 2: QUESTION PAPER 2

QUESTION 1: CONCLUSIONS

QUESTION PAPER 2 OVERVIEW

This question paper has a total mark allocation of 28 marks. This is 26% of the overall course assessment.

This question paper allows candidates to demonstrate application of the following higher order thinking skills; detecting and explaining the degree of selectivity using a range of sources of information; drawing and supporting complex conclusions using a range of sources of information; evaluating the trustworthiness of a range of sources of information.

This question paper will have three questions. You should complete each of them.

Question 1 – You will be asked to answer a question which assesses the skill of detecting and explaining the degree of selectivity or accuracy of a view. This question consists of between two and four sources of information. Sources may be written, numerical, graphical or pictorial. This question is worth 10 marks.

Question 2 – You will be asked to answer a question which assesses the skill of drawing and supporting conclusions. This question consists of between two and four sources of information. Sources may be written, numerical, graphical or pictorial. This question is worth 10 marks.

Question 3 – You will be asked to answer a question which assesses the skill of evaluating the reliability or trustworthiness of sources of information. This question consists of three sources of information. Sources may be written, numerical, graphical or pictorial. This question is worth 8 marks.

You will have 1 hour and 15 minutes to complete the Question Paper.

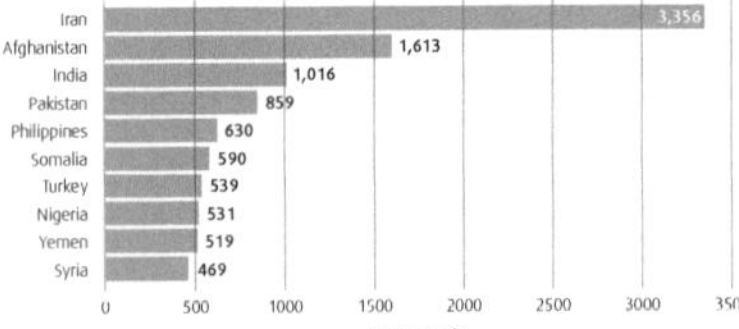

Source B: i) The Location of Known Terrorist Attacks 2016

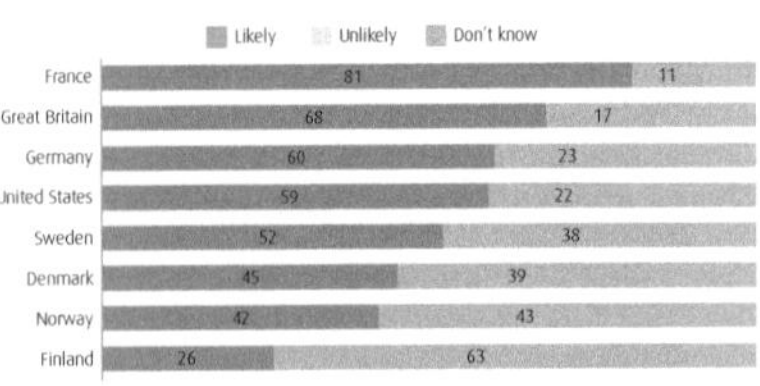

Source B: ii) Expectation of Terrorist Attacks in selected countries (2016–17)

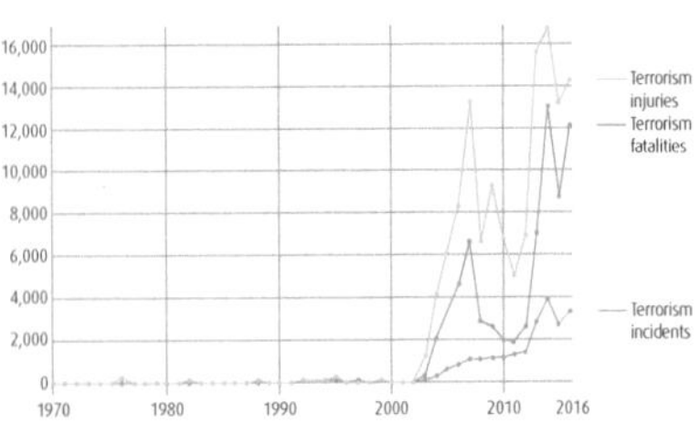

Source C: i) Terrorist Attacks 1970-2016 in Iraq

CONCLUSIONS QUESTION

Source A: Terrorist Attacks in 2016

In July 2016, a truck drove into crowds assembled to watch Bastille Day fireworks in Nice, France. ISIS claimed responsibility for the attack, which killed 86 and wounded 433. But for all the news coverage of the event, it is in a small minority. Events like Nice represent a mere 2.5 percent of all terror attacks (one of only 36 fatal attacks in 2016 in the West). "Those attacks [in the West] remain a very small minority of attacks we see," said Erin Miller, of the Global Terrorism Database (GTD). "Obviously, these major attacks get so much attention because they're unusual and they're newsworthy, and the Middle East blurs into the background." Kidnapping and hostage taking (both a rarity in the West) remain a much bigger problem than fatal attacks.

The deadliest terror attack in 2016 took place in the Karrada district of Baghdad in Iraq on July 3. In a shopping centre filled with people buying presents before the festival of Eid al-Fitr, an ISIS suicide bomber detonated a truck full of explosives, killing 382 and wounding 200 more. Sayad Jiyad, an Iraqi political analyst at the Al-Bayan Center in Baghdad, was at a nearby hotel watching a football match on the night of the bombing. In a blog post, he described living in a country where terrorism is a daily threat. "As we were still discussing the result, we suddenly felt the shockwave of a bomb and the loud sound of an explosion accompanying it, meaning it was nearby," Jiyad wrote. "Living in Baghdad means you learn to tell the difference between [the many different types of bombs]."

Mass terror attacks — those killing 50 or more people — are extremely rare, only half a percent of all incidents in 2016. There were 72 attacks that caused 50 or more fatalities. Only two — the attack in Nice and the Pulse nightclub shooting in Orlando, Florida, where 50 people died — took place in the West. Out of 36 fatal attacks in the West, 70 percent resulted in one death, and in nine out of 26 cases, it was only the terrorist who was killed.

Overall, 75 percent of 2016 terrorist attacks listed in the GTD took place in just 10 countries: Iraq, Afghanistan, India, Pakistan, the Philippines, Somalia, Turkey, Nigeria, Yemen and Syria. Iraq, the deadliest place in the world for terror, was home to 35 percent of all deaths worldwide, an average of 33 deaths every day. Six out of the 10 deadliest terror attacks in 2016 took place in Iraq, all of which were by ISIS.

Source A: Adapted from the website: The World (https://www.pri.org/stories/2017-07-14/more-75-percent-terrorist-attacks-2016-took-place-just-10-countries)

contd

Attempt the following question, using only the information in Sources A, B and C.

What conclusions can be drawn about terrorism in 2016? You must draw conclusions about: terrorism in Iraq compared to other countries in 2016; the effects of terrorist attacks on victims; the fear of terrorist attacks versus the likelihood of terrorist attacks in the Western world. You must also make an overall conclusion on terrorism in 2016. **(10 marks)**

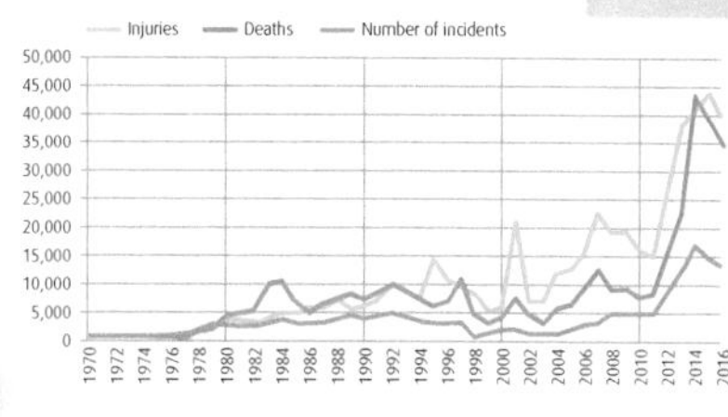

Source C: ii) Terrorist Attacks 1970-2016 worldwide)

HOW TO LAY OUT YOUR ANSWER

Remember, a conclusion is a statement about an issue, which is supported by evidence. You should write a conclusion based on each bullet point. The information you give as evidence should be linked and can come from different sources **or** from within the same source. A well-developed conclusion is worth up to **three** marks. In the model answers below, the conclusions are shown in *italics*.

Terrorist attacks were much more common and deadly in Iraq than in countries in the West in 2016. Evidence to support this conclusion is shown in Source A, which states that six out of the ten deadliest attacks took place in Iraq, and that it also had 35% of all deaths worldwide whilst attacks like the one in Nice represent a mere 2.5% of all terror attacks. This is supported by Source B i) which shows Iraq had 3,356 terrorist attacks in 2016, the highest in the world. The only Western country in the top 10 was Turkey with 539 terrorist attacks. Finally, Source C i) shows that in 2016 Iraq had around 12,000 terrorist fatalities whilst worldwide there were 35,000 deaths clearly showing that terrorism affects Iraq much more than other countries. **(3 marks)**

Terrorist attacks are more likely to cause injuries to the victims rather than deaths. Source A states that out of 36 fatal attacks in the West, 70% resulted in one death, and in nine out of 26 cases, it was only the terrorist who was killed. Sources C i) and ii) show that both in Iraq and worldwide, injuries from terrorist attacks are higher than deaths. For example, worldwide there were 40,000 injuries from terrorist attacks but only 35,000 deaths. **(2 marks)**

Fear of terrorist attacks in Western countries is far greater than the possibility of an actual attack. Evidence to support this conclusion is shown in Source A which states that "Those attacks [in the West] remain a very small minority of attacks we see," said Erin Miller, of the Global Terrorism Database (GTD). Source A also states that the Nice terrorist attack was 1 of only 36 fatal terrorist attacks in the West in 2016. However, Source B ii) shows that fear of terrorist attacks is very high in Western countries. In five out of eight countries (France, Great Britain, Germany, the USA and Sweden), a majority of people surveyed expected a terrorist attack in 2017 with France the highest with 81% of people believing a terrorist attack was 'likely'. **(3 marks)**

For the full ten marks, you **must** also write an overall conclusion. The overall conclusion should **not** simply repeat what you said in your first three conclusions. Look again at the sources.

Overall, although there were 72 mass terror attacks including in Nice and Florida, the number of terrorist attacks actually fell from 2014-2016 worldwide. The number of incidents fell from around 13,000 in 2014 to around 8,000 in 2016 (Source C ii)). *Mass terror attacks in the West remain rare and are much more likely to happen in countries in the Middle East, particularly Iraq* where six out of ten of the deadliest attacks in 2016 occurred (Source A). **(2 marks)**

QUESTION 2: SELECTIVITY

QUESTION

Study Sources A, B and C below then answer the question which follows.

Source A: Dundee – An Economic and Social Profile 2018

Dundee is the fourth largest city in Scotland, with a population of 148,710. The city accounts for 2.7% of the total population of Scotland – within a population of 5,404,700.

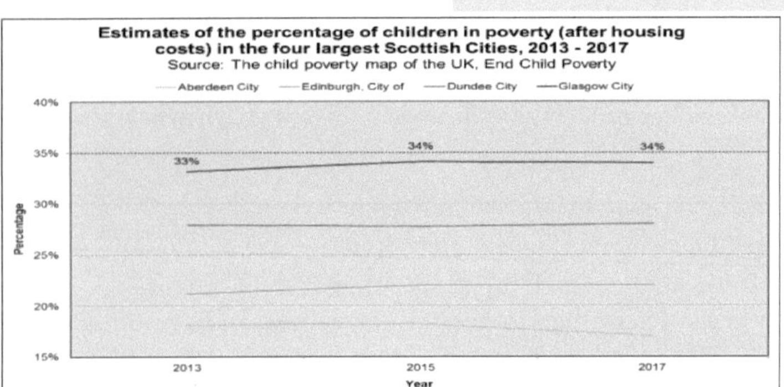

An analysis of employment in the city revealed that employee numbers have increased from 59,000 in 2013 to 62,000 in 2017. Additionally, official figures indicate that full-time employees (FTE) increased from 42,000 to 44,000, with part-time employees (PTE) increasing from 17,000 to 18,000. In the same way, unemployment has also fallen across Dundee, although the announcement of the closure of the Michelin factory in November 2018, with the loss of 850 well-paid tyre manufacturing jobs, will hit the city hard.

In terms of average gross annual earnings, Dundee does not do as well as Scotland's other three largest cities – Glasgow, Edinburgh and Aberdeen. Sadly, the city remains short of high-paid, professional employment opportunities. However, the development of the city's Waterfront area, which includes the Victoria and Albert Museum (V&A) museum, and the signing of the Tay Cities deal, a multi-million investment project across the Tayside area (which includes Dundee), aims to significantly increase high-paid employment opportunities in the future.

Poverty remains a serious problem in Dundee. Compared to other large cities, Dundee has a high rate of low-income households with many people struggling. There is evidence of increased use of foodbanks in recent years. Also, the levels of child poverty have remained high and are largely unchanged despite the city council's best efforts to improve the life circumstances of all its young people.

Finally, Dundee has maintained its unenviable reputation for having one of the lowest life expectancies of any local authority in Scotland. At present, men in Dundee are expected to live for around three years less than the Scottish average. Women do not fare much better in the city, with a life expectancy that is two years less. However, there is evidence to show life expectancy rates for both men and women have increased which is to be welcomed.

Source: Adapted from various economic and social profiles of Dundee City

Attempt the following question using **only** the information in Sources A, B and C.

To what extent is it accurate to state that *Dundee is one of the most deprived cities in Scotland and there is no sign of improvement?* **(10 marks)**

MARKING INSTRUCTIONS OBJECTIVITY QUESTIONS – 10 MARKS

- Award up to **3 marks** for a single developed point depending on the use of the evidence in the sources and the quality of the analysis or evaluation.
- Award marks where candidates synthesise information both within and between sources.
- For **full marks** candidates must refer to all sources in their answer.
- Candidates must also make an overall judgement as to the extent of the accuracy of the given statement. Award a **maximum of 8 marks** if no overall judgement provided.

Note: It is important to use **evaluative language** when supporting/opposing a viewpoint.

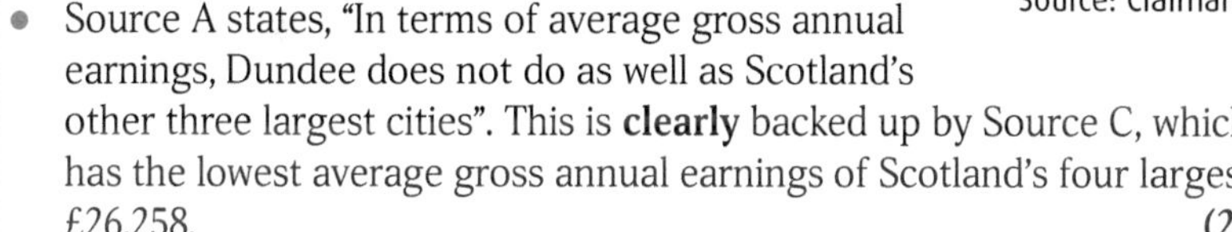

	Dundee count	Dundee rate	Scotland rate
2013	5,195	5.3%	3.7%
2014	4,065	4.1%	2.8%
2015	3,310	3.4%	2.3%
2016	3,455	3.5%	2.2%
2017	3,245	3.3%	2.3%

Source: Claimant Count (2018)

Evidence that **supports** the view "Dundee is one of the most deprived cities in Scotland" includes:

- Source A states, "In terms of average gross annual earnings, Dundee does not do as well as Scotland's other three largest cities". This is **clearly** backed up by Source C, which shows Dundee has the lowest average gross annual earnings of Scotland's four largest cities at £26,258. **(2 marks)**
- Also, Source A states, "compared to other large cities, Dundee has a high rate of low-income households." This is **mainly** backed up by Source B which shows that in 2015, after Glasgow, Dundee had the next highest percentage of households with an income below £10,000. **(2 marks)**
- Thirdly, Source A states, "the levels of child poverty have remained high and are largely unchanged". This is **wholly accurate** as Source B shows the rate of child poverty in Dundee (28%) is second only to Glasgow (about 34%) and has remained largely unchanged 2013–17 (28%). **(3 marks)**
- Finally, Source A states, "Dundee has maintained its unenviable reputation for having one of the lowest life expectancies of any local authority in Scotland." This is **statistically** proven by Source B which shows Dundee's life expectancy for men and women is lowest after Glasgow at men 74.5 years and women 79.2 years respectively. **(2 marks)**

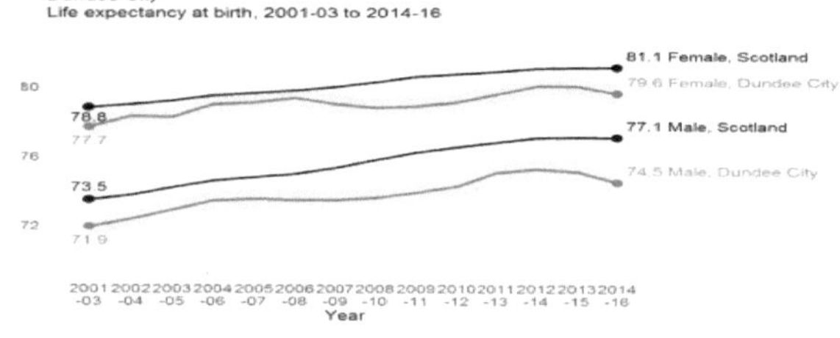

Evidence that **opposes** the view "there is no sign of improvement" includes:

- Source A states "employee numbers in the city are increasing from 59,000 (2013) to 62,000 (2017)". Also, "unemployment has also fallen". This is **accurately** backed up Source C which shows Dundee's unemployment rate fell from 5.3% in 2013 to 3.3% in 2017. **(3 marks)**
- Source A states "life expectancy rates for both men and women have increased" and this is **statistically** backed up by Source C, as male life expectancy in Dundee has increased from 71.7 to 74.5 years (2001–03 to 2014–16) and female life expectancy from 79.6 to 81.1 in the same period. **(3 marks)**
- Overall, the evidence **partly** supports the view. Dundee is clearly one of the most deprived cities in Scotland (along with Glasgow, which is arguably worse) with relatively low-income levels, low earnings, high child poverty rates and low life expectancy compared to Edinburgh and Aberdeen. However, there are signs of improvement in the city as life expectancy and employment rates are increasing and unemployment falling. **(2 marks)**

QUESTION 3: RELIABILITY

QUESTION

Study Sources A, B and C and attempt the question that follows.

Source A: Scotsman Newspaper Online Article (Adapted)

Violent Crime Higher Than Official Reports

(15 September 2018) By Chris Marshall

The new head of an internationally recognised police unit credited with helping Glasgow shed its image as the murder capital of western Europe has warned violent crime continues to go unreported. Niven Rennie, who took the helm at the Violence Reduction Unit (VRU) in the summer, told the Scotsman newspaper that parts of the country still experience "unacceptable" levels of violence, with A&E departments dealing with far higher numbers of serious assaults than those reported to police. The VRU, which has pioneered a public health approach to tackling violence in the west of Scotland, believes violent crime could be significantly higher than the official recorded crime statistics suggest. Its work has received international attention since the turn of the year after 80 people were stabbed to death in London in 2017, a quarter of them in their teens.

Source: https://www.scotsman.com/news/politics/violent-crime-in-scotland-higher-than-official-reports-1-4800625

Source B: Scottish Government Website

Non-sexual crimes of violence account for 3% of all crimes recorded in Scotland in 2017-18. Between 2016-17 and 2017-18, the number of non-sexual crimes of violence recorded by the police in Scotland increased by 1%, from 7,164 to 7,251. Updated October 2018.

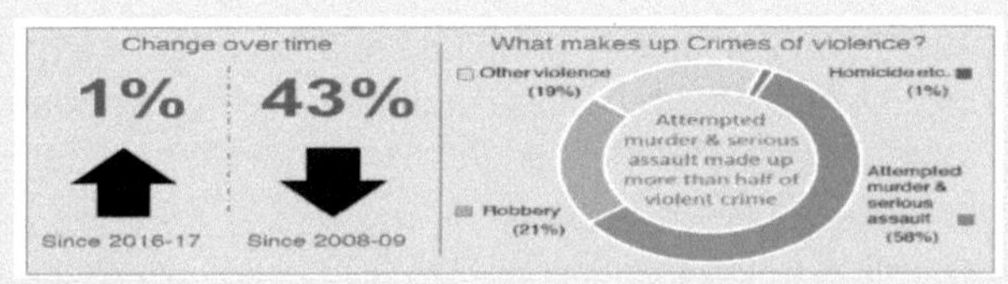

Source C: Public Opinion Survey: What Scotland Thinks

Question: How good or bad a job do you think the SNP has done in the last five years regarding tackling crime?

Published: 15 April 2016

"What Scotland Thinks" is a polling organisation that states on its website that it provides non-partisan information on attitudes to how Scotland and the UK should be governed.

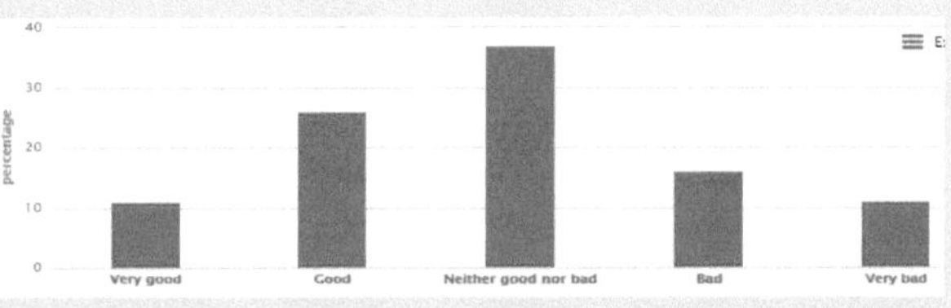

Source: http://whatscotlandthinks.org/questions/how-good-or-bad-a-job-do-you-think-the-snp-has-done-in-the-last-five-years-reg-2

Attempt the following question, using **only** the information in Sources A, B and C.

To what extent are Sources A, B and C reliable? You must provide an overall conclusion on the **most** reliable source of information. **(8 marks)**

MARKING INSTRUCTIONS RELIABILITY QUESTIONS (8 MARKS)

- Award up to **2 marks** for a single developed point depending on the use of the evidence in the sources and the quality of the analysis and/or evaluation.
- For **full marks** candidates must refer to all sources in their answer.
- Candidates must also make a judgement based on the evidence on the most reliable source.
- Award a **maximum of 6 marks** if candidates do not provide an overall judgement.
- Award a **maximum of 2 marks** for an overall judgement.

Source A

Examples of evidence to support reliability:

- The source is an article from a recognised quality Scottish newspaper, and it is up-to-date.
- It provides a weblink to the source and the email of the author.
- The article quotes the head of the Violence Reduction Unit, which improves the quality of source.

Examples of evidence that makes the source less reliable:

- The article is adapted, so it may be subject to change or omission.
- It is a secondary source; the newspaper can be selective in its use of information.

Source B:

Examples of evidence to support reliability:

- The source is taken from the Scottish Government website, so the expectation is that the statistics are compiled and presented accurately; up-to-date.
- It provides a weblink to the source.

Examples of evidence that makes the source less reliable:

- Not all statistics are provided here to support the graphics.

Source C:

Examples of evidence to support reliability:

- It provides information on the polling organisation that conducted the survey.
- It provides a weblink to the source.

Examples of evidence that makes the source less reliable:

- The source doesn't state how many people were surveyed, over what period or where.
- The statistics were published in 2016 so most out-of-date resource of three provided.

Any other valid point.

EXAMPLE OF HIGH SCORING RESPONSE

It can be argued that Source A is a **partly reliable** source because although it comes from a quality newspaper and has been adapted (secondary source and changed which could misinform readers), there is an email by which to contact the author for more information and there is a weblink which allows a researcher to check the original article. Importantly, the article cites the head of the VRU, a person obviously informed, and someone the researcher could then contact directly.

Source B is arguably the **most reliable** source. Coming directly from the Scottish Government's website and quoting data from National Statistics, this source also has a weblink to allow a researcher to check the information for themselves.

Source C appears the **least reliable** as it comes from an opinion poll and opinion polls can and do change quickly, making them at best only a rough guide to what the public think at any one time on any issue. However, Source C has some value to a researcher as it comes from a recognised polling organisation (which it states is non-partisan and whose research methodology will probably be explained on its website), and it contains a weblink to check the information.

Overall, Source B is **clearly the most reliable** as it is based on Scottish Government and National Statistics, there is a weblink and, most importantly, there is an expectation that the website will be accurate, up-to-date and trustworthy, with data that has been compiled using recognised research methodologies.

INDEX